International Medical Law

International Medical Law

Second Edition

Mohammad Naseem
Saman Naseem

This book was originally published as a monograph in the International Encyclopaedia of Laws/Medical Law.

Founding Editor: Roger Blanpain
General Editor: Frank Hendrickx
Volume Editor: Herman Nys

Wolters Kluwer

Published by:
Kluwer Law International B.V.
PO Box 316
2400 AH Alphen aan den Rijn
The Netherlands
E-mail: lrs-sales@wolterskluwer.com
Website: www.wolterskluwer.com/en/solutions/kluwerlawinternational

Sold and distributed by:
Wolters Kluwer Legal & Regulatory U.S.
7201 McKinney Circle
Frederick, MD 21704
United States of America
E-mail: customer.service@wolterskluwer.com

ISBN 978-94-035-4750-3

e-Book: ISBN 978-94-035-4760-2
web-PDF: ISBN 978-94-035-4770-1

The Author

Mohammad Naseem, born and brought up in Sardarnagar of Pilibhit district, Uttar Pradesh, India, is a Science graduate and a Master of Laws, with a specialization in Commercial Law, from Aligarh Muslim University, India. He is an ex-Deputy General Manager (Legal) of ONGC Limited, where he joined in 1985. He was also the Vice President—Legal in ONGC Videsh Limited for seven years. At present he is the Chairman and Managing Partner of Global Law and Liaison Services, New Delhi. In his professional career, spanning over more than three decades, he has dealt with a large number of high-value commercial matters, domestic and international arbitration, and litigation. He has been part of a large number of negotiation teams, having successfully negotiated various types of contracts worth billions of dollars, including acquisitions of petroleum properties in a number of countries. He is the author of monographs/books on Energy Law, Environmental Law, Sports Law, Religion Law, and Medical Law of India and also on International Energy Law and International Environmental Law for Wolters Kluwer International, the Netherlands and has had to his credit a number of papers published in national and international journals of repute. He is the coauthor of *Fuel and Energy II (Petroleum and Natural Gas)* of Halsbury's Laws of India Series (volume 21) published by LexisNexis Butterworth's India Limited. Edward Elgar Publishing Limited has published a chapter authored by him, by the title "World Petroleum Regimes" in the *Hand Book on International Energy Law* and another article on "Natural Gas Provisions in Host Government Contracts—Regulatory and Contractual Aspects in India" published by Oil, Gas and Energy Law Intelligence (OGEL), United Kingdom (UK). He is a visiting faculty and a guest expert speaker at the Indian Academy of International Law and Diplomacy, The International Centre for Alternate Dispute Resolution, the University of Petroleum and Energy Studies, Dehradun and the Indian School of Petroleum, New Delhi. He has traveled extensively throughout the world in relation to negotiations and conducting training programs. He has spoken in seminars organized by IBC Asia Limited in Singapore; by Oil and Gas IQPC in Bangkok, Thailand and Kuala Lumpur, Malaysia; and Tehran, Iran in a seminar conducted by OIPF, Iran. For conducting negotiations he has visited Myanmar, Singapore, Vietnam, Japan, South Korea, Hong Kong, Thailand, Iran, the UAE, Iraq, Jordan, Syria, Turkey, Egypt, Libya, Sudan, South Sudan, Italy, Russia, Kazakhstan, Denmark, Netherlands, Switzerland, France, the UK, the US,

The Author

Canada, Ecuador, Venezuela, and Uzbekistan. He is a lifetime member of the Indian Society of International Law and a permanent member of the India International Law Foundation, which are very prestigious bodies. With more than thirty years of varied practical and on-the-job legal experience in negotiations, drafting, interpretation and vetting of legal documents and dealing with arbitration and litigation, on the one hand, and acting as a trainer, speaker, and author, on the other, Naseem has been part of an exclusive team of trainers, negotiators, advisers, and strategists and is a legal luminary of international repute in his own right.
Eimail: naseem_md@yahoo.com
Mobile: +91-9958160213/9410397786

Coauthor

Saman Naseem holds a post-graduation in Commercial Law from Aligarh Muslim University and is a graduate of Symbiosis International University, India. She is the Founder Partner of Global Law and Liaison Services, a firm providing professional advice in the field of law. She is an active participant in seminars and conferences and has presented research papers on various topics. She is the coauthor of monographs on *Environmental Law*, *Medical Law*, and *Religion Law of India* and also on *International Environmental Law and International Energy Law* for Wolters Kluwer International, the Netherlands. Edward Elgar Publishing Limited has published an article coauthored by her, by the title "World Petroleum Regimes" and another article on "Natural Gas Provisions in Host Government Contracts—Regulatory and Contractual Aspects in India" published by OGEL, UK. She has been connected with NGOs, namely the Madad Foundation, and supports various social causes like the Leprosy Eradication Drive by the Indian Leprosy Foundation and helps in the collection of funds for Help Age India, the poor, needy, and for the blind, to name a few.

E-mail: saman1492@gmail.com
Mobile: +91-9911386011

Coauthor

Table of Contents

Table of Contents

List of Abbreviations

AA	Appropriate Authority
ACLM	The American College of Legal Medicine
ADR	Adverse Drug Reactions
ADR	Alternate Dispute Resolution
AHIMA	American Health Information Management Association
AIA	Advance Informed Agreement
AIDS	Acquired Immune Deficiency Syndrome
AMA	American Medical Association
B.C./BCE	Before Christ/Before the Common Era
BWC	Biological Weapons Convention
CCPCJ	Commission on Crime Prevention and Criminal Justice
CD-P-TO	Council of Europe European Committee on Organ Transplantation
CIO	Contribution to International Organization
CHIP	Country Health Intelligence Portal
CRPD	Convention on the Rights of Persons with Disabilities
CME	Continuing Medical Education
CNS	Central Nervous System
CRC	Convention on the Rights of the Child
CRVS	Civil Registration and Vital Statistics
CWC	Chemical Weapons Convention
DBS	Deep Brain Stimulation
DICG	Declaration of Istanbul Custodian Group
DNA	Deoxyribonucleic Acid
DNR	Do Not Resuscitate Status
DOI	Declaration of Istanbul
DTCA	Direct-to-Consumer Advertising
ECDD	Expert Committee on Drug Dependence
ECME	European Charter of Medical Ethics
ECMO	European Council of Medical Orders

List of Abbreviations

ERISA	Employee Retirement Income Security Act
EU	European Union
FAO	United Nations Food and Agriculture Organization
FCO	Foreign and Commonwealth Office
FDA	Food and Drug Administration
FSMB	Federation of State Medical Boards of the United States
GDP	Gross Domestic Product
GHO	Global Health Observatory
GNI	Gross National Income
HIPAA	Health Insurance Portability and Accountability Act
HIV	Human Immunodeficiency Virus
HMO	Health Maintenance Organization
IAMLA	International Association of Medical Licensing Authorities
IAMRA	International Association of Medical Regulatory Authorities
ICC	International Criminal Court
ICCPR	International Covenant on Civil and Political Rights
ICESCR	International Covenant on Economic, Social and Cultural Rights
ICD	International Classification of Diseases
ICF	International Classification of Functioning, Disability and Health
ICHI	International Classification of Health Intervention
ICN	International Council of Nurses
ICNP	International Classification for Nursing Practice
ICPO/INTERPOL	International Criminal Police Organization
ICSI	Intracycoplasmic Sperm Injection
ICJ	International Court of Justice
ICU	Intensive Care Unit
IDLO	International Development Law Organization
IHR	International Health Regulations, 2005
IMA	International Medical Corps
INCB	International Narcotics Control Board
INN	International Nonproprietary Name
IRCT	International Rehabilitation Council for Torture Victims
ISN	International Society of Nephrology
ISR	International Sanitary Regulations
IVF	In Vitro Fertilization
JCI	Joint Commission International
LAI	Laboratory-Acquired Infection

LSD	Lysergic Acid Diethylamide
MDG	United Nations Millennium Development Goals
MRA	Medicine Regulatory Authorities
NGO	Nongovernmental Organization
NMD	Neurosurgery for Mental Disorder
NPT	Treaty on the Non-Proliferation of Nuclear Weapons
NRx	New Prescriptions
OCD	Obsessive-Compulsive Disorder
ODA	Official Development Assistance
OECD	Organization for Economic Cooperation and Development
PGD	Preimplantation Genetic Diagnosis
PHR	Physicians for Human Right
SAGE	Study of Global Aging and Adult Health
SARA	Service Availability and Readiness Assessment
SARS	Severe Acute Respiratory Syndrome
SPS	Agreement, 1994 WTO Agreement on the Application of Sanitary and Phytosanitary Measures
TB	Tuberculosis
TBT	Agreement, 1994 the WTO Agreement on Technical Barriers to Trade
THB	Trafficking in Human Beings
THBOR	Trafficking of Human Beings for the purpose of Organ Removal
TRx	Total Prescriptions
UAE	United Arab Emirates
UN	United Nations
UNAIDS	Joint United Nations Programme on HIV/AIDS
UNCLOS	UN Convention on the Law of the Sea
UNDP	United Nations Development Programme
UNDCP	United Nations International Drug Control Programme
UNEP	United Nations Environmental Programme
UNESCO	United Nations Educational, Scientific and Cultural Organization
UNFPA	United Nations Population Fund
UNICEF	United Nations Children's Fund
UNIDO	United Nations Industrial Development Organization
UNODC	United Nations Office on Drugs and Crime
UNOS	United Network for Organ Sharing of the United States
UNRRA	United Nations Relief and Rehabilitation Administration
UNSCR	United Nations Security Council Resolution 1540

List of Abbreviations

UNTOC	United Nations Convention against Transnational Organized Crime
WCO	World Customs Organization
WHA	World Health Assembly
WHO	World Health Organization
WHOQOL	WHO Quality of Life Investment
WMA	World Medical Association
WMD	Weapons of Mass Destruction
WMO	World Meteorological Organization

Acknowledgments

We would like to thank and express our sincere gratitude to Mrs. Rana Naseem and Mr. Faraz Naseem, who have not only spared us to take time out of their share but also helped in the collection of valuable material on Medical Law International, typographic help, and in all other respects so that this task could be completed successfully.

Mohammad Naseem
Saman Naseem
New Delhi 2022

Acknowledgments

General Introduction

1. Medical law incorporates the spirit of two main professions of the world, i.e., Medicine and Law. These professions interact in everyday life, but, in general, lawyers know very little about medical law and, similarly, there may be a lack of understanding among physicians to comprehend the law, except for those doctors who deal with medico-legal cases. While dealing with such cases, doctors have a chance to deal with injury reports, autopsy, or, when, as the treating doctor, as a witness in a personal injury lawsuit or as an expert in connection, with claims that another member of his profession has been negligent. A doctor may be required to render governmental reports or to preserve physical evidence for the benefit of a law enforcement agency, which will use it during prosecution.

2. So, international medical law deals with medico-legal issues having global legal implications or regulation of medical practice, which is controlled and monitored by legislation, treaties, conventions, court decisions, professional regulations, etc. Medical law may also consist of forensic medicine, law relating to sexology, psychiatry, psychology, dentistry, nursing law, pharmaceutical law, medical ethics, clinical criminology, drugs, problem of alcoholism, child abuse, medical experimentation, genetic engineering, organ transplantation, organ trafficking, abortion, contraception, sterilization, euthanasia, religion, Acquired Immune Deficiency Syndrome (AIDS), etc. Medical law also concerns the rights and responsibilities of medical professionals and their patients and ethical standards. The areas of focus for medical law include confidentiality, negligence, and other torts related to medical treatment.

3. The doctors, as medical professionals, are held in high esteem and to a higher standard of ethics than any other professional as they deal with one's body. Medical malpractice is one of the key focuses of medical law and relates to the liability of a medical professional for negligence in the treatment of a patient resulting in injury or death. But other torts are also present in the field of medical law. For example, it is possible for a medical professional to defame a patient if they wrongfully disclose untrue information about the patient's health. Another example is battery when one performs a treatment on someone who has declined such treatment, maybe for religious reasons.

Part I. History and Development of International Medical Law

Chapter 1. Human Civilization and the Evolution of Medical Treatment

4. Early medical traditions included those of Babylon, China, Egypt, Greece, and India. The Greeks introduced the concepts of medical diagnosis, prognosis, and advanced medical ethics. The Hippocratic Oath, still taken by doctors, was written in Greece in the fifth century B.C. The first known dentistry dates back to around 7000 B.C., in Baluchistan, where Neolithic dentists used flint-tipped drills and bowstrings. The first known trepanning operation was carried out around 5000 B.C. in modern-day France. The earliest known surgery, an amputation, was carried out around 4900 B.C., also in France. During the Renaissance, understanding of the human anatomy improved, and the microscope was invented. The "germ theory of discasc," in the nineteenth century, led to cures for many infectious diseases. Military doctors advanced the methods of trauma treatment and surgery. Public health measures were developed in the nineteenth century as the rapid growth of cities required systematic sanitary measures. The mid-twentieth century was characterized by new biological treatments, such as antibiotics. These advancements, along with developments in chemistry, genetics, and lab technology (such as the X-ray), led to the evolution and development of modern medicine.

§1. Ancient Egyptian Medicine

5. Imhotep, of the third Egyptian dynasty, is credited with being the founder of ancient Egyptian medicine and was the original author of the Edwin Smith Papyrus, detailing cures, ailments, and anatomical observations. The Edwin Smith Papyrus is regarded as a copy of several earlier works and was written in circa 1600 B.C. However, medical information in the Edwin Smith Papyrus dates to a time as early as 3000 B.C. The Kahun Gynaecological Papyrus deals with women's health complaints, including problems with conception. Thirty-four cases, detailing diagnosis and treatment, are suggested, some of them fragmentarily. Dating back to 1800 B.C., it is the oldest surviving medical text relating to gynecological medicine in the world. The earliest known physician is also credited to Ancient Egypt: Hesy-Ra, "Chief of Dentists and Physicians" for King Djoser in the twenty-seventh century

B.C. The earliest known woman physician, Peseshet, practiced in Ancient Egypt at the time of the 4th dynasty. Her title was "Lady Overseer of the Lady Physicians."

§2. Babylonian Medicine

6. The oldest Babylonian texts on medicine date back to the Old Babylonian Period in the first half of the 2nd millennium B.C. The most extensive Babylonian medical text is the Diagnostic Handbook, written by the *ummânū*, or chief scholar, Esagil-kin-apli of Borsippa during the reign of the Babylonian king Adad-apla-iddina (1069–1046 B.C.). Along with the Egyptians, the Babylonians introduced the practice of diagnosis, prognosis, physical examination, and remedies. There was little development after the medieval era. Major European treatises on medicine took 200 years to reach the Middle East, where local rulers sometimes consulted Western doctors to get the latest treatments. Medical works in Arabic, Turkish, and Persian, as late as A.D. 1800, were based on medieval Islamic medicine.

§3. System of Medicine in India

7. The Ayurveda and Siddha are ancient systems of medicine that originated and developed in India, whereas the Unani system was brought and developed after the advent of Turks and other central Asians in India.

I. Ayurveda

8. The Atharvaveda, dating from the Early Iron Age, is one of the first Indian texts dealing with medicine and contains prescriptions of herbs for various ailments and the use of herbs to treat ailments. Ayurveda, meaning the "complete knowledge for long life" is a medical system of India. Its two most famous texts belong to the schools of Charaka and Sushruta. The foundations of Ayurveda were built on a synthesis of traditional herbal practices together with the addition of theoretical concepts and new therapies dating from around 600 B.C. onward, coming out of the communities of thinkers who included the Buddha and others.

II. Siddha System of Medicines

9. Siddha is an ancient Indian system of medicine that originated in South India which derives its name from the term, "Siddha" which means an achievement. The practitioners of this system of medicine, called the Siddhars, are required to attain physical and spiritual excellence to be able to treat people. Many ingredients used for preparing Siddha medicines are the same as used in Ayurveda. According to history, the Dravidians were the first inhabitants of India, among whom the Tamils were quite prominent and made considerable progress in the civilization than the other ancient people. During those times, the languages of India were grouped largely into two classes: Sanskrit in the northern regions and Dravidian language in the southern regions. The Siddha books of medical science were written in the Dravidian, Tamil language.

III. Unani Medicines

10. The Unani system of medicine originated in Greece (Unan or Yunan in the Arabic language), and Aesculapius is credited as the originator of this system. Buqrat (better known as Hippocrates, 460–377 B.C.) is said to be a descendant of Aesculapius and is recognized as "father of Unani medicine." According to Unani medicine, health is considered a state of the body when the "humors" are in equilibrium and the body functions normally. Classical diagnosis in the Unani system is based on examination of pulse, stool, and urine in addition to routine physical checkup.

11. Unani medicine in India progressed during the Sultanate and Mughal periods. Unani medicine is very close to Ayurveda. Both are based on the theory of the presence of the elements of nature (in Unani, they are considered to be fire, water, earth, and air) in the human body. According to followers of Unani medicine, these elements are present in different fluids and their balance leads to health and their imbalance leads to illness. Muslim rulers built large hospitals in 1595 in Hyderabad and in Delhi in 1719.

§4. Chinese Medicine

12. The basic text of Chinese medicine is the Huangdi Neijing (or Yellow Emperor's Inner Canon) written during the fifth century to third century B.C. The Jin Dynasty practitioner and advocate of acupuncture and moxibustion, Huangfu Mi (A.D. 215–282), also quotes the Yellow Emperor in his Jiayi Jing, circa A.D. 265. During the Tang Dynasty, the Suwen was expanded and revised and formed the foundational roots of traditional Chinese medicine, which is based on the use of herbal medicine, acupuncture, massage, and other forms of therapy, practiced in China for thousands of years.

13. In the eighteenth century, during the Qing Dynasty, there was a proliferation of popular books, as well as more advanced encyclopedias on traditional medicine. Jesuit missionaries introduced Western science and medicine to the Chinese royal court. In the nineteenth century, Western medicine was introduced at the local level by Christian medical missionaries from the London Missionary Society (Britain), the Methodist Church (Britain), and the Presbyterian Church (USA). Benjamin Hobson (1816–1873), in 1839, set up a highly successful Wai Ai Clinic in Guangzhou, China. The Hong Kong College of Medicine for Chinese was founded in 1887 by the London Missionary Society, with its first graduate (in 1892) being Sun Yat-sen, who later led the Chinese Revolution (1911). Because of the social custom that men and women should not mix together, the women of China were reluctant to be treated by male doctors. The missionaries sent women doctors, such as Dr. Mary Hannah Fulton (1854–1927). Supported by the Foreign Missions Board of the Presbyterian Church (USA) she, in 1902, founded the first medical college for women in China, the Hackett Medical College for Women, in Guangzhou.

§5. Medicine in Ancient Greece

14. Around 800 B.C., Homer, in The Iliad, had given the descriptions of wound treatment by the two sons of Asklepios, the admirable physicians Podaleirius and Machaon and one acting doctor, Patroclus. Because Machaon is wounded and Podaleirius is in combat Eurypylus asks Patroclus to cut out the arrow from his thigh, wash off the blood with warm water, and spread soothing ointment on the wound. Asklepios, like Imhotep, becomes the god of healing over time. Temples dedicated to the healer-god Asclepius, known as Asclepieia, functioned as centers of medical advice, prognosis, and healing. At these shrines, patients would enter a dream-like state of induced sleep known as *enkoimesis*, not unlike anesthesia, in which they either received guidance from the deity in a dream or were cured by surgery.

I. Hippocrates

15. A towering figure in the history of medicine was the physician, Hippocrates of Kos (circa 460–370 B.C.), considered the "father of Western medicine." The Hippocratic Corpus is a collection of around seventy early medical works from Ancient Greece strongly associated with Hippocrates and his students. Most famously, Hippocrates invented the Hippocratic Oath for physicians, which is still relevant and in use. Hippocrates and his followers were the first to describe many diseases and medical conditions. He is given credit for the first description of clubbing of the fingers, an important diagnostic sign in chronic suppurative lung disease, lung cancer, and cyanotic heart disease. For this reason, clubbed fingers are sometimes referred to as "Hippocratic fingers."

II. Galen

16. The Greek physician, Galen (A.D. 129–circa 216), was one of the greatest physicians of the ancient world, studying and traveling widely in Ancient Rome. He dissected animals to learn about the body and performed many operations, which included brain and eye surgeries, not tried again for almost two millennia. In *Ars Medica* ("Arts of Medicine"), he explained mental properties in terms of specific mixtures of the bodily parts. Galen's medical works were regarded as authoritative until well into the Middle Ages. Galen left a physiological model of the human body that became the mainstay of the medieval physician's university anatomy curriculum. The Renaissance rediscovered Galen and, in 1523, Galen's "On the Natural Faculties" was published in London.

§6. Medicine in Ancient Rome

17. The Romans invented numerous surgical instruments, including the first instruments unique to women, as well as the surgical uses of forceps, scalpels, cautery, cross-bladed scissors, the surgical needle, the sound, and specula. Romans also performed cataract surgery. The Roman army physician, Dioscorides (circa A.D. 40–90), was a Greek botanist and pharmacologist. He wrote the encyclopedia *De Materia Medica* describing over 600 herbal cures, forming an influential pharmacopeia which was used extensively for the following 1,500 years.

§7. Medicine in the Medieval Islamic world

18. The Islamic civilization rose to primacy in medical science as its physicians contributed significantly to the field of medicine, including anatomy, ophthalmology, pharmacology, pharmacy, physiology, surgery, and the pharmaceutical sciences. The Arabs were influenced by ancient Indian, Greek, Roman and Byzantine medical practices and developed them further. Galen and Hippocrates were preeminent authorities for this development. The translation of 129 of Galen's works into Arabic by the Nestorian Christian Hunayn ibn Ishaq and his assistants, and, in particular, Galen's insistence on a rational systematic approach to medicine, set the basis for Islamic medicine, which rapidly spread throughout the world.

§8. Medieval Medicine of Western Europe

19. As the practice of medicine declined in the Western Roman Empire, most of the writings of Galen and Hippocrates were lost to the West, with the summaries and compendia of St. Isidore of Seville being the primary channel for transmitting Greek medical ideas. The Carolingian Renaissance brought increased contact with Byzantium and a greater awareness of ancient medicine, but only with the twelfth-century Renaissance and the new translations coming from Muslim and Jewish sources in Spain and the fifteenth-century flood of resources after the fall of Constantinople moved the tide of information and the West recovered its acquaintance with classical antiquity. The Renaissance brought an intense focus on scholarship to Christian Europe. A major effort to translate the Arabic and Greek scientific works into Latin emerged. Europeans gradually became experts not only in the ancient writings of the Romans and Greeks but also in the contemporary writings of Muslim scientists.

I. Paracelsus

20. Paracelsus (1493–1541) rejected Galen and bookish knowledge, calling for experimental research and looked for cures in nature. He preached and pioneered the use of chemicals and minerals in medicine. His hermetical views were that sickness and health in the body relied on the harmony of man (microcosm) and nature (macrocosm). He took an approach different from those before him that humans must have certain balances of minerals in their bodies and that certain illnesses of the body had chemical remedies that could cure them. Paracelsus is a highly controversial figure in the history of medicine but left a lasting influence in the field of medicine, with most experts hailing him as a "father of Modern medicine."

II. Padua and Bologna

21. University training of physicians began in the thirteenth century. The University of Padua was founded in around 1220 by walkouts from the University of Bologna and began teaching medicine in 1222. It played a leading role in the identification and treatment of diseases and ailments, specializing in autopsies and the inner workings of the body. Starting in 1595, Padua's famous anatomical theatre drew in artists and scientists studying the human body during public dissections. At the University of Bologna, the training of physicians began in 1219. The Italian city attracted students from across Europe. Taddeo Alderotti built a tradition of medical education that established the characteristic features of Italian-learned medicine and was followed by medical schools in other parts of the world.

§9. Age of Enlightenment

22. During the Age of Enlightenment, the eighteenth century, science was held in high esteem and physicians upgraded their social status by becoming more scientific. The health field was crowded with self-trained barber surgeons, apothecaries, midwives, drug peddlers, and charlatans. Across Europe medical schools primarily relied on lectures and readings. Laboratory work was uncommon and dissections were rarely done because of legal restrictions on cadavers. Most schools were small, and only Edinburgh, Scotland, with 11,000 alumni, produced large numbers of graduates.

I. Britain

23. In Britain, there were three small hospitals after 1550. Pelling and Webster estimate that in London, in the 1580–1600 period, out of a population of nearly 200,000 people, there were about 500 medical practitioners. The London Dispensary opened in 1696, the first clinic in the British Empire to dispense medicines to poor, sick people. The innovation was slow to catch on, but new dispensaries were opened in the 1770s. In the colonies, small hospitals were started in Philadelphia in 1752, New York in 1771, and Boston in 1811. English physician Thomas Percival (1740–1804) wrote a comprehensive system of medical conduct, "Medical Ethics, or a Code of Institutes and Precepts, Adapted to the Professional Conduct of Physicians and Surgeons" (1803) that set the standard for many subsequent textbooks.

II. Spain and the Spanish Empire

24. In the Spanish Empire, the viceregal capital of Mexico City was a site of medical training for physicians. Epidemic diseases had decimated indigenous populations, starting in the early sixteenth century. The Spanish conquest of the Aztec empire, a black auxiliary in the armed forces, with an active case of smallpox, set off a virgin land epidemic among indigenous peoples, Spanish allies and enemies alike. Aztec emperor Cuitlahuac died of smallpox. Medical education was instituted at the Royal and Pontifical University of Mexico, and their clientele were the urban elites. The Spanish Crown began regulating the medical profession just a few years after the conquest, setting up the Royal Tribunal of the Protomedicato, a board for licensing medical personnel in 1527.

III. Japan

25. European ideas of modern medicine were spread widely throughout the world by medical missionaries and the dissemination of textbooks. Japanese elites enthusiastically embraced Western medicine. Highly influential was the 1765 edition of Hendrik van Deventer's pioneer work *Nieuw Ligt* ("A New Light") on Japanese obstetrics, especially on Katakura Kakuryo's publication in 1799 of *Sanka Hatsumo* ("Enlightenment of Obstetrics"). A cadre of Japanese physicians began to interact with Dutch doctors, who introduced smallpox vaccinations. By 1820 Japanese medical practitioners not only translated Dutch medical texts but also integrated their readings with clinical diagnoses.

§10. Rise of Modern Medicine

26. The practice of medicine changed with the rapid advances in science as well as new approaches by physicians. Among the more powerful new techniques were anesthesia and the development of both antiseptic and aseptic operating theatres. Actual cures were developed for certain endemic infectious diseases. Medicine was revolutionized in the nineteenth century and beyond by advances in chemistry and laboratory techniques and equipment. The previous ideas of infectious disease epidemiology were replaced with bacteriology and virology.

I. The US Civil War

27. In the American Civil War (1861–1865), more soldiers died of disease than in battle, and an even larger number were temporarily incapacitated by wounds, diseases and accidents. The war had a dramatic long-term impact on medicine in the US, from surgical techniques to hospitals to nursing and to research facilities. Hygiene in the training and field camps was poor because men, who had never been far from home, were brought together for training with thousands of strangers. First came epidemics of chicken pox, mumps, whooping cough, and, especially, measles.

Harsh weather, contaminated water, inadequate shelter in winter quarters, poor policing of camps, and dirty camp hospitals took their toll. The government responded by building army hospitals in every state which led to the emergence of skilled, well-funded medical organizers, especially in the much enlarged United States Army Medical Department and the United States Sanitary Commission. Numerous other new agencies also targeted the medical and morale needs of soldiers, including the United States Christian Commission and, ultimately, the US Army in August 1886 established the Hospital Corps.

II. Germ Theory and Bacteriology

28. In the 1830s, in Italy, Agostino Bassi traced the silkworm disease muscardine to microorganisms. Meanwhile, in Germany, Theodor Schwann led research on alcoholic fermentation by yeast and proposed that they were alive—i.e., microorganisms. In 1847, in Vienna, Ignaz Semmelweis (1818–1865), by requiring physicians to clean their hands before attending childbirth, dramatically cut new mothers' death rate due to childbed fever. Starting in 1857, by confirming Schwann's fermentation experiments, Louis Pasteur, in France, placed his eminent reputation behind the belief that yeast is a microorganism and indicated that such a process might also explain contagious diseases. In 1860, Pasteur's report on bacterial fermentation to butyric acid motivated fellow Frenchman Casimir Davaine to establish a similar species, which he called *bacteridia*, as the pathogen of the disease anthrax, costly to the cattle industry.

III. Statistical Methods

29. A major breakthrough in epidemiology came with the introduction of statistical maps and graphs which allowed careful analysis of seasonality issues in disease incidents, and the maps allowed public health officials to prepare literature for the dissemination of disease. John Snow, in London, observed that the symptoms of cholera were vomiting and diarrhea. He concluded that the source of contamination must be through ingestion rather than inhalation, as was previously thought. English nurse Florence Nightingale pioneered the analysis of large amounts of statistical data, using graphs and tables, regarding the condition of thousands of patients in the Crimean War to evaluate the efficacy of hospital services. By the late nineteenth- and early twentieth-century English statisticians, led by Francis Galton, Karl Pearson, and Ronald Fisher, developed the mathematical tools, such as correlations and hypothesis tests, that made possible the much more sophisticated analysis of statistical data.

§11. Women in Medical Field

30. Catholic women played major roles in health and healing in medieval and early modern Europe. A life as a nun was a prestigious role, and wealthy families provided dowries for their daughters, and these funded the convents. The nuns provided free nursing care for the poor. The local officials recognized the public value of hospitals and some were continued in Protestant lands, but without monks or nuns and in the control of local governments. In London, the government allowed two hospitals to continue their charitable work, under the nonreligious control of city officials.

I. Women as Nurses

31. Florence Nightingale triggered the professionalization of nursing. Women had always served in ancillary roles and as midwives and healers. They were trained in traditional methods of physical care that involved little knowledge of medicine.

The "Nightingale model" was widely copied. Linda Richards (1841–1930) studied in London and became the first professionally trained American nurse. She established nursing training programs in the US and Japan and created the first system for keeping individual medical records for hospitalized patients. The Russian Orthodox Church sponsored seven orders of nursing sisters in the late nineteenth century. They ran hospitals, clinics, almshouses, pharmacies, and shelters, as well as training schools for nurses.

II. Women as Physicians

32. Elizabeth Blackwell (1821–1910) became the first woman to formally study and practice medicine in the US. She was a leader in women's medical education. At a deeper level of disagreement, Blackwell felt that women would succeed in medicine because of their humane female values, but Jacobi believed that women should participate as the equals of men in all medical specialties using identical methods, values, and insights. In the Soviet Union although the majority of medical doctors were women, they were paid less than the mostly male factory workers.

§12. Medical Schools

33. The first medical schools were opened in the ninth century, most notably the Schola Medica Salernitana at Salerno in Southern Italy. The cosmopolitan influences from Greek, Latin, Arabic, and Hebrew sources gave it an international reputation as the Hippocratic City. Students from wealthy families came for three years of preliminary studies and five years of medical studies. In the twentieth-century universities were founded in Italy, France, and England which soon developed into schools of medicine. The University of Montpellier in France and Italy's University of Padua and University of Bologna were leading schools. Nearly all the learning was from lectures and readings in Hippocrates, Galen, Avicenna, and Aristotle. There was little clinical work or dissection.

I. Paris Medical Center

34. Paris and Vienna were the two leading medical centers in 1750–1914. In the 1770–1850 period Paris became a world center of medical research and teaching. The "Paris School" emphasized that teaching and research should be based in large hospitals and promoted the professionalization of the medical profession with emphasis on sanitation and public health. Louis Pasteur (1822–1895) was one of the most important founders of medical microbiology. His discoveries reduced mortality from puerperal fever, and he created the first vaccines for rabies and anthrax. He was best known for inventing a method to treat milk and wine in order to prevent it from causing sickness, a process that came to be known as "pasteurization." He is regarded as one of the three main founders of microbiology, together with Ferdinand Cohn and Robert Koch. He worked chiefly in Paris and, in 1887, founded the Pasteur Institute there to perpetuate his commitment to basic research and its practical applications.

II. Viennese School

35. The First Viennese School of Medicine, 1750–1800, was led by the Dutchman Gerard van Swieten (1700–1772), who aimed to put medicine on new scientific foundations. When the Vienna General Hospital opened in 1784, it, at once, became the world's largest hospital and physicians acquired a facility that gradually developed into the most important research center. Vienna, long known as the capital of a diverse empire, attracted not just Germans but Czechs, Hungarians, Jews, Poles, and others to its world-class medical facilities. After 1820 the Second Viennese School of Medicine emerged. Basic medical science expanded and specialization advanced. Furthermore, the first dermatology, eye, as well as ear, nose, and throat clinics in the world were founded in Vienna.

III. Berlin

36. After 1871, Berlin, the capital of the new German Empire, became a leading center for medical research. Robert Koch (1843–1910) was a representative leader. He became famous for isolating *Bacillus anthracis* (1877), the tuberculosis bacillus, *Mycobacterium tuberculosis* (1882) and *Vibrio cholerae* (1883) and for his development of the Koch's postulates. He was awarded the Nobel Prize in Physiology or Medicine in 1905 for his tuberculosis findings. Koch is one of the founders of microbiology, inspiring such major figures as Paul Ehrlich and Gerhard Domagk.

Chapter 2. Development of International Medical Law

37. In early civilizations, primitive legal codes, religious doctrines, and social obligations were not distinguished. Ecclesiastical courts and canon law were not only applicable to religious matters but also to medicine—for example, sterility, pregnancy, abortion, period of gestation, and sexual deviations were dealt with as per religious beliefs. The oldest of these written records, the Code of Hammurabi, included legislation pertaining to the practice of medicine, dating back to 2200 B.C. It covered the topic of medical malpractice and set out, for the first time, the concept of civil and criminal liability for improper and negligent medical care. Penalties not only included monetary compensation but also to the extent of cutting off the surgeon's hand. The fees of medical practitioners were also fixed. The Code discussed various diseases of a slave that would invalidate a contract. References to incest, adultery, and rape were also included in the Code.

§1. Historical Development of Medical Law

38. In Ancient Egypt, the acts of the medical man were prescribed and covered by law. Stab wounds were differentiated in the seventeenth century B.C. The Egyptians had a thorough knowledge of poisons. There is evidence that priests made determinations regarding the cause of death and whether it was natural or not.[1] The Chinese published information about poisons, including arsenic and opium, in around 3000 B.C. In ancient Persia, wounds were put into one of seven classes, ranging from simple to mortal. In Ancient Greece, there was knowledge of poisons and laws against abortions. However, autopsies were not performed since a dead body was regarded as sacred.

I. Development in Rome

39. In 600 B.C, a law was passed in Rome requiring that a woman who died in confinement should be immediately "opened" to save the child. When Julius Caesar was assassinated in 44 B.C. (March 15), the physician Antistius examined his body and concluded that only one of the twenty-three stab wounds was fatal.[2]

II. Development in Greece

40. The legal code in Ancient Greece (around 460 B.C.) was very elaborate. In addition, it was a time of great advances in medicine. Though there is no clear evidence that medical knowledge was officially made use of in establishing proof in courts of law. However, it is known that Hippocrates and others discussed many

1. J.R. Oliver, *Legal Medicine in Europe and America,* 18 Am. Bar Assoc. J. 405–411 (1932).
2. W.H. Spitz (e.), *Medico-legal Investigation of Death* (Charles C Thomas 3rd ed. 1993).

genuine medico-legal questions. These questions included the relative fatality of wounds in different parts of the body, the average duration of pregnancy, and other matters.

III. Development in Egypt

41. A papyrus was found in Egypt, dated from pre-Christian times, in which a medical officer in Alexandria submitted a report on a suicide about which there had been some suspicion of murder. The Justinian Code, which made its appearance in Rome between A.D. 529 and 564, included within its provisions an indication that a medical expert would not be used to proper or greatest advantage if he were to be simply regarded as an ordinary witness, appearing for one side or the other. The Code stated that the function of such an expert was really to assist the judiciary by impartial interpretation and opinion, based on his specialized knowledge.[3]

IV. Development in China

42. In China, in around A.D. 1236, a volume entitled the Hsi Yuan Lu (freely translated, "Washing Away of Wrongs") was compiled which outlined procedures to be followed in investigating suspicious deaths. The book urged the medical examiner to make a thorough examination of every corpse, however unpleasant its condition. The book discussed the difficulties caused by decomposition and even advised the examiner about the problems associated with counterfeit wounds. Sections were devoted to wounds caused by blows from fists or from kicking and to deaths caused by strangulation or drowning. Means for distinguishing between the bodies of drowned persons and those thrown into the water after death were discussed, as were the distinctions between antemortem and postmortem burning. The examiner was also cautioned that nothing in the inquest should be regarded as being unimportant.

V. Development in Europe

43. In 1553 the Germanic Emperor, Charles V, published and proclaimed the Caroline Code, which stated that expert medical testimony must be obtained for the guidance of the judges in cases of murder, wounding, poisoning, hanging, drowning, infanticide, and abortion and in other circumstances involving injury to a person.[4] France also had an early start among European nations in the development of a medico-legal system. From 1570 to 1692, France enacted laws that favored the development of legal medicine as an academic discipline. However, by 1690,

3. S. Smith, *The History and Development of Legal Medicine*, in *Legal Medicine* 1–19 (Gradwohi RBH ed., CV Mosby 1954).
4. W.U. Spitz (ed.), *Medico-legal Investigation of Death* (Charles C Thomas 3rd ed. 1993).

medico-legal offices became corrupt, and progress in legal medicine actually regressed, not to start on a forward march again until after the French Revolution in the next century.[5]

44. In Italy, physician Fortunato Fedele published a comprehensive volume on forensic medicine entitled "*De Relationes Medicorum*" in 1602. Another Italian, Paola Zacchia, a Papal physician, published the *Questiones Medico-Legales*, which overshadowed Fedele's work. Zacchia's book discussed the questions of age, legitimacy, pregnancy, death during delivery, resemblance of children to their parents, dementia, poisoning, impotence, feigned diseases, miracles, rape, mutilation, and the matters concerning public health. The book also contains sections on the different methods of torture then in existence, and it also has a section that deals with miracles.[6]

45. A good development was that medical law was not treated as only a theoretical matter but was brought into the courtroom. For example, in 1667, Schwammerdamm, in Germany, claimed that the lungs of a newborn baby would float in water if the baby had actually breathed. That is, if it was not stillborn and had lived and subsequently died, either by natural causes or by homicide. In 1681, the German physician Schreger used this test, forensically, and secured the acquittal of a girl who had been accused of murdering her illegitimate child.[7] Germany established the first known medico-legal clinic in Vienna in about 1830 and the second one in Berlin in 1833. France established its first clinic in 1840. France has also provided, since 1803, that judges appoint medical experts who must be graduates in medicine and must have attended a course and have passed an examination in legal medicine. France established its first professional Chair in Legal Medicine in 1794. Great Britain, in 1803, established its Chair of Forensic Medicine at the University of Edinburgh. By 1876, there were chairs in legal medicine in all of its medical schools.

46. In the fifth century, the Germanic and Slavic peoples took over Western Europe and they instituted a system of indemnity to replace the system of personal vendetta. The person responsible for the injury would pay an amount to the injured party or, in the case of death, to his relative. Since the payment varied with the severity of the wound, it was important to classify the wounds in the code and to be able to call on experts to testify as to the damages. In the Visigothic and Bavarian Codes, mention has been made of injury to pregnant women, to the child in utero, poisoning of prisoners, and penalties of negligent doctors if the patient died. Charlemagne attempted to give some unity to the laws of the empire. There was recognition of the necessity of adducing all relevant evidence in judicial cases. There were articles discussing the direct intervention of physicians and instructions to judges to seek all relevant medical evidence, especially in cases involving questions

5. S.E. Chaille, *Origin and Progress of Medical Jurisprudence*, 40 J Crim L. Criminol 397–402 (1949).
6. S.S. Sanbar, *Legal Medicine: Historical Roots and Current Status*, in *Legal Medicine* 3–11 (S.S. Sander ed., CV Mosby 6th ed. 2004).
7. J.R. Oliver, *Legal Medicine in Europe and America*. 18 Am. Bar Assoc. J. 405–411 (1932).

of wounds, infanticide, suicide, rape, bestiality, and divorce on the grounds of impotence. The assizes of Jerusalem, in 1100, provided for the courts to order medical examinations. In the case of murder, the corpse had to be examined and a report made as to what had been found, the location of the injuries, and the likely mechanism that had caused them.[8]

47. In Italy, in 1249, Hugo de Lucca took his oath as a medico-legal expert. Medical reports show that autopsies were performed to determine the cause of death. Pope Innocent III, in 1209, provided for appointment of doctors to the courts for the determination of wounds. In Germany, in 1507, a penal code was established calling for proof of cause in all violent deaths. It allowed for the opening of bodies and represented progress toward the practice of medico-legal autopsies and the development of legal medicine as a separate professional discipline. It became a subject for special instruction in the seventeenth century. By the start of the eighteenth century, designated chairs in legal medicine were created in German universities.

48. The first book on legal medicine written in English was authored by Samuel Farr in 1788 and was entitled "Elements of Medical Jurisprudence," containing a description of findings in the human body that were required for judgment by coroners and courts of law in cases of divorce, rape, murder, etc. The first British teacher of legal medicine was Andrew Duncan, a professor of physiology, who gave lectures on legal medicine and public health, beginning in 1789. His son, "Andrew Duncan, the younger," became the first professor on this subject at the University of Edinburgh, the seat of the first Chair in Legal Medicine in the English-speaking world. Alfred Taylor (1806–1880), Professor of Medical Jurisprudence at Guy's Hospital Medical School, wrote Principles and Practice of Medical Jurisprudence. The British Association in Forensic Medicine was established in 1950, and later the British Academy of Forensic Sciences was created in 1960.

VI. Developments in America

49. For medical students and physicians, medical jurisprudence assumed importance in US schools of medicine throughout most of the 1800s. During the course of the nineteenth century, the institutions, laws, and judicial decisions in America reflected the influence of sound medico-legal principles, especially those pertaining to mental disease and criminal lunacy. The first lecturer on legal medicine was Dr. J. S. Stringham, giving lectures in New York beginning at around 1804. In 1813, the first Chair of Medical Jurisprudence was established by the College of Physicians and Surgeons of New York City. In 1815, the College of Physicians and Surgeons of the Western District of New York appointed Dr. T. R. Beck as the Professor

8. S.S> Sanbar SS, *Legal Medicine: Historical Roots and Current Status*, in *Legal Medicine* 3–1 (S.S. *Sander* ed., CV Mosby 6th ed. 2004).

of the Institutes of Medicine and Lecturer on Medical Jurisprudence. In the same year, the Medical Department of Harvard University appointed Dr. Walter Channing as the Professor of Midwifery.

50. Dr. Benjamin Rush is credited with emphasizing the significance of the relationship between law and medicine in the early 1800s. As America's first *surgeon general* and a signatory of the Declaration of Independence, Rush established American legal medicine with his published lecture "On the Study of Medical Jurisprudence," which he delivered to medical students at the University of Pennsylvania in Philadelphia in 1811. The lecture dealt with homicide, mental disease, and capital punishment.[9]

51. These developments inspired the teaching of medical jurisprudence in other American medical schools. Among the early teachers were Dr. Charles Caldwell in Philadelphia and Dr. Walter Channing at Harvard. In 1819, Dr. Cooper, a legal officer of distinction and president of the College of South Carolina, published "Tracts on Medical Jurisprudence." This volume contained almost all the available literature written in English on legal medicine.[10] In 1815 Dr. T. Romeyn Beck was appointed lecturer of medical jurisprudence at Western Medical College in New York State. In 1823, Beck published the Elements of Medical Jurisprudence, which defined the field of legal medicine for about half a century of American medical practice. Beck's two volumes included impressive topics, such as rape, impotence and sterility, pregnancy and delivery, infanticide and abortion, legitimacy, presumption of survivorship, identity, mental alienation, wounds, poisons, persons found dead, and feigned and disqualifying diseases.

52. In 1838, Isaac Ray published "A Treatise on Medical Jurisprudence of Insanity."[11] In 1855, the year that Beck died, Francis Wharton, an attorney, and Dr. Moreton Stille, a physician, collaborated to publish "A Treatise on Medical Jurisprudence." In 1860, Dr. John J. Elwell, a physician and an attorney, published a book entitled "A Medico-Legal Treatise on Malpractice, Medical Evidence, and Insanity Comprising the Elements of Medical Jurisprudence," highlighting the issue of malpractice in the medical jurisprudence literature. Elwell's book presented excerpts from contemporary cases for the purpose of teaching physicians what to expect from malpractice litigation. Dr. John Odronaux, also a physician and an attorney, published Jurisprudence of Medicine in 1867 and Judicial Aspects of Insanity in 1878. In 1894, Randolph A. Witthaus and Tracy C. Becker published Medical Jurisprudence, Forensic Medicine and Toxicology.

53. After the Civil War, however, things changed and legal medicine became temporarily dormant. The teaching of medical jurisprudence deteriorated and in some medical colleges the course dropped out altogether. In others, it was attached

9. B. Rush, *Introductory Lectures Upon the Institutes and Practices of Medicine* 363 (Bradford and Innskeep 1811).
10. T. Cooper, *Tracts on Medical Jurisprudence* (James Webster 1819).
11. I. Ray, *A Treatise on the Medical Jurisprudence of Insanity* (Little Brown Company 1860).

to some other subjects. In the early twentieth century, the teaching of medical jurisprudence was relegated to a position of an occasional subject taught outside the mainstream. The situation changed and by the middle of the twentieth century, legal medicine underwent a renaissance. The American College of Legal Medicine (ACLM) and the Law-Medicine Institute at Boston University were established.

54. In 1867, the Medico-Legal Society was organized in New York. It was the first society in the world to be organized for the purpose of promoting the principles that an attorney could not be fully equipped for the prosecution or the defense of an individual indicted for homicide without knowledge of anatomy and pathology and that no physician or surgeon could be a satisfactory expert witness without some knowledge of the law. Harvard University established a separate professorship in legal medicine in 1877.

Chapter 3. Sources of International Medical Law

55. There are various sources of international medical law and these are generally the same as the sources of international law but specific to the medical field.

Under Article 8(1) of the Statute of International Court of Justice (ICJ), for resolving disputes among nations the court is directed to apply the following:

(i) International treaties (These are described as International conventions, whether general or particular, establishing rules expressly recognized by the contesting States).
(ii) International custom, as evidence of a general practice accepted as law.
(iii) The general principles of law recognized by civilized nations.
(iv) Judicial decisions and teaching of the most highly qualified publicists of the various countries as subsidiary means for the determination of rule of law.

§1. Conventions and Treaties

56. International conventions and treaties are one of the important sources of international medical law. Treaties are known by many names, like conventions, agreements, pacts, general acts, charters, and covenants. These signify written instruments in which the participants agree to be bound by the negotiated terms. Some agreements are governed by the municipal law (e.g., commercial accords between states and international enterprises). Informal, nonbinding political statements or declarations are excluded from the category of treaties. Treaties may be bilateral or multilateral, and multilateral treaties are more likely to have international significance. A number of treaties, such as the Geneva Conventions (1949) and the Law of the Sea treaty (1982), have more than 150 parties to them, reflecting both their importance and the evolution of the treaty as a method of general legislation in international law. Other significant treaties include the Convention on the Prevention and Punishment of the Crime of Genocide (1948), the Vienna Convention on Diplomatic Relations (1961), the Antarctic Treaty (1959), and the Rome Statute establishing the International Criminal Court (ICC) (1998). Some treaties create international organizations and provide their constitutions (e.g., the UN Charter of 1945).

I. Treaty Provisions Forming Basis of Custom

57. Treaty provisions may form the basis of an international custom in certain circumstances, provided that the provision in question is capable of such generalization or is "of a fundamentally norm-creating character," as the ICJ termed the process in *North Sea Continental Shelf* (1969). A treaty is based on the consent of the parties to it, is binding, and must be executed in good faith. The concept known by the Latin formula *pacta sunt servanda* ("agreements must be kept") is the oldest principle of international law. Without such a rule, no international agreement would be binding or enforceable. There is no prescribed form or procedure for making or concluding treaties. They may be drafted between heads of state or between government departments. The most crucial element in the conclusion of a treaty is the signaling of the state's consent, which may be done by signature, an exchange of instruments, ratification, or accession. Ratification is the usual method of declaring consent—unless the agreement is a low-level one, in which case a signature is usually sufficient. Ratification procedures vary, depending on the country's constitutional structure.

II. Reservations in Treaties

58. A treaty may allow signatories to opt out of a particular provision, a tactic that enables countries that accept the basic principles of a treaty to become a party to it even though they may have concerns about peripheral issues. These concerns are referred to as "reservations," which are distinguished from interpretative declarations, which have no binding effect. States may make reservations to a treaty where the treaty does not prevent doing so, provided that the reservation is not incompatible with the treaty's object and purpose. Other states may accept or object to such reservations. In the former case, the treaty as modified by the terms of the reservations comes into force between the states concerned. In the latter case, the treaty comes into force between the states concerned except for the provisions to which the reservations relate and to the extent of the reservations. An obvious defect of this system is that each government determines whether the reservations are permissible, and there can be disagreement regarding the legal consequences if a reservation is deemed impermissible.

59. In cases where the treaty is also the constitutional document of an international organization, a more programmatic or purpose-oriented approach is used in order to assist the organization in coping with change. A purpose-oriented approach also has been deemed appropriate for what has been described as "living instruments," such as human rights treaties that establish an implementation system. In the case of the European Convention on Human Rights of 1950, this approach has allowed the criminalization of homosexuality to be regarded as a violation of human rights in the contemporary period despite the fact that it was the norm when the treaty was signed.

III. Kinds of Treaties

60. Treaties are of two kinds, namely law-making treaties and treaty contracts.

A. *Law-Making Treaties*

61. Law-making treaties lay down general rules which are binding on the majority of the states. These are multilateral treaties, but every multilateral treaty is not necessarily a law-making treaty. According to *Briefly*, "Law-making treaties are those which a large number of States have concluded for the purpose either of declaring their understanding of what the law is on a particular subject, or of laying down a new general rule for future conduct, or of creating some international situation." Since the middle of the nineteenth century there has been an astonishing development of law-making treaties. As the customary rules of international law proved inadequate to meet the demands of industrial and economic changes, therefore, after the World Wars a large number of treaties were concluded relating to and dealing with weights and measures, the protection of submarine cables, the suppression of slave trade, etc.

B. Treaty Contracts

62. Treaty contracts are not directly a source of international medical law. Such treaties are generally bilateral treaties applicable between the signatories. But, sometimes, they also lead to the formation of international law through the operation of the principles governing the development of customary rules in the following circumstances:

(i) A series or a recurrence of treaties laying down a similar rule may produce a principle of customary international law. Such treaties are thus a step in the process whereby a rule of international custom emerges.
(ii) It may happen with a treaty originally concluded between a limited number of parties and it may make a rule to be generalized by subsequent independent acceptance or imitation. Instances of this nature are "free-ships, free goods." This rule is now generalized but it was concluded for the first time in 1650 between Spain and the United Provinces.
(iii) A treaty may be of considerable evidentiary value as to the existence of a rule crystallized into law by an independent process of development.

IV. Evolution of International Law on Drugs and Narcotic Substances

63. The League of Nations adopted several drug control treaties prior to World War II specifying uniform controls on addictive drugs such as cocaine, opium, and its derivatives. However, the list of substances to be controlled was fixed in the treaties' text; consequently, the conventions had to be periodically amended or superseded by new treaties in order to keep up with advances in chemistry. The work of consolidating the existing international drug control treaties into one instrument began in 1948, but it was 1961 before an acceptable third draft was ready. In the same year, the UN Economic and Social Council (ECOSOC) convened a plenipotentiary conference of seventy-three nations for the adoption of a single convention on narcotic drugs. That meeting was known as the United Nations Conference on Narcotic Drugs. These developments have resulted in the evolution of international law on drugs and narcotic substances.

§2. Customary Law

64. The customs followed by the international community have given rise to certain rules making it the oldest source of international law. These customary laws had generally evolved after a long historical process culminating in their recognition by the international community. The importance of custom lies in the fact where there is no permanent legislative machinery to enact international law, custom plays an important part in laying down the rules of international law. The customary rules have evolved out of a long and continued practice and they have, thus, become so mature and perfect that states do not hesitate in accepting the custom as a source of law. It was held in *Paquete Habana* hat customary rules of international law grant immunity to small fishing vessels from belligerent action in times of war. In the *Lotus* case the court again resorted to the customary rules and held that there was no customary rule conferring exclusive jurisdiction in maritime collision cases on the contrary of the ship's flag as regards all incidents on the ship.

I. ICJ Statute

65. The ICJ's statute refers to "international custom, as evidence of a general practice accepted as law," as a second source of international law. Custom, to become a law, involves two fundamental elements: the actual practice of states and the acceptance by states of that practice as law. The actual practice of states covers various elements, including the duration, consistency, repetition, and generality of a particular kind of behavior by the states. All such elements are relevant in determining whether a practice may form the basis of a binding international custom.

66. The ICJ has required that practices amount to a "constant and uniform usage" or be "extensive and virtually uniform" to be considered binding. Although all states may contribute to the development of a new or modified custom, they are not all equal in the process. The major states generally possess a greater significance in the establishment of customs. For example, during the 1960s, the US and the USSR played a crucial role in the development of customs relating to space law than did the states that had little or no practice in this area. After a practice has been established, a second element converts a mere usage into a binding custom—the practice must be accepted as *opinio juris sive necessitatis* (Latin: "opinion that an act is necessary by rule of law"). In *North Sea Continental Shelf*, the ICJ stated that the practice in question must have "occurred in such a way as to show a general recognition that a rule of law or legal obligation is involved."

67. Once a practice becomes a custom, all states in the international community are bound by it whether or not individual states have expressly consented—except in cases where a state has objected from the start of the custom, a stringent test to demonstrate. A particular practice may be restricted to a specified group of states (e.g., the Latin American States) or even to two states, in which cases the standard for acceptance as a custom is generally high. Customs can develop from a generalizable treaty provision, and a binding customary rule and a multilateral treaty provision on the same subject matter may exist at the same time.

§3. General Principles of Law

68. Another source of international law identified by the ICJ's statute is "the general principles of law recognized by civilized nations." These principles provide a mechanism to address international issues not already subject either to treaty provisions or to binding customary rules. Such general principles may arise either through municipal law or through international law, and many are, in fact, procedural or evidential principles or those that deal with the machinery of the judicial process; for example, the principle, established in Chorzow Factory (1927–1928), that the breach of an engagement involves an obligation to make reparation. Accordingly, in the *Chorzow Factory* case, Poland was obliged to pay compensation to Germany for the illegal expropriation of a factory.

69. The ICJ has been authorized to apply principles of law recognized by civilized states. These general principles of law are equity, natural justice, and good conscience. General principles also include the principles of private law administered in national courts. In the *Mavromattes Palestine Concessions* case, the court referred to the general principle of subjugating, and in the case of the diversion of water from the Meuse, the court held that it might apply Anglo-American equitable doctrines as being general principles. In order to deal with certain questions relating to the mandates and trusteeship systems, Judge MacNair applied the general private law doctrine of trusts. In the *Mazina and Naulila* case the arbitrators held that in the absence of the express rules of international law, it was their duty to apply the principles of equity to fill the gap left by the express principles of international law.

§4. Decisions of International and Other Courts and Tribunals

70. The decisions of international and domestic courts and tribunals may sometime mature and can be taken into consideration as subsidiary sources of international medical law. The state judicial decision and decisions of international arbitral tribunals may be treated as weighty precedents or even as binding authorities.

I. Evolution of Medical Law Through Court Decisions

71. Article 38(1) of the ICJ's statute also recognizes judicial decisions and scholarly writings as subsidiary means for the determination of the law. Both municipal and international judicial decisions can serve to establish new principles and rules. In municipal cases, international legal rules can develop through their consistent application by the courts of a number of states. A clearer method of evolution of international law is constituted by the international judicial decisions of bodies, such as the ICJ at The Hague, the UN International Tribunal for the Law of the Sea at Hamburg in Germany, and international arbitral tribunals. The following state court decisions on medical negligence and duty of care have immensely helped in the development of international medical law.

A. *Standard of Care*

72. The concept of "the standard of care" is often discussed among physicians, and yet the legal definition of this term is frequently not understood. Emergency physicians are on the front lines of medicine and are involved in medical malpractice cases. Thus, it is important to know how the legal system defines the standard of care and to what standards we, as physicians, are being held.

Negligence, in general, is legally defined as "the standard of conduct to which one must conform … [and] is that of a reasonable man under like circumstances." In law, medical malpractice is considered a specific area within the general domain of negligence. Prior to several important cases in the 1900s, the standard of care was defined by the legal concept of "custom." As quoted in the 1934 case of *Garthe v. Ruppert*, when "certain dangers have been removed by a customary way of doing things safely, this custom may be proved to show that [the one charged with the dereliction] has fallen below the required standard."[12] Put another way, if others in the business are commonly practicing a certain way that eliminates hazards, then this practice can be used to define the standard of care. A jury still needed to decide, however, whether this "custom" was reasonable and whether the deviation from this "custom" was so unreasonable as to cause harm.

73. Two cases changed the legal definition of the standard of care as it is applied in medical malpractice law. The case of *The T.J. Hooper* in 1932 helped to alter how the legal profession thought about custom and the standard of care. In this case, the owner of the tugboat T.J. Hooper was sued for the value of two barges. The tugboat had been caught in a storm and the two barges it was transporting sunk. The owners of the barges charged that the T.J. Hooper was unsafe for duty at sea as it did not have a radio receiver to review important storm warnings. In addition, they charged that it was "customary" for tugboats to have this radio receiver. They claimed that if the T.J. Hooper had a radio, they could have been warned of the storm and avoided it. In reviewing the case during appeal, Justice Learned Hand ruled in favor of the barge owners; however, he did not do so based on custom. He indicated that it was not, in fact, customary for tugboats to be outfitted with the receivers but that, since the practice was reasonable, the owners of the T.J. Hooper could be held liable for damages. He stated, "In most cases reasonable prudence is in fact common prudence; but strictly it is never its measure; a whole calling may have unduly lagged in the adoption of new and available devices. It never may set its own tests, however persuasive be its usages. Courts must, in the end, say what is required; there are precautions so imperative that even their universal disregard will not excuse

---

12. *Garthe v. Ruppert*, 264 N.Y. 290, 296, 190 N.E. 6430.

their omission."[13] In other words, if there is a practice that is reasonable but not universally "customary" it may still be used as a measure of the standard of care.

74. The case of *The T.J. Hooper* set the stage for an important development in medical malpractice that occurred in 1974. In *Helling v. Carey*, the plaintiff (Helling) sued her ophthalmologist (Carey) for the loss of her eyesight due to glaucoma. The defendant won both during the original trial and the appeal, but when the case made it to the Supreme Court of Washington State the verdict was overturned in favor of the plaintiff. During the initial trials, the expert witnesses indicated that as the patient was under the age of 40 and the incidence of glaucoma in this group was only 1 in 25,000, it was not the standard to test patients under 40 with tonometry. The Supreme Court decided, however, that the test was inexpensive and harmless and should have been offered to the patient. Justice Hand's decision in *The T.J. Hooper* case was quoted in the decision.[14]

75. *Helling v. Carey* set a bad precedent for medical malpractice cases. The court essentially ruled that even though the customary practice at the time was followed, the physician was still liable. They cited the case of *The T.J. Hooper* and also referenced a decision by Justice Oliver Wendell Holmes in 1903 that stated: "what usually is done may be evidence of what ought to be done, but what ought to be done is fixed by a standard of reasonable prudence, whether it usually is complied with or not."[15] These two cases legally established that while great weight is given to customary practices with regard to the standard of care, custom is not the definitive factor in determining negligence. In essence, the two cases suggest that what is commonly done (i.e., custom) may not be enough and that there are some considerations that may not be standard but are still reasonable for the physician to perform. Unfortunately, for the physician, these cases suggest that it is up to the legal profession and the jury, and not the medical profession, to decide what is "reasonable" and what is not.

76. The ruling in *Helling v. Carey* prompted state legislatures to pass statutes that defined the standard of care in their jurisdiction. The State of Washington was the first to pass this type of legislation when they stated that the standard of care is not met when "the defendant or defendants [fail] to exercise that degree of skill, care and learning possessed by other persons in the same profession … ."[16]

B. Perfection in Practice

77. In recent cases there appears an effort to ensure that jurors understand that the standard of care does not mean perfection in practice. While old cases in law tend to be more powerful as they have stood the test of time, these more recent cases

13. *The T.J. Hooper*, 60 F:2d 737 (2d Cir.), cert. denied, 287 U.S. 662 (1932).
14. *Helling v. Carey*, 83 Wash. 2d 514, 519 P.2d 981 (1974).
15. *Texas & P. Ry. v. Behymer*, 189 U.S. 468, 470, 47 L. Ed. 905, 23 S. Ct. 622 (1903).
16. Revised Code of Washington. Section 4.24.290.

show a trend toward keeping jury expectations realistic. In the 1985 case of *Hall v. Hilbun*, a patient (Mrs. Hall) presented to her physician for abdominal pain. Dr. Hilbun, a general surgeon, was consulted and operated on the patient for a small bowel obstruction. He observed the patient in the recovery room and left for the night. Details from the case indicate that there were abnormal vital signs and Mrs. Hall had pain throughout the night, but Dr. Hilbun was not notified. She died of respiratory failure in the morning. During the night, Dr. Hilbun had been notified about another patient but he did not checkup on Mrs. Hall. In addition, his orders never indicated what things should be called for by the nursing staff. Initially, he won the case because the testimony of two witnesses that discussed the national standard of care for a surgeon was excluded. On appeal, however, Dr. Hilbun was found liable as their testimony was allowed. Even though the physician lost in this case, the court's discussion was very important in defining the standard of care in the modern era. Chief Justice C.J. Robertson stated:

> Medical malpractice is a legal fault by a physician or surgeon. It arises from the failure of a physician to provide the quality of care required by law. When a physician undertakes to treat a patient, he takes on an obligation enforceable at law to use minimally sound medical judgment and render minimally competent care in the course of services he provides. A physician does not guarantee recovery … A competent physician is not liable per se for a mere error of judgment, mistaken diagnosis or the occurrence of an undesirable result.[17]

78. In this case, Dr. Hilbun did not provide "minimally competent care," but the good news from a physician's standpoint is that the law only requires "minimal competence." The care does not even have to be "average," which makes sense; otherwise, 50% of all medical care would be malpractice by definition.

79. In a similar case, *McCourt v. Abernathy*, the physicians again lost due to their substandard care. Mrs. McCourt presented for several complaints over the course of three days but was found to have an infection on her finger from a pin stick while working with manure. Over the course of these three days, she was seen by Dr. Abernathy and his partner Dr. Clyde, who simply cleaned the wound. When she became increasingly ill, they gave her oral antibiotics, but she subsequently became septic. An internist who was consulted diagnosed septicemia and the patient died despite aggressive care. Again, the physicians acted below the standard of care, but the trial judge gave an important set of instructions to the jury. He stated:

> The mere fact that the plaintiff's expert may use a different approach is not considered a deviation from the recognized standard of medical care. Nor is the standard violated because the expert disagrees with a defendant as to what is the best or better approach in treating a patient. Medicine is an inexact science,

17. *Hall v. Hilbun*, 466 So. 2d 856 (Miss. 1985).

> and generally qualified physicians may differ as to what constitutes a preferable course of treatment. Such differences due to preference ... do not amount to malpractice.
>
> I further charge you that the degree of skill and care that a physician must use in diagnosing a condition is that which would be exercised by competent practitioners in the defendant doctors' field of medicine ... .
>
> Negligence may not be inferred from a bad result. Our law says that a physician is not an insurer of health, and a physician is not required to guarantee results. He undertakes only to meet the standard of skill possessed generally by others practicing in his field under similar circumstances.[18]

80. The judge reinforced that the care provided by a physician be minimally competent may differ from the care of other physicians and that a bad outcome does not mean that the standard of care was not met.

81. A final case that helped define the modern definition of the standard of care is *Johnston v. St. Francis Medical Center.*[19] In this case, a 79-year-old male, who presented with abdominal complaints, was evaluated with radiographs and labs, but his examination was equivocal. Two physicians examined him during the course of the day and found him to be in mild distress. Additional studies to include computed tomography and ultrasound were ordered, but the patient became hypotensive and was sent to the intensive care unit (ICU). The ICU physician thought he might have an aortic aneurysm, which was confirmed during laparotomy. The patient died in the operating room. The plaintiffs argued that the physicians should have diagnosed the aneurysm earlier. All of the experts, except one, in the case indicated this was a difficult diagnosis. The court ruled in favor of the physicians. More importantly, however, the court made it clear that while the aneurysm was obvious on radiograph and labs once the diagnosis was made, hindsight cannot be used for evaluating the conduct and judgment of the physician. In this case the diagnosis of the aneurysm was "possible" but difficult enough that missing the diagnosis did not amount to not providing the standard of care. This is in sharp contrast to the prior case of *Helling v. Carey*.

82. The concept of the standard of care has evolved over the years and will continue to change as legal theory in this area develops. Hopefully, this will allow for increased certainty and clarity, which is the stated goal of all laws. The bad news is that there are several important cases where the suggestion is that even if a practice is not the standard, if it is reasonable, a physician can be found culpable for not pursuing that course of action. However, in more recent cases the courts have frequently upheld that the standard of care is what a minimally competent physician in the same field would do in the same situation, with the same resources. Thus court cases have also contributed to the development of international medical law.

---

18. *McCourt v. Abernathy*, 457 S.E.2d 603 (S.C. 1995).
19. *Johnston v. St. Francis Medical Center, Inc.*, No. 3 5, 236-CA, Oct. 31, 2001.

§5. Other Sources

83. International medical law can arise indirectly through other mechanisms. UN General Assembly resolutions, for example, are not binding—except with respect to certain organizational procedures—but they can be extremely influential. Resolutions may assist in the creation of new customary rules, both in terms of state practice and in the process of establishing a custom by demonstrating the acceptance by states of the practice "as law" (the *opinio juris*). For this to occur, a resolution must contain generalizable provisions and attract substantial support from countries with diverse ideological, cultural, and political perspectives. Examples of such resolutions include the Declaration on the Granting of Independence to Colonial Countries and Peoples (1960), the Declaration on the Legal Principles Governing Activities of States in the Exploration and Use of Outer Space (1963), and the Declaration on Principles of International Law Concerning Friendly Relations and Co-operation among States (1970).

84. Unilateral actions by a state may give rise to legal obligations when it is clear that the state intends to be bound by the obligation and when its intention is publicly announced. An example of such a case was France's decision to stop atmospheric nuclear testing during litigation at the ICJ between it and Australia and New Zealand (1974) concerning the legality of such testing. Unilateral statements may also constitute evidence of a state's views on a particular issue. Even when an instrument or document does not entail a legal obligation, it may be influential within the international community. The Helsinki Accord (1975), which attempted to reduce tensions between the USSR and the US during the Cold War, was expressly not binding but had immense political effects. In certain areas, such as environmental law and economic law, a range of recommendations, guidelines, codes of practice, and standards may produce what is termed "soft law"—i.e., an instrument that has no strict legal value but constitutes an important statement.

§6. Hierarchies of Sources and Norms

85. General principles of international law are complementary to treaty law and custom. Sources that are of more recent origin are generally accepted as more authoritative and specific rules take precedence over general rules. *Jus cogens* (Latin: "compelling law") rules are peremptory norms that cannot be deviated from by states; they possess a higher status than *jus dispositivum* (Latin: "law subject to the dispensation of the parties"), or normal international rules, and can be altered only by subsequent norms of the same status. Rules in the former category include the prohibitions against genocide, slavery, and piracy and the outlawing of aggression. Other examples of *jus cogens* rules are more controversial. The Vienna Convention on the Law of Treaties provides (Article 53) that a treaty will be void if, at the time of its conclusion, it conflicts with a peremptory norm of general international law. Further, the wrongfulness of a state action is precluded if the act is required by a peremptory norm of general international law. For a *jus cogens* norm to be created, the principle must first be established as a rule of international law and then recognized by the international community as a peremptory rule of law from which no derogation is permitted.

86. International law also has established a category of *erga omnes* (Latin: "toward all") obligations which apply to all states. Whereas in ordinary obligations the defaulting state bears responsibility toward particular, interested states (e.g., other parties to the treaty that has been breached), in the breach of *erga omnes* obligations, all states have an interest and may take appropriate actions in response.

Part II. Role of International Institutions and Bodies

Chapter 1. International Medical Institutions and Bodies

§1. World Health Organization

87. The World Health Organization (WHO) is a specialized agency of the UN established in 1948 to further international cooperation for improved public health conditions. It inherited specific tasks relating to epidemic control, quarantine measures, and drug standardization from the Health Organization of the League of Nations (set up in 1923) and the International Office of Public Health at Paris (established in 1907); the WHO was given a broad mandate under its constitution to promote the attainment of "the highest possible level of health" by all people. Each year the WHO celebrates its date of establishment, April 7, 1948, as World Health Day. The mandate of WHO includes working for universal health care, monitoring public health risks, coordinating responses to health emergencies, and promoting human health and wellbeing. It provides technical assistance to countries, sets international health standards and guidelines, and collects data on global health issues through the World Health Surveys.

WHO has played an important role in eradication of smallpox, polio, and the development of a vaccine for Ebola. Its current priorities include communicable diseases, particularly HIV/AIDS, Ebola, COVID-19, malaria and tuberculosis; non-communicable diseases such as heart disease and cancer; healthy diet, nutrition, and food security; occupational health; and substance abuse.

I. World Health Assembly

88. With its administrative headquarters in Geneva, governance of the WHO operates through the World Health Assembly (WHA), which meets annually as the general policymaking body, and through an Executive Board of health specialists elected for three-year terms by the assembly. The WHO Secretariat, which carries out routine operations and helps implement strategies, consists of experts, staff, and field workers who have appointments at the central headquarters or at one of the six regional WHO offices or other offices located in countries around the world. The organization is led by a director general nominated by the Executive Board and appointed by the WHA. The director general is supported by a deputy director general and multiple assistant directors general, each of whom specializes in a specific area within the WHO framework, such as family, women's, and children's health or health systems and innovation. The organization is financed primarily from annual contributions made by member governments on the basis of their relative ability to pay. In addition, after 1951 the WHO was allocated substantial resources from the Expanded Program of Technical Assistance of the UN. WHA is part of the United Nations Sustainable Development Group. It is composed of representatives from all the 194 Member States and serves as the agency's supreme decision-making body. It also elects and advises an executive board made up of 34 health specialists.

§2. World Medical Association

89. The World Medical Association (WMA) is an idea born in the House of the British Medical Association in 1945, officially started in Paris in 1947, and now it has become the recognized authority to speak for the doctors in international affairs. The purpose of the WMA is to serve humanity by endeavoring to achieve the highest international standards in "Medical Education, Medical Science, Medical Art and Medical Ethics, and Health Care" for all people in the world. As an organization promoting the highest possible standards of medical ethics, the WMA provides ethical guidance to physicians through its "Declarations, Resolutions and Statements." These are far-reaching, including an International Code of Medical Ethics, the rights of patients, research on human subjects, care of the sick and wounded in times of armed conflict, torture of prisoners, the use and abuse of drugs, family *planning*, and pollution. The Declaration of Helsinki is the WMA's best-known policy statement. The WMA promotes health-related human rights for all people around the globe. Physicians play a key role in providing the best quality care to patients without discrimination and promoting health-related human rights worldwide. But physicians, as well as patients, can also be victims of human rights abuses. The WMA intervenes to support them and denounce such violations. The main areas of service of the WMA are:

(i) Health-related human rights.
(ii) Medical education—helping physicians to continuously improve their knowledge and skills.
(iii) Human resources planning for health care services.
(iv) Patient safety.
(v) Public health policy and projects.
(vi) Democracy building for new medical associations.
(vii) Leadership and career development.
(viii) Advocacy for physicians and patients' rights.
(ix) Occupational health and safety.

90. WMA takes up the issues on behalf of health personnel. For example, it condemned violence against health personnel during the COVID-19 pandemic, which witnessed a dramatic increase in cases of violence against medical personnel worldwide. As the outbreak continued to spread, a rise in attacks against physicians and nurses was reported by the members of WMA, other health organizations and individual physicians. In some countries, physicians became victims of reprisals for denouncing bad and dangerous working conditions, the lack of medical equipment, or for criticizing their governments' pandemic responses. Violence included threats, insults, stigmatization by communities and the state as well.

I. The WMA and Ethical Issues

91. Since its establishment, a central objective of the WMA has been to establish and promote the highest possible standards of ethical behavior and care by physicians. In pursuit of this goal, the WMA has adopted global policy statements on a range of ethical issues related to medical professionalism, patient care, research on human subjects, and public health. The WMA Council and its standing committees regularly review and update existing policies and continually develop new policies on emerging ethical issues.

92. The WMA serves as a clearinghouse of ethics information resources for its members. To achieve this goal, the WMA cooperates with academic institutions, global organizations, and individual experts in the field of medical ethics. The WMA has adopted numerous policies that are recognized internationally as the global ethical standard for the topics they address.

§3. Physicians for Human Rights

93. Physicians for Human Rights (PHRs) was founded in 1986 on the idea that health professionals, with their specialized skills, ethical duties, and credible voices, are uniquely positioned to investigate the health consequences of human rights violations and work toward stopping them. PHR mobilizes health professionals to advance health, dignity, and justice and promotes the right to health for all. It is headquartered in Cambridge, Massachusetts, and it maintains an office in Washington, DC. PHR is a nonprofit, nonsectarian organization funded through private foundations and by individual donors. PHR is a 1997 co-recipient of the Nobel Peace Prize. It emphasizes poor and marginalized populations, evidence-based approaches, health system strengthening, and a right to health.

I. Main Activities

94. PHR's Global Health Action Campaign promotes the "right to health" as the framework governments use to implement health programs to meet their obligations to their people. The campaign addresses global health issues, such as: health workforce and systems, Human Immunodeficiency Virus (HIV)/AIDS, women's health, and harm reduction. PHR emphasizes equity and participation of those who best understand their own needs. It has a strong tradition of mobilizing health workers for research, education, and advocacy. There are many groups that focus on gender health inequalities in Africa, but few focus on mobilizing and training health professionals to use their knowledge for policy change.

95. PHR applies the skills, knowledge, and ethical commitments of health professionals to a wide range of issues. Over the past seven years, PHR's Health Action AIDS campaign has:

(i) built a network of nearly 8,000 health care professionals and students to influence international policymakers;
(ii) advanced policies to address the global workforce crisis;
(iii) partnered with health professionals in Kenya, Uganda, and Rwanda to expand local advocacy capacity; and
(iv) raised attention on the need to strengthen health systems.

96. In the fight against COVID-19, PHR is supporting doctors, nurses, public health specialists, and others on the front lines of this pandemic. PHR and its global network of health professionals are working to strengthen the world's response to COVID-19 and to better prepare for what lies ahead. It has joined the call to realize equitable vaccine allocation and distribution that prioritize at-risk populations and communities that have disproportionately suffered high rates of infection and death and that face high barriers to vaccine access. In addition to prioritizing health care professionals and essential workers around the world, it is imperative that global cooperation allows vaccines to effectively reach people in conflict zones, as well as refugees and displaced populations. PHR advocates for vaccines to be provided to all marginalized groups, including people in immigration, criminal, or any other form of detention, and all migrants, such as refugees, asylum seekers, and undocumented immigrants. PHR has joined the Campaign for a People's Vaccine, a movement demanding that vaccines be free, fair, and accessible.

§4. International Rehabilitation Council for Torture Victims (IRCT)

97. The IRCT is a private, nonpartisan, nonprofit, nongovernmental organization (NGO) being governed by democratic structures. It evolved as a response to the pervasive use of torture around the world and helped the hundreds of thousands of torture victims whose pain and suffering are the responsibility of the perpetrating states. The notion of torture victims' right to construct or reconstruct their autonomy led to the development of a health-based approach to torture rehabilitation. Health professionals in different parts of the world embraced this approach, which resulted in the creation of medical groups and centers dedicated to the treatment of torture victims. One such place was Copenhagen where, in 1974, Inge Genefke and three fellow doctors responded to a call by Amnesty International to help diagnose torture victims and produce forensic evidence that could help hold torturers to account in a court of law. In 1980, Dr. Genefke and her colleagues were given permission to admit torture victims to the University Hospital in Copenhagen, Denmark and, in

1981, she became one of the founders of the Rehabilitation and Research Centre for Torture Victims. Around the same time other rehabilitation centers were created across the world and, soon, there was the foundation of a global network. The IRCT was established in 1985 to articulate the voice and aspirations of this movement and also to support the foundation and financing of new centers. Since then, it has grown to become an organization of more than 160 member centers in over 76 countries.

98. As a network of more than 160 torture rehabilitation centers spread over 76 countries, the IRCT is the world's largest membership-based civil society organization specializing in the field of torture rehabilitation. The work of the IRCT provides context to health-based rehabilitation within all pillars of the global fight against torture: prevention, accountability, and reparation. This movement is effective in fighting torture across the globe. The core strength of the movement stems from a triad of values, namely Solidarity, Equality and Democracy.

99. IRCT supports torture victims to rebuild their lives through health-based rehabilitation services by helping them to overcome the physical, psychological and social consequences of torture. More than 50,000 torture survivors are supported in IRCT member centers each year. The impact of rehabilitation efforts on society is far-reaching. Torture is a political act, and the rehabilitation of torture survivors is also considered political. Rehabilitation centers play a key role in promoting democracy, co-existence, and respect for human rights. They provide support and act as a symbol of hope to the victims over the man-made terror of torture. According to IRCT, the rehabilitation should be:

(i) Holistic, taking into account all aspects of the individual's existence.
(ii) Available, appropriate, accessible and provided in a way that guarantees the safety and personal integrity of the victims, their family and their caretakers.
(iii) Provided at the earliest possible point in time after the torture event, without a requirement for the victim to pursue judicial remedies, but solely based on recommendations by a qualified health professional.
(iv) Provided in close consultation with the victim and tailored to meet the specific needs of each individual victim.
(v) Adequately funded by national governments.

100. The IRCT uses the definition of "Torture" as provided in the UN Convention against Torture, according to which "torture means any act by which severe pain or suffering, whether physical or mental, is intentionally inflicted on a person for such purposes as obtaining from him or a third person information or a confession, punishing him for an act he or a third person has committed or is suspected of having committed, or intimidating or coercing him or a third person, or for any reason based on discrimination of any kind, when such pain or suffering is inflicted by or at the instigation of or with the consent or acquiescence of a public official or other person acting in an official capacity. It does not include pain or suffering arising only from, inherent in or incidental to lawful sanctions."

The IRCT has a pool of world-class experts providing support not only in terms of rehabilitation but also for forensic evidence gathering and training through the

UN Istanbul Protocol as a cornerstone document for gathering torture evidence, documenting and presenting them to the courts and also using for advocacy purposes.

§5. International Association of Medical Regulatory Authorities

101. In May 1994, the Federation of State Medical Boards of the United States (FSMB), under contract with the US Department of Health and Human Services, planned and hosted the first International Conference on Medical Regulation in Washington, D.C. Participants included representatives of Australia, Canada, Ireland, New Zealand, South Africa, the United Kingdom and the United States. Observers attended from Egypt, Israel, Mexico and Taiwan. This conference was designed to initiate dialog among the attendees and the conference focused on the status of medical regulation in the participating nations, examined current research and identified future research needs. The conference resulted in a consensus in favor of continuing international dialog and concluded that the issues faced in the field of regulation, licensure and discipline are not unique to any one nation. It was decided to hold a second conference in Australia in 1996, beginning a pattern of biennial conferences that still continues.

102. In September 2000, medical regulatory authorities from Australia, Canada, Ireland, New Zealand, South Africa, Sweden, the United Kingdom and the United States formed the International Association of Medical Licensing Authorities (IAMLA), which was formally incorporated in 2004 in the State of Texas as the International Association of Medical Regulatory Authorities (IAMRA).

103. IAMRA does not promote or endorse any particular model of medical regulation but rather recognizes that there are many different structures and approaches. IAMRA supports effective regulatory systems that provide the foundation for patient safety and public protection, relevant to the environment in which they operate. Given the increasing mobility of the medical workforce, IAMRA recognizes that the impacts of medical regulation can be felt across the world.

I. Functioning of the IAMRA

104. At present IAMRA has over one hundred members from all regions of the world and promotes effective medical regulation worldwide by supporting best practice, innovation, collaboration, and knowledge sharing in the interest of public safety and in support of the medical profession. The challenge for medical regulators is to create relevant and effective systems that can respond to the rapidly changing environments in which physicians work, changes in both health care and communication technologies, and evolving health care delivery systems.

II. Goals of the IAMRA

105. The IAMRA supports the purposes of medical regulation through scientific, educational and collaborative activities, which include the furtherance of the following objects and purposes:

(i) To support medical regulatory authorities worldwide in protecting the public interest by promoting high standards for physician education, licensure, regulation, and professional conduct and facilitating the ongoing exchange of information among medical regulatory authorities.
(ii) To advocate for and promote high standards of medical education, physician evaluation and assessment, licensure, medical practice and professional conduct.
(iii) To facilitate international cooperation and collaboration among medical regulatory authorities, including establishing a network for the regular exchange of medical licensing and disciplinary information.
(iv) To provide a forum for the development and sharing of new concepts and new approaches in the regulation of medical practice.
(v) To encourage and support research, policy analysis and policy development related to medical licensure and regulation.
(vi) Serve as an information source to medical regulatory authorities, the public, and national and international organizations.

106. The IAMRA is a membership organization with the purpose to promote effective medical regulation worldwide by supporting best practise, innovation, collaboration, and knowledge sharing in the interest of public safety and in support of the medical profession. Its vision is that everyone around the world is treated and cared for by safe and competent doctors. IAMRA encourages and facilitates international cooperation and understanding and provides opportunities and platform for members to share information and discuss common problems.

107. The challenge for medical regulation in the twenty-first century is to create a relevant, effective medical regulatory system that can address the dynamics of the global and rapidly changing medical practice environments, technologies, and health care delivery systems. International cooperation is the key to enhancing the role of medical regulatory authorities as to the primary vehicle for public protection in health care.

§6. The International Development Law Organization

108. The International Development Law Organization (IDLO) has been working with WHO and others to build capacity and promote greater understanding of public health law in the world. IDLO's work includes strengthening the legal response to HIV and AIDS in developing nations; fostering awareness of public health goals and human rights among government officials, and among those communities most at risk of HIV infection; and building lawmakers capacity for reform based on evidence, international law and best practice. It also works with the United Nations agencies to scale up joint efforts toward zero HIV discrimination. Developed in partnership with UNAIDS and UNDP, Scaling up HIV-Related Legal Services toolkit has been distributed.

109. Falsified and substandard (FS) medicines undermine global health gains as these can be toxic and may lead to drug resistance. Falsified products include medicines for the treatment of cancer, diabetes, bacterial and fungal infections, malaria and other medical conditions. The problem is most acute in low- and middle-income countries, where oversight is often minimal or nonexistent. IDLO is tackling this challenge of FS with partners in the World Bank's Global Forum on Law, Justice and Development. A consortium led by the organization is developing an assessment tool to assist and strengthen the national legal frameworks to respond to this emerging challenge.

§7. International Council of Nurses

110. The International Council of Nurses (ICN) is a federation of national nurses associations in more than 130 countries. Operated by nurses and leading nursing internationally, the ICN works to ensure quality nursing care for all and sound health policies globally. Founded in 1899, the ICN is the world's first and widest reaching international organization for health professionals and is headquartered in Geneva, Switzerland.

I. Key Program Areas

111. The ICN has identified three programs for the betterment of nursing and health. These are known as the ICN's Pillars and they are: "Professional Practice, Regulation, and Socioeconomic Welfare." The International Classification for Nursing Practice (ICNP®)—a common code language for data globally—and Leadership for Change ™ are two significant ICN projects which come under the professional practice pillar. Leadership in Negotiation is a project which falls under the socioeconomic welfare pillar. The ICN's International Centre for Human Resources in Nursing is dedicated to strengthening nursing through the development, ongoing monitoring and dissemination of information, standards, and tools on nursing human resources policy, research, and practice.

112. Quality Workplaces for Quality Care is promoted by the health professions (ICN, International Pharmaceutical Federation, World Confederation for Physical Therapy, World Dental Federation and WMA), together with the International Hospital Federation. The multiyear campaign promotes safe, cost-effective, and healthy workplaces which strengthen the health systems and improves patient safety.

§8. International Medical Corps

113. The establishment of International Medical Corps (IMC) in 1984 ushered in a new and different kind of relief and development organization. IMC based in California is a global, humanitarian, nonprofit organization dedicated to saving lives and relieving suffering through health care training and relief and development programs. It delivers emergency medical and related services to those affected by conflict, disaster and disease. IMC also trains people in their communities, providing them with the skills they need to recover, chart their own path to self-reliance and become effective first responders themselves. It responds to emergencies and also tackles the world's most difficult challenges, such as poverty, hunger and disease.

§9. Red Cross and Red Crescent

114. The International Red Cross and Red Crescent Movement was founded to protect human life and health, to ensure respect for all human beings, and to prevent and alleviate human suffering. It is a worldwide humanitarian movement with approximately ninety-seven million volunteers, members and staff. It consists of three distinct organizations that are legally independent of each other but are united within the movement through common basic principles, objectives, symbols, statutes and governing organizations.

The International Committee of the Red Cross (ICRC), a private humanitarian institution founded in 1863 in Geneva, Switzerland, in particular by Henry Dunant and Gustave Moynier. It functions under international humanitarian law to protect the life and dignity of the victims of international and internal armed conflicts. The ICRC was awarded the Nobel Peace Prize in 1917, 1944 and 1963.

115. The International Federation of Red Cross and Red Crescent Societies (IFRC) were founded in 1919. IFRC coordinates between the 192 National Red Cross and Red Crescent Societies internationally in close cooperation with the National Societies and relief assistance missions and responds to large-scale emergencies. The International Federation Secretariat is based in Geneva, Switzerland. In 1963, the Federation (then known as the League of Red Cross Societies) was awarded the Nobel Peace Prize jointly with the ICRC.

Chapter 2. World Health Organization

116. After World War II, countries of the world came together to form the United Nations and voted to create a global health agency as a U.N. arm. Thus, in 1948, the WHO was founded with the objective to attain the highest possible level of health by the people of the world. WHO replaced many regional health authorities that had been established in Europe and the America in the early 1900s to help prevent the spread of diseases such as smallpox and typhus. As a specialized agency of the U.N., WHO acts as a directing and coordinating authority on international health work. WHO started with 55 Member States and now has 194 Member States and 2 associate members. WHO has a staff of 7,000 that includes scientists, medical doctors and public health specialists, as well as experts in economics, statistics and emergency relief. The agency is headquartered in Geneva and has offices in more than 150 countries around the world.

117. The WHO officials periodically review and update the organization's leadership priorities. The WHO's leadership priorities are aimed at:

(i) assisting countries that seek progress toward universal health coverage;
(ii) helping countries establish their capacity to adhere to International Health Regulations (IHR);
(iii) increasing access to essential and high-quality medical products;
(iv) addressing the role of social, economic, and environmental factors in public health;
(v) coordinating responses to noncommunicable disease;
(vi) promoting public health and well-being in keeping with the Sustainable Development Goals set forth by the UN.

118. The work encompassed by those priorities is spread across a number of health-related areas. For example, the WHO has established a codified set of international sanitary regulations (ISR) designed to standardize quarantine measures without interfering unnecessarily with trade and air travel across national boundaries. The WHO also keeps member countries informed of the latest developments in cancer research, drug development, disease prevention, control of drug addiction, vaccine use, and health hazards of chemicals and other substances.

119. The WHO sponsors measures for the control of epidemic and endemic diseases by promoting mass campaigns involving nationwide vaccination programs, instruction in the use of antibiotics and insecticides, the improvement of laboratory and clinical facilities for early diagnosis and prevention, assistance in providing pure water supplies and sanitation systems, and health education for people living in rural communities. These campaigns have had some success against AIDS, tuberculosis, malaria, and a variety of other diseases. In May 1980 smallpox was globally eradicated, a feat due largely to the efforts of the WHO.

§1. STRUCTURE OF WHO

I. World Health Assembly and Executive Board

120. The World Health Assembly (WHA) also based in Geneva, Switzerland was inaugurated in 1966. It is the legislative and supreme body of the WHO. WHO Member States appoint delegations to the World Health Assembly which is the WHO's supreme decision-making body. All UN Member States are eligible for WHO membership and a country may be admitted as a member when her application has been approved by a simple majority vote of the World Health Assembly. The World Health Assembly is attended by delegations from all Member States, and determines the policies of the organization. It votes on matters of policy and finance of WHO, including the proposed budget. The Assembly elects 34 members, technically qualified in the field of health, to the executive board for a three-year term. The main functions of the board are to carry out the decisions and policies of the Assembly, to advise it, and to facilitate its work. The WMA also works against all forms of stigmatization, criminalization and discrimination based on the sexual orientation of the people and asserts that psychiatric or psychotherapeutic approaches to treatment must not focus upon homosexuality itself but rather upon the conflicts which arise between homosexuality and religious, social and internalized norms and prejudices.

A. *Director General*

121. The Director General elected by the World Health Assembly is the head of WHO. The Director General is typically appointed in May with a term of five years, when the Assembly meets.

B. *Executive Board*

122. The executive board is composed of members technically qualified in health matters and gives effect to the decisions and policies of the World Health Assembly. In addition, the UN observer organizations International Committee of the Red Cross and International Federation of Red Cross and Red Crescent Societies have entered into "official relations" with WHO and are invited as observers. In the World Health Assembly, they are seated alongside the other NGOs.

123. The WHO is financed by contributions from Member States and outside donors. As of 2020, the biggest contributor was the United States, which gives over USD 400 million annually. U.S. contributions to the WHO are funded through the U.S. State Department's account for Contributions to International Organizations (CIO). In 2018 the largest contributors (USD 150+ each) were the United States, Bill & Melinda Gates Foundation, United Kingdom, Germany and GAVI, the Vaccine Alliance.

§2. Vision and Mission of WHO

124. WHO establishes global standards and gives advice to countries regarding rational public health measures. To achieve these goals, WHO does not typically give out grants or loans or send doctors and others from its staff to countries to provide hands-on medical treatments. It gets on the ground to provide direction, advice, help trace disease outbreaks and provide additional support when needed.

125. The basic and primary objective for creation of WHO is the attainment by all people of the highest possible level of health. The WHO fulfills this objective through its functions as defined in its Constitution: (a) to act as the directing and coordinating authority on international health work; (b) to establish and maintain effective collaboration with the United Nations, specialized agencies, governmental health administrations, professional groups and such other organizations as may be deemed appropriate; (c) to assist Governments, upon request, in strengthening health services; (d) to furnish appropriate technical assistance and, in emergencies, necessary aid upon the request or acceptance of Governments; (e) to provide or assist in providing, upon the request of the United Nations, health services and facilities to special groups, such as the peoples of trust territories; (f) to establish and maintain such administrative and technical services as may be required, including epidemiological and statistical services; (g) to stimulate and advance work to eradicate epidemic, endemic and other diseases; (h) to promote, in cooperation with other specialized agencies where necessary, the prevention of accidental injuries; (i) to promote, in cooperation with other specialized agencies where necessary, the improvement of nutrition, housing, sanitation, recreation, economic or working conditions and other aspects of environmental hygiene; (j) to promote cooperation among scientific and professional groups which contribute to the advancement of health; (k) to propose conventions, agreements and regulations, and make recommendations with respect to international health matters and to perform.

I. Role of WHO in Public Health

126. The WHO encourages the strengthening and expansion of the public health administrations of member nations. The organization, on request, provides technical advice to governments in the preparation of long-term national health plans, sends out international teams of experts to conduct field surveys and demonstration projects, helps set up a local health center, and offers aid in the development of national training institutions for medical and nursing personnel. Through various education support programs, the WHO is able to provide fellowship awards for doctors, public health administrators, nurses, sanitary inspectors, researchers, and laboratory technicians.

127. As of 2012, the WHO has defined its role in public health as follows:

(a) providing leadership on matters critical to health and engaging in partnerships where joint action is needed;

(b) shaping the research agenda and stimulating the generation, translation, and dissemination of valuable knowledge;
(c) setting norms and standards and promoting and monitoring their implementation;
(d) articulating ethical and evidence-based policy options;
(e) providing technical support, catalyzing change, and building sustainable institutional capacity; and monitoring the health situation and assessing health trends. CRVS (civil registration and vital statistics) to provide monitoring of vital events (birth, death, wedding, divorce).

128. WHO has been moving toward acceptance and integration of traditional medicine and traditional Chinese medicine (TCM). In 2022, the new International Statistical Classification of Diseases and Related Health Problems, ICD-11, will attempt to enable classifications from traditional medicine to be integrated with classifications from evidence-based medicine. Though Chinese authorities have pushed for the change, this and other support of the WHO for traditional medicine has been criticized by the medical and scientific community, due to lack of evidence and the risk of endangering wildlife hunted for traditional remedies.

§3. Regional Approach

I. Regional Structure of WHO

129. As of January 2021, the WHO has 194 Member States. All Member States of the United Nations except for Liechtenstein (192 countries), plus the Cook Islands and Niue. A state becomes a full member of WHO by ratifying the treaty known as the Constitution of the WHO. As of May 2019 and January 2021, it also had two associate members, Puerto Rico and Tokelau. Palestine is an observer as a "national liberation movement" recognized by the League of Arab States under United Nations Resolution 3118. The Sovereign Military Order of Malta (or Order of Malta) also attends as an observer. The Holy See attends as an observer, and its participation as "non-Member State Observer" was formalized by an Assembly resolution in 2021.

130. One of WHO's primary roles is to provide countries with science-based recommendations for health policy. There are guidelines on what kind of essential medicines there should be, what kind of essential diagnostics there should be, what might be the regimens to use in relation to HIV in different countries, taking into account available resources. Countries are not under any obligation legally to follow these guidelines, but many do in relation to epidemics. WHO is governed by its Member States — it does not have the legal authority to enter countries without permission or to force countries to take its advice. WHO persuades through science, through evidence, by demonstrating what other countries are doing and showcasing good examples of good practice. Beyond that, WHO has no power to enforce, no power to put any form of pressure on the country to change what is their sovereign will.

II. Regional Offices

131. The regional divisions of WHO were created between 1949 and 1952 and are based on Article 44 of the WHO's constitution, which allowed the WHO to establish a regional organization to meet the special needs of the area. Many decisions are made at the regional level, including important discussions over WHO's budget, and in deciding the members of the next assembly, which are designated by the regions. Each region has a regional committee, which generally meets once a year, normally in the autumn. Representatives attend from each member or associative member in each region, including those states that are not full members. For example, Palestine attends meetings of the Eastern Mediterranean Regional Office. Each region also has a regional office headed by a director, who is elected by the Regional Committee.

132. Each regional committee of the WHO consists of all the Health Department heads in all the governments of the countries that constitute the region. Aside from electing the regional director, the regional committee is also in charge of setting the guidelines for the implementation, within the region, of the health and other policies adopted by the World Health Assembly. The regional committee also serves as a progress review board for the actions of WHO within the region. The regional director is the head of WHO for his or her region. The RD manages and/or supervises a staff of health and other experts at the regional offices and in specialized centers. The RD is also the direct supervising authority—concomitantly with the WHO Director General—of all the heads of WHO country offices, known as WHO Representatives, within the region.

III. Country and Liaison Offices

133. The WHO operates 150 country offices in 6 different regions. It also operates several liaison offices, including those with the European Union, United Nations and a single office covering the World Bank and International Monetary Fund. It also operates the International Agency for Research on Cancer in Lyon, France, and the WHO Centre for Health Development in Kobe, Japan. Additional offices include those in Pristina; the West Bank and Gaza; the US-Mexico Border Field Office in El Paso; the Office of the Caribbean Program Coordination in Barbados; and the Northern Micronesia office. There will generally be one WHO country office in the capital, occasionally accompanied by satellite offices in the provinces or sub-regions of the country in question. The country office is headed by a WHO Representative (WR). The country office consists of the WR, and several health and other experts, both foreign and local, as well as the necessary support staff. The main functions of WHO country offices include being the primary adviser of that country's government in matters of health and pharmaceutical policies.

IV. Partnerships

134. At the beginning of the twenty-first century, the WHO's work involved increasing collaboration with external bodies. As of 2002, a total of 473 NGOs had some form of partnership with WHO. There were 189 partnerships with international NGOs in formal "official relations"—the rest being considered informal in character. Partners include the Bill and Melinda Gates Foundation and the Rockefeller Foundation.

135. The WHO along with the World Bank constitutes the core team responsible for administering the International Health Partnership (IHP+). The IHP+ is a group of partner governments, development agencies, civil society, and others committed to improving the health of citizens in developing countries. Partners work together to put international principles for aid effectiveness and development cooperation into practice in the health sector.

136. The organization relies on contributions from renowned scientists and professionals to inform its work, such as the WHO Expert Committee on Biological Standardization, the WHO Expert Committee on Leprosy, and the WHO Study Group on Inter-professional Education & Collaborative Practice. WHO collaborates with The Global Fund to Fight AIDS, Tuberculosis and Malaria, UNITAID, and the United States President's Emergency Plan for AIDS Relief to spearhead and fund the development of HIV programs.

V. Goodwill Ambassadors

137. The WHO operates "Goodwill Ambassadors"; members of the arts, sports, or other fields of public life aimed at drawing attention to WHO's initiatives and projects.

VI. Medical Society of the WHO

138. Since the beginning, the WHO has had the Medical Society of the WHO. It has conducted lectures by noted researchers and published findings.

VII. International Agency for Research on Cancer

139. The WHO sub-department, the International Agency for Research on Cancer (IARC), conducts and coordinates research into the causes of cancer. It also collects and publishes surveillance data regarding the occurrence of cancer worldwide. Its Monographs Programme identifies carcinogenic hazards and evaluates environmental causes of cancer in humans.

VIII. Civil Society Reference Group on HIV

140. WHO created the Civil Society Reference Group on HIV, which brings together other networks that are involved in policymaking and the dissemination of guidelines. WHO, a sector of the United Nations, partners with UNAIDS to contribute to the development of HIV responses in different areas of the world. WHO facilitates technical partnerships through the Technical Advisory Committee on HIV, which they created to develop WHO guidelines and policies.

§4. Work and Contribution of WHO

I. Health Policy

141. WHO addresses government health policy with two aims: first, to address the underlying social and economic determinants of health through policies and programs that enhance health equity and integrate pro-poor, gender-responsive, and human rights-based approaches and second to promote a healthier environment, intensify primary prevention and influence public policies in all sectors so as to address the root causes of environmental threats to health. In terms of health services, WHO looks to improve governance, financing, staffing and management and the availability and quality of evidence and research to guide policy. It also strives to ensure improved access, quality and use of medical products and technologies.

142. WHO develops and promotes the use of evidence-based tools, norms and standards to support Member States to inform health policy options. It oversees the implementation of the International Health Regulations and publishes a series of medical classifications; of these, three are over-reaching reference classifications: the International Statistical Classification of Diseases (ICD), the International Classification of Functioning, Disability and Health (ICF) and the International Classification of Health Interventions (ICHI). Other international policy frameworks produced by WHO include the International Code of Marketing of Breast-Milk Substitutes (adopted in 1981), Framework Convention on Tobacco Control (adopted in 2003), the Global Code of Practice on the International Recruitment of Health Personnel (adopted in 2010) as well as the WHO Model List of Essential Medicines and its pediatric counterpart. An international convention on pandemic prevention and preparedness is being actively considered.

II. Environment and WHO

143. The WHO estimates that 12.6 million people died as a result of living or working in an unhealthy environment in 2012 which accounts for nearly 1 in 4 of total global deaths. Environmental risk factors, such as air, water, and soil pollution, chemical exposures, climate change, and ultraviolet radiation, contribute to more than 100 diseases and injuries. This can result in a number of pollution-related diseases.

144. In 2018 (30 October–1 November) WHO's first global conference on air pollution and health (improving air quality, combatting climate change—saving lives) was organized in collaboration with UN Environment, World Meteorological Organization (WMO), and the secretariat of the UN Framework Convention on Climate Change (UNFCCC). WHO works to reduce morbidity and mortality and improve health during key stages of life, including pregnancy, childbirth, the neonatal period, childhood and adolescence, and improve sexual and reproductive health and promote active and healthy aging for all individuals.

III. Drug Control

145. WHO also works to prevent or reduce risk factors for health conditions associated with the use of tobacco, alcohol, drugs and other psychoactive substances, unhealthy diets and physical inactivity and unsafe sex. The WHO works to improve nutrition, food safety and food security and to ensure this has a positive effect on public health and sustainable development.

146. WHO is mandated under two international drug control conventions (Single Convention on Narcotic Drugs, 1961 and Convention on Psychotropic Substances, 1971) to carry out scientific assessments of substances for international drug control. Through the WHO Expert Committee on Drug Dependence (ECDD), it can recommend changes to scheduling of substances to the United Nations Commission on Narcotic Drugs. The ECDD is in charge of evaluating the impact of psychoactive substances on public health and their dependence producing properties and potential harm to health, as well as considering their potential medical benefits and therapeutic applications.

IV. Public Health Education and Action

147. In 2014, WHO released the Global Atlas of Palliative Care at the End of Life in a joint publication with the Worldwide Hospice Palliative Care Alliance, an affiliated NGO working collaboratively with the WHO to promote palliative care in national and international health policy. Each year, the organization marks World Health Day and other observances focusing on a specific health promotion topic. World Health Day falls on 7 April each year, timed to match the anniversary of WHO's founding. Recent themes have been vector-borne diseases (2014), healthy aging (2012) and drug resistance (2011).

In April 2019, WHO released new recommendations stating that children between the ages of 2 and 5 should spend no more than one hour per day engaging in sedentary behavior in front of a screen and that children under 2 should not be permitted any sedentary screen time.

148. The WHO promotes road safety as a means to reduce traffic-related injuries. It has also worked on global initiatives in surgery, including emergency and essential surgical care, trauma care, and safe surgery. The WHO Surgical Safety

Checklist is in current use worldwide in the effort to improve patient safety. The other official global public health campaigns marked by WHO are World Tuberculosis Day, World Immunization Week, World Malaria Day, World No Tobacco Day, World Blood Donor Day, World Hepatitis Day, and World AIDS Day.

149. As part of the United Nations, the WHO supports work toward the Millennium Development Goals. Of the eight Millennium Development Goals, three—reducing child mortality by two-thirds, reducing maternal deaths by three-quarters, and halting and beginning to reduce the spread of HIV/AIDS—relate directly to WHO's scope; the other five inter-relate and affect world health.

V. Data Handling and Publications

150. The WHO works to provide the needed health and well-being evidence through a variety of data collection platforms, including the World Health Survey and the Study on Global Aging and Adult Health (SAGE). The Country Health Intelligence Portal (CHIP) has also been developed to provide an access point to information about the health services that are available in different countries. The information gathered through this portal is used by countries to set priorities for future strategies or plans, so as to implement, monitor, and evaluate it.

151. The WHO has published *various* tools for measuring and monitoring the capacity of national health systems and health workforces. The Global Health Observatory (GHO) has been the WHO's main portal which provides access to data and analyses for key health themes by monitoring health situations around the globe.

152. The WHO Assessment Instrument for Mental Health Systems (WHO-AIMS), the WHO Quality of Life Instrument (WHOQOL), and the Service Availability and Readiness Assessment (SARA) provide guidance for data collection. Collaborative efforts between WHO and other agencies, such as through the Health Metrics Network, also aim to provide sufficient high-quality information to assist governmental decision-making. WHO promotes the development of capacities in Member States to use and produce research that addresses their national needs, including through the Evidence-Informed Policy Network (EVIPNet). The Pan American Health Organization (PAHO/AMRO) became the first region to develop and pass a policy on research for health approved in September 2009.

153. On 10 December 2013, a new WHO database, known as MiNDbank, went online. The database was launched on Human Rights Day and is part of WHO's Quality Rights initiative, which aims to end human rights violations against people with mental health conditions. The new database presents a great deal of information about mental health, substance abuse, disability, human rights, and the different policies, strategies, laws, and service standards being implemented in different countries. It also contains important international documents and information. The database allows visitors to access the health information of WHO Member States and other partners. Users can review policies, laws, and strategies and search for the best practices and success stories in the field of mental health.

154. The WHO publishes a World Health Report, its leading publication, including an expert assessment of a specific global health topic. Other publications of WHO include the *Bulletin of the World Health Organization*, the *Eastern Mediterranean Health Journal* (overseen by EMRO), the *Human Resources for Health* (published in collaboration with BioMed Central), and the *Pan American Journal of Public Health* (overseen by PAHO/AMRO).

155. In 2016, the WHO drafted a global health sector strategy on HIV. The draft outlines its commitment to ending the AIDS epidemic by 2030 with interim targets for 2020. To make achievements toward these targets, the draft lists actions that countries and the WHO can take, such as a commitment to universal health coverage, medical accessibility, prevention and eradication of disease, and efforts to educate the public. Some notable points made in the draft include addressing gender inequity where females are nearly twice as likely as men to get infected with HIV and tailoring resources to mobilized regions where the health system may be compromised due to natural disasters, etc. Among the points made, it seems clear that although the prevalence of HIV transmission is declining, there is still a need for resources, health education, and global efforts to end this epidemic. The WHO has a Framework Convention on Tobacco implementation database which is one of the few mechanisms to help in enforcing compliance with the FCTC. However, there have been reports of numerous discrepancies between it and the national implementation reports on which it was built.

§5. Handling of Outbreak of Pandemic

156. WHO's handling of the SARS (severe acute respiratory syndrome) outbreak in 2003 was considered a success. WHO acted quickly and issued guidance to restrict travel. The epidemic did not extend to all countries in the world. Effects of the SARS outbreak were concentrated in Asia, where 8,000 people were sickened, and around 800 died before the epidemic ended in 2004. In the 2009 H1N1 swine flu pandemic, WHO received mixed reviews. In post-pandemic analysis requested by WHO, an international committee found that WHO provided useful guidance to countries on how to slow pandemic flu transmission and helped monitor the virus' spread. However, its messaging around the severity of the pandemic was unclear, and its failure to coordinate effective vaccine distribution led to countries receiving them too late to be truly helpful.

And the WHO's response to the 2014 Ebola outbreak in West Africa was criticized for not responding quickly enough in declaring a public health emergency of international concern. WHO initially dismissed the scale of the problem, then lacked the staff and funds to lead an effective response, NPR reported in 2015.

I. Communicable Diseases

157. The 2012–2013 budget of WHO identified five areas among which funding was distributed. Two of those five areas are related to communicable diseases: the first, to reduce the "health, social and economic burden" of communicable diseases in general; the second is to combat HIV/AIDS, malaria and tuberculosis in particular.

158. As of 2015, the WHO has worked within the UNAIDS network and strives to involve sections of society other than health to help deal with the economic and social effects of HIV/AIDS. In line with UNAIDS, WHO has set itself the interim task between 2009 and 2015 of reducing the number of those aged 15–24 years who are infected by 50%; reducing new HIV infections in children by 90%; and reducing HIV-related deaths by 25%.

II. Noncommunicable Diseases

159. One of the thirteen WHO priority areas is aimed at the prevention and reduction of disease, disability and premature deaths from chronic noncommunicable diseases, mental disorders, violence and injuries, and visual impairment which are collectively responsible for almost 71% of all deaths worldwide.

§6. COVID-19 Pandemic and WHO

160. Under the International Health Regulations, a global legal agreement revised in 2005 and signed by all WHO members, countries are required to report to WHO any disease outbreaks that are unexpected or of unknown cause and have a significant risk of international spread. The pandemic designation is an official alert that triggers a set of responses. WHO helps guide the country and gauge whether its response is effective. And it can bring in international assistance for training, surveillance and other measures at the request of a state party.

161. China reported a cluster of pneumonia cases to WHO on December 31, 2019. WHO declared the coronavirus a pandemic in January 30, 2020, when there were no reported deaths outside of China but a sharp increase in the number of countries, which were reporting such cases. Later on, WHO officially named the disease COVID-19. WHO requested information that countries are bound to provide under international health regulations — for instance, explanations of why travel bans are needed to stop disease spread. WHO has also asked countries — including China — for timely and accurate outbreak data that they are required to provide under the international health regulations.

162. Drawing from publications and discussions with researchers globally, WHO has published COVID-related public health advice on topics ranging from diagnostic tests and the public use of masks to how religious leaders can assess the risks of holding social and religious gatherings and how countries can manage risks as they lift their lockdowns. The agency has also developed online courses to train health care workers to diagnose and treat COVID-19 patients.

163. WHO has sent teams of response coordinators, epidemiologists and other advisers into countries to help guide COVID-19. It is also raising money for and organizing a global COVID-19 supply chain to get diagnostic tests, medical equipment and aid workers to places that need them. WHO is helping to organize global research into treatment *drugs* and potential coronavirus vaccines. WHO brought medical doctors, virologists, modelers and epidemiologists together in a global research forum to establish a unified set of priorities and timelines for conducting research on COVID-19.

164. The WHO created an Incident Management Support Team on January 1, 2020, one day after Chinese health authorities notified the organization of a cluster of pneumonia cases of unknown etiology. On January 5, 2020 WHO notified all Member States of the outbreak and subsequently provided guidance to all countries on how to respond, and confirmed the first infection outside China. The organization warned of limited human-to-human transmission on January 14, 2020, and confirmed human-to-human transmission one week later. On January 30, 2020, the WHO declared a Public Health Emergency of International Concern considered a "call to action" and "last resort" measure for the international community and a pandemic on March 11, 2020.

165. While organizing the global response to the COVID-19 pandemic and overseeing "more than 35 emergency operations" for cholera, measles and other epidemics internationally, the WHO has been criticized for praising China's public health response to the crisis while seeking to maintain a "diplomatic balancing act" between the United States and China.

I. Criticism on Handling of COVID-19

166. The WHO faced criticism from the United States administration while guiding the world in how to tackle the deadly COVID-19 pandemic. On 14 April 2020, the United States pledged to halt its funding to the WHO while reviewing its role in mismanaging and covering up the spread of the coronavirus. The United States had paid half of its annual assessed fees to the WHO as of 31 March 2020; it would ordinarily pay its remaining fees in September 2020.

167. WHO defended its actions in alerting the world to the emergence of COVID-19. On 8 May 2020, the United States blocked a vote on a U.N. Security Council resolution aimed at promoting nonviolent international cooperation during the pandemic and mentioning the WHO. On 7 July 2020, the USA formally notified the UN of its intent to withdraw the United States from the WHO. However, new President Joe Biden canceled the planned withdrawal and announced that the U.S. would resume funding the organization.

Part III. Public Health Law and the Spread of Disease

Chapter 1. Public Health Law

168. Public health law broadly includes laws dealing with health interventions, laws defining the powers, duties, and boundaries of health agencies and systems, and, in general, laws with an impact on health. As the role of public health practitioners and researchers in the law has grown, a transdisciplinary public health law has emerged integrating legal and scientific expertise. Public health law focuses on legal practice, scholarship, and advocacy on issues involving the government's legal authorities and duties "to ensure the conditions for people to be healthy" and how to balance these authorities and duties with "individual rights to autonomy, privacy, liberty, property and other legally protected interests." Public health law issues range from questions of legal interpretation to complex matters involving public health policy, social justice, and ethics. Therefore, the scope of public health law is broad.

§1. Public Health Law in International Arena

169. The scope of public health law in the international field encompasses the legal norms, processes, and institutions needed to attain the highest possible level of physical and mental health. The field seeks to facilitate health-promoting norms that influence the public's health, including international organizations, governments, businesses, foundations, the media, and civil society. The mechanisms of global health law required to stimulate investment in research and development, mobilize resources, set priorities, monitor progress, create incentives, and enforce standards. The development in public health law should be guided by the values of social justice, requiring equitable distribution of health services, particularly to benefit the poorest populations of the world.

I. Scope of Public Health Law

170. The public health law in the international sphere is primarily concerned with:

(i) sources of public international law, including, for example, treaties establishing the authority and responsibility of states for the health of their populations and duties for global cooperation; and
(ii) subjects of international law, which include states, individuals and public international organizations.

The international health law aims at effective collective health action among governments, businesses, civil societies, etc. and set out the sort of international legal framework needed to empower the world community to advance global health. International law pertaining to public health has evolved gradually in response to developments within the community of the nations. Considerable development in the nature of international law has taken place, for example, as a result of the recognition, in the twentieth century, of universal human rights. The evolution of international law envisioned in the concept of global health law is consistent with the progressive, historical development of international law.

II. State Public Health Law

171. The stage of legal development of an individual state is also very important and may act as an important influence on the health of the population or as a barrier to action. Although in most countries the texts of laws are theoretically available, identifying specific laws can be difficult in practice. Many nations either lack the basic laws and regulations needed to comply with basic obligations and to support effective public health systems or have laws that are outdated or poorly designed and implemented. Therefore, promoting a robust health infrastructure in every country is the most effective long-term preparedness strategy for global health emergencies. Health infrastructure includes the physical structures of public health agencies, clinics and hospitals, and the human resources to operate them. But it operates when legal infrastructure is properly developed, like laws and policies that empower, obligate, and limit government action, and when private action concerning the health of the general public is not restricted.

172. The regulatory system is tested in an emergency and reveals how effectively regulatory strategies, health regulations, and human rights norms have been embodied in the laws of a country when these are practically applied. Governments are also obliged to protect the human rights of individuals affected by an outbreak. Laws are central, for example, to a country's strategy to improve road safety and manage lifestyle-related chronic diseases. Virtually, all the major public health achievements of the last century, from universal immunization to narcotic drugs control, depended on effective legal interventions. Nations have made firm commitments to action for health in instruments, such as the Constitution of the WHO, the IHR, and the Framework Convention on Tobacco Control.

173. On 8 July 2021 a report was published by the International Federation of Red Cross and Red Crescent Societies (IFRC) which contains extensive findings and recommendations based on an analysis of the legal and policy frameworks used to respond to COVID-19 and other public health emergencies such as those caused by the Ebola, Zika and SARS viruses. As per this report, there was an overall lack of legal preparedness or strong legislation for public health emergencies like COVID-19. The lessons learned from the COVID-19 pandemic may be used to review law and policy for public health emergencies. The IFRC has called for urgent action to strengthen domestic legal and policy frameworks for public health emergencies, so that states can be better prepared. The legal issues and preparedness are very important in an emergency as laws and policies enable states of emergency to be declared, lockdowns to be imposed and vaccine approvals may be expedited. As per the report, in many cases, states were not legally prepared to deal with COVID-19 situation. Old laws, policies and contingency plans were taken out, often proving to be outdated or inadequate, requiring the rapid development of new laws. Never before have so many laws been made in so many countries in respect of one event, in such a short span of time.

III. Globalization and Public Health Law

174. Globalization has created new challenges for international medical law and policy. The spread of infectious diseases in a changing and interdependent world is much more prevalent and have assumed dangerous proportions, given increased human migration, congregation, travel, and trade. Another aspect is that multinational corporations have significant influence and power over global consumption of food, tobacco, pharmaceuticals, and consumer products. The production and delivery of these goods and services pose health hazards that span national borders but often escape scrutiny under national laws. International trade and intellectual property laws affect the ability of low- and middle-income countries to ensure access to essential drugs and vaccines. Access to antiretroviral medications for poor people living with HIV/AIDS offers an illustration of the political and humanitarian implications of intellectual property protection. At the same time, through unethical recruitment practices and the "push and pull" of market forces, doctors and nurses are migrating to developed countries, leaving the poor without adequate human resources needed for the proper functioning of public health care systems of poor and least developed countries.

175. Some of the most significant impacts of globalization on health are: creating global inequity by compelling poor countries to, *inter alia*, privatize, impose user fees and adopt trade liberalization policies in health services and pharmaceutical distribution. The United Nations Development Programme (UNDP) and the World Bank have both highlighted the spiraling problem of inequity. The UNDP reported "unprecedented reversals" in human development of the world's poorest countries which registered lower scores in the human development index. As income is the primary determinant of health in poor countries, today's inequalities present the most critical global health threat. Overall, the increasing integration and the internationalization of the determinants of health have contributed to the rapid decline in the capacity of sovereign states to protect the health of their populations through unilateral national action and, thus, intensified the need for international cooperation among states.

176. The world community's growing appreciation of the scope and scale of the challenges in global health is reflected in the multiplication of actors in global health since the founding of the UN in 1945. Within the UN system, organizations with involvement in health include the WHO, the UN Children's Fund, the UN Food and Agricultural Organization, the UN Environment Programme, the UN Population Fund, the International Labor Organization, and the World Bank. The non-state actors in international health, particularly foundations, religious organizations, non-governmental agencies, and for-profit organizations, for example, the pharmaceutical industry, have a powerful influence.

IV. The Challenges of Global Health Law

177. The global health law faces major challenges in its formation and implementation. The population of a state is to be cared for by the local government so far as public health is concerned, so even international laws become state-centric. The emphasis on sovereignty by the states prevents any direct action by the international community as well as international institutions. Further, the main challenge is posed by the poor–rich divide.

A. *State-Centric International Law and Health Law*

178. The state-centric nature of international law also poses obstacles to the use of global health law as an effective tool to advance international global health cooperation. The idea that sovereign states are the organizing principle of international relations and, thus, are the focus of international law has a number of implications. The principle of sovereignty makes international law different from domestic law. International law is largely voluntary as there is generally no authority to enforce the law against sovereign states. In treaties, the primary source of global health law, states establish international legal rules by expressly consenting to them. Because states are reluctant to sacrifice their freedom of action through the codification of binding international law, treaties are most often far from sufficiently comprehensive and tend to incorporate limited obligations with numerous exceptions. Moreover, the drive to establish universal consensus in treaty negotiations leads to the codification of weak treaty commitments.

B. *Overriding Principle of Sovereignty*

179. In the present-day scenario, states are generally unwilling to develop international legal instruments that create binding and meaningful obligations and incentives and provide adequate funding or services for the protection of the poor people.

As a consequence of the voluntary nature of international law and the overriding principle of sovereignty, states have established only a limited legal framework for national action and international cooperation to advance domestic and global public health. Pursuant to international human rights law, governments have the primary responsibility to protect and promote the health of their own populations. But, if a state is unable or unwilling to meet its responsibilities because of poverty, political instability, ineffectual management, corruption, or the absence of political will, the international community cannot force it to meet the commitment.

C. Rich and Poor Divide

180. The poor states that bear the main burden of disease have the least financial capacity to overcome them. And the states that have the capability are resistant to expending the economic resources necessary to make a difference to improve health outside their borders. When rich countries do act, it is often more to protect national interests or humanitarian instinct than a full sense of ethical or legal obligation. The result is deterioration of health in the poorest regions, with manifest global consequences apart from others for cross-border disease transmission. The vicious cycle of poverty, disease, and political instability is the primary reason that low-income states are not able to create healthy living conditions. Besides, many countries, including developing countries, spend a very small percentage of their Gross Domestic Product (GDP) on health, preferring to spend on armaments or other perceived needs so as to gain political advantage. Furthermore, some governments misappropriate foreign health assistance, whether by excessive bureaucracy, incompetence, or graft. Yet, as a consequence of the operation of the principle of sovereignty in international law, states have not created an effective legal framework to establish and hold governments accountable for investing in the health of their own populations.

D. Basic Survival Needs Not Addressed

181. There has been no support to concretize and codify the norms of the United Nations Millennium Development Goals (MDGs) which address issues in global health relating to basic survival needs, including sanitation and sewage, pest control, clean air and water, diet and nutrition, essential medicines and vaccines, and well-functioning health systems. The rich states do not feel accountable to provide sufficient and stable international health assistance to states that lack the capacity. Developed countries have not even fulfilled their pledges made in 1975 of giving 0.7% of their Gross National Income (GNI) per annum on Official Development Assistance (ODA). A small number of wealthy donors currently wield considerable influence in setting the global health spending agenda—such as OECD (Organization for Economic Cooperation and Development) countries, the Gates Foundation, and the Global Fund, which tend to prioritize specific diseases rather than larger problems, such as failing health systems, that could influence outcomes from all diseases.[20]

182. The cloning negotiations and other recent global health law initiatives suggest that states are not up to the task of using international law as an effective tool for health improvement. The few legal instruments that are in place are inadequate to lift countries out of their perpetual state of poor health. In a fractured environment where states, NGOs, intergovernmental organizations, and foundations all fund and prioritize different health interventions and states engage in international law-making that does not address the core of global health needs, establishing mechanisms to set global health law-making priorities is an essential task for the global community.

20. L. Garrett, Midway in the Journey. How to Promote Global Health: A Foreign Affairs Roundtable (Special Web Feature) (2007b), available at http://www.foreignaffairs.org/special/global health/garrett.

Chapter 2. International Spread and Prevention of Diseases

183. The international disease control measures were started in Europe in the fourteenth century to prevent the spread of the bubonic plague. Subsequently, cholera became the main target of international disease control efforts. The first International Sanitary Conference was held in Paris in 1851 and, thereafter, periodically until 1944. Several international health organizations, including the Health Organization of the League of Nations, were established to oversee the various international regulations on disease control. The United Nations Relief and Rehabilitation Administration (UNRRA) was created in 1943 to provide economic assistance to war-ravaged European nations, assist refugees, and conduct public health functions. The public health responsibilities included the oversight of international quarantine activities delineated in the updated International Sanitary Conventions of 1944, which contained yellow fever control measures. Specific provisions for national governments included quarantining a traveler from an endemic area who did not possess a valid vaccination certificate. This provision, which directed countries how to deal with unvaccinated travelers who may have been exposed to yellow fever virus, was the precursor to formal yellow fever vaccination requirements.

§1. International Sanitary Convention

184. The areas where yellow fever was endemic were identified for implementing provisions of the Sanitary Conventions of 1944. The conventions delegated this responsibility to the UNRRA, which appointed the Expert Commission on Quarantine which created the first official map of yellow fever endemic areas in 1945. Soon after the end of World War II, the responsibilities of the UNRRA were assumed by the newly formed WHO, which appointed the Yellow Fever Panel. In 1949, the Yellow Fever Panel modified the original UNRRA map and issued its first report, which recommended that "measures may be applied permanently against arrivals from endemic areas."

185. The ISR, drafted by the WHO to replace the International Sanitary Conventions, were adopted by the WHA in 1951. The ISR stipulated that vaccination against yellow fever is required of any person leaving an infected area on an international voyage and proceeding to a yellow fever receptive area. This was the first regulatory language that clearly mandated yellow fever vaccination requirements for entry into a country. The ISR were modified and renamed the IHR in 1969 and, thereafter, completely revised in 2005. The IHR (2005) stipulated that "Vaccination against yellow fever may be required of any traveler leaving an area where the Organization has determined that a risk of yellow fever transmission is present."

§2. Venereal Diseases

186. Various methods are used for preventing the spread of diseases in the world, like isolation through confinement, quarantine, and development of a surveillance system. Isolating persons who have or may have been exposed to a serious contagious disease, in order to prevent transmission, is a long-established public health strategy. Where an outbreak of a serious, contagious disease occurs, it may be impractical or impossible to accurately identify cases and carriers of the disease. For this reason, public health laws authorize officials to evacuate or to order the closure of premises where a large number of people gather and to prevent access to public spaces. Since the closure of premises can affect businesses and livelihoods, it is important for the operation of public health orders to be reviewed regularly and to be based on public health considerations, without discrimination on the grounds of race, gender, racial background, or other inappropriate criteria.

I. Closure of Premises

187. Public health orders for the evacuation or closure of premises may be coupled with orders to disinfect and decontaminate premises or to remove noxious articles contaminated with an infectious agent. In case the confiscation or destruction of private property causes economic loss, public health laws should require reasonable compensation to be paid to the owner. This principle can have an important benefit that public health laws which provide for just compensation are more likely to secure the trust and voluntary cooperation of those who are poor and economically vulnerable.

II. Isolation and Confinement

188. The domestic public health laws should authorize public health officials to make orders for the isolation of infected individuals and the quarantine of those who have been exposed to a serious contagious disease. As with treatment orders, however, these restrictions on autonomy should only be used as a last resort and should be minimally restrictive. For example, an infectious individual who does not require medical attention may be effectively quarantined within his or her home rather than being confined in a hospital or other facility used as a detention center. The vital role of mandatory confinement must ensure that basic needs are met, like shelter, provision for treatment, and health care, and respect the cultural or religious expectations of quarantined or isolated individuals. National laws should also include procedural safeguards by giving individuals who are the subject of a quarantine or isolation order the right to seek review by a court within a reasonable time.

A. Authorization

189. A state or local public health agency and not a private individual is authorized to isolate or quarantine an individual or group of individuals, pursuant to rules or regulations promulgated by the state public health agency.

B. Conditions and Principles

190. The state or local public health agency shall adhere to the following conditions and principles when isolating or quarantining individuals or groups of individuals:

(i) Isolation and quarantine must be by the least restrictive means necessary to prevent the spread of a contagious or possibly contagious disease to others and may include, but are not limited to, confinement to private homes or other private and public premises.
(ii) Isolated individuals must be confined separately from quarantined individuals.
(iii) The health status of isolated and quarantined individuals must be monitored regularly to determine if they continue to require isolation or quarantine.
(iv) If a quarantined individual subsequently becomes infected or is reasonably believed to have become infected with a contagious or possibly contagious disease, he or she must promptly be removed to isolation.
(v) Isolation and quarantine must be terminated when an individual poses no substantial risk of transmitting a contagious or possibly contagious disease to others.
(vi) The needs of individuals who are isolated or quarantined should be addressed in a systematic and competent fashion, including, but not limited to, providing adequate food, clothing, shelter, means of communication with those in isolation or quarantine and outside these settings, and medical care.
(vii) Outside premises used for isolation and quarantine shall be maintained in a safe and hygienic manner and be designed to minimize the likelihood of further transmission of infection or other harms to individuals isolated and quarantined.
(viii) To the extent possible, cultural and religious beliefs shall be respected in addressing the needs of individuals and establishing and maintaining isolation and quarantine premises.

C. Entry into Isolation or Quarantine Premises

191. The state or local public health agency may authorize physicians, health care workers, or others access to individuals in isolation or quarantine.

§3. Surveillance System for Disease Outbreak

192. The WHO's Health Systems and Innovation Cluster released its WHO Guidelines on Ethical Issues in Public Health Surveillance. This was the first attempt to develop a framework to guide public health surveillance systems on the conduct of surveillance and reporting in public health emergencies. In the public health context, surveillance—monitoring for disease outbreaks—must be done in a manner that assures the privacy and safety of the individuals concerned. Safety is also a priority to ensure that those who are infected are not vulnerable to attack or discrimination based on their illness. Privacy and safety, however, depend upon more than just the ethical practice of surveillance; it relies upon the social and political environments in which surveillance occurs—in particular, upon good governance and respect for human rights. In many countries the conditions of good governance are not met either because individual rights cannot be protected or because the government is not open to public scrutiny or both. When good governance is missing then individuals and health practitioners who identify and want to report disease outbreaks can be put at risk by their government's attempts to keep the extent of the outbreak concealed.

I. States to Develop Surveillance and Response Capabilities

193. Since 2007, when the IHR came into force, states have been expected to meet eight IHR core capacity requirements to contain public health threats under the new framework. These core capacity requirements include: (i) national legislation; (ii) policy and financing; (iii) coordination and National Focal Point (NFP) communications; (iv) surveillance and response; (v) preparedness; (vi) risk communication; (vii) human resources; and (viii) laboratories.

194. So, under the IHR, states agreed to develop surveillance or detection and response capacities, including the creation of the post of an IHR NFP, available throughout day and night in every country to communicate outbreak events with the WHO. In the revised IHR, the WHO has been given the right to receive reports of disease outbreak events from sources other than the affected state. There is a general reluctance on the part of states to intimate the outbreak. The individuals who report against the wishes of the state about the outbreak may face problems like loss of employment, deportation, threat of imprisonment, and sometimes actual imprisonment. The WHO makes efforts to balance supporting a state in its conduct of public health surveillance and risk communication against supporting non-state actors' right to report relevant and necessary outbreak information. Under Article 9, the WHO has the right to receive reports from non-state actors.

§4. TRANSMISSION OF HIV

195. The Joint United Nations Programme on HIV/AIDS (UNAIDS) and the Global Commission on HIV and the law require that countries should only prosecute HIV transmission in cases of intentional and actual transmission with a high standard of evidence and proof. The Global Commission recommended that countries should repeal provisions that explicitly criminalize HIV transmission and rely on existing laws against assault, laws against causing bodily harm, or laws that permit public health officials to intervene when a person's behavior creates a serious risk of transmission of communicable disease.

I. Transmission of HIV and Criminal Law

196. The role of criminal law in national efforts to prevent transmission of HIV and other sexually transmissible infections is controversial. Public health laws may contain penalties for failing to comply with public health orders made by authorities or for engaging in behaviors that place public health at risk. However, the potential for unintended consequences arising from laws that create criminal offenses cannot be ignored for recklessly exposing another person to HIV or for failing to disclose one's HIV status to a sexual partner. Laws like these may be intended to encourage personal responsibility in the hope that individuals will modify their behavior in order to avoid criminal penalties. They may also be motivated by the belief that those who fail to protect others from HIV transmission or from the risk of transmission deserve punishment. The state criminal laws against HIV in many countries are overly broad, carry harsh penalties, and may not be enforced with fairness.

197. The criminal penalties also create disincentives for individuals to come forward for HIV testing and treatment for fear of criminal penalties or official investigation. This is counterproductive since it is important to encourage individuals to monitor their HIV status and to seek treatment as soon as they are diagnosed, both because those who acquired the virus will have a higher viral load and will be more likely to transmit it and because effective treatment with therapy lowers viral load and makes it less likely that HIV positive individuals will pass on the virus to others. An additional concern that relates to mandatory disclosure laws is the potential for such laws to undermine disease control efforts by weakening the assumption that individuals are primarily responsible for protecting themselves from the risks of transmission of HIV and other sexually transmissible diseases. In countries where large numbers of the population are infected, relying on voluntary disclosure by sexual partners is unrealistic. Individuals may not know their status or may be ashamed, fearful, or, otherwise, unwilling to reveal information about themselves.

§5. COVID-19 and Pandemic Preparedness

198. The rapid spread of the COVID-19 revealed the fact that human rights, the rule of law, democratic institutions and global solidarity are essential to effective public health emergency preparedness and response. It was reiterated in the World Health Assembly (WHA) held between 24 and 31 May 2021 and there was consensus on the need to strengthen international legal standards to ensure future global pandemic preparedness. There was also support for a proposed Pandemic Treaty. But there is a danger that in the guise of emergency actions, rights of the people may not be curtailed.

I. Restrictive Measures in Violation of Human Rights

199. While States and WHO have to be empowered to quickly respond to a public health emergency, there is a danger that States may resort to the "precautionary principle" providing some governments excuse for discriminatory, fear-based, and xenophobic health measures, and unnecessary or disproportionate emergency rules restricting the enjoyment of human rights and fundamental freedoms. The public health measures must be proportionate, nondiscriminatory and based on scientific principles and available scientific evidence. Rather than encouraging nations to turn inwards, a Pandemic Treaty should encourage States to collaborate to better understand the effectiveness and consistency with human rights of various public health measures.

200. The application of the precautionary principle in the event of a pandemic can be no substitute for pandemic preparedness commitments that prioritize a comprehensive public health system and infrastructure internationally. Adequate preparation can only be achieved through global solidarity in compliance with States' obligations to realize the right to health through cooperation and assistance of the countries of the world. To be properly and adequately prepared for the next pandemic, or to overcome continued damage from the current one, States must focus efforts on providing access to quality universal health coverage, education, food, water, sanitation, housing, social security, and other economic and social rights for the people.

II. Access to Health Care

201. The countries must take steps to ensure vaccine equity and access to necessary health care services and products needed to respond to the COVID-19 pandemic. But States have made half-hearted attempts and prioritized national interests and the interests of the powerful, even as the pandemic has deepened inequalities both within and between societies and imposed disproportionate impacts on the most marginalized. States must take coordinated action through global governance to enhance manufacturing and production capacities for vaccines and other essential medicines and health care services and products in all regions of the world. The

States must build an international legal instrument that promotes measures such as sharing data, sharing information, sharing pathogens, sharing resources and sharing technology. They must also maintain a sense of urgency while engaging in thoughtful, sustained and good-faith deliberation. They must also ensure the full participation of civil society, including independent public health and human rights experts, to improve the effectiveness and legitimacy of efforts for emergency pandemic preparedness.

§6. Compulsory Treatment

202. The right to consent to medical treatment is a fundamental individual human right but there can be circumstances where public health authorities may be justified in ordering compulsory treatment. Public health laws should authorize compulsory treatment orders only in circumstances where the person in question is unable or unwilling to consent to a diagnostic procedure or treatment and where such behavior creates a significant risk of transmission of a serious disease to others.

203. A treatment order should clearly state the grounds on which it has been made, set out any restrictions or limitations on behavior, and should take into account the principle that individual liberty only be restricted to the extent necessary to reduce risks to public health. Public health laws should also include procedural rights to protect the interests of individuals subject to treatment orders. This may include the requirement for a court to review each compulsory treatment order within a specified period of time. Public health officials must ensure that laws authorizing treatment without consent are never used to discriminate against or to marginalize vulnerable populations and minority groups.

Part IV. Dimensions of Ethics in the Medical Field

204. "Medical Ethics" is the study of moral values and judgments as they apply to medicine. Ethical principles govern the practice of medicine and ethical theories form the basis of ethical argument. With high-profile cases regarding malpractice of doctors and medical advances in technology, more and more clinical practices are coming under the scrutiny of both the media and the general public. However, medical ethics is not an exact science so in certain situations it may be difficult to know what is ethically "correct."

Chapter 1. Medical Ethics

205. Since the beginning of human history, concern for medical ethics has been expressed in the form of laws, decrees, and "oaths" prepared for or by physicians. Among the oldest of these are the Code of Hammurabi of Babylonia (approximately 1750 B.C.), Egyptian papyri, Indian and Chinese writings, and early Greek writers, most notably Hippocrates (who lived between 460 and 377 B.C.). Early medical ethical codes were written by individuals or by small groups of people, usually physicians. The "Oath of Hippocrates" is considered, historically, to be the first such code written in an organized and logical way, which describes the proper relationship between a physician and patient. During the Middle Ages, other medical codes were written. In recent times, the writings of Thomas Precival, disseminated in 1803, represent one of the first ethical codes in the US and the Western world.

206. Beginning in the second half of the nineteenth century, medical organizations began writing codes of medical ethics. The first ethics code of the American Medical Association (AMA) was published in 1847. This was the first ethical code of a professional organization that outlined the rights of patients and caregivers. Over the years many revisions and additions to this original code have been made. The latest edition of the AMA Code of Medical Ethics (1997) contains four parts, which include general principles, opinions on specific issues, and special reports. The AMA established the Council on Ethical and Judicial Affairs to advise it on legal and ethical issues and to prepare position papers on these issues for the AMA. The British Medical Association published its first Code of Medical Conduct of Physicians in 1858. The Code has subsequently undergone numerous changes. The WHO issued the Declaration of Geneva in 1948. This is the first worldwide medical ethical code and is modeled after the Oath of Hippocrates.

207. Modern medical ethics, as a separate field, began to develop in the 1950s. One of the major innovations of modern Western medical ethics involves the physician–patient relationship with the dramatic change from paternalism to autonomy and its resultant requirement for informing the patient, obtaining informed consent, and relating to the patient as an active partner in decision-making. A physician should not release confidential information about the patient unless it is required by the law. The sex determination test shall not be undertaken with the intent to terminate the life of a female fetus developing in her mother's womb unless there are other justifiable reasons for termination of pregnancy.

208. Ethical theories can be seen as schools of thought when judging the rightness or wrongness of a proposed action or when choosing from a number of proposed actions. There are two main ethical theories that apply to medical practice. The first theory is "Consequentialism," referring to those moral theories which hold that the consequences of a particular action form the basis for any valid moral judgment about that action. The second is "Deontology," which is an approach to ethics that focuses on the rightness or wrongness of actions themselves, as opposed to the rightness or wrongness of the consequences of those actions.

§1. ETHICAL PRINCIPLES

209. The ethical principles that govern medical practice should act as a framework when making medical decisions. When ethical dilemmas arise the best approach is to think through these ethical principles logically and methodically.

I. Beneficence and Nonmaleficence

210. Beneficence is the act of "doing good" while nonmaleficence is the act of "not doing bad." In practical terms, medical practitioners have an ethical responsibility to strive to do what is in the best interests of their patients. However, it is important to remember that some medical interventions may seem beneficial but may also carry with them the possibility of causing harm. In fact, nearly all medical treatments and procedures harm the patient in some way, but it is more to do with the magnitude of the benefit versus the magnitude of potential risks.

II. Autonomy and Consent

211. Autonomy is the right of a patient to make an informed and free decision about their own health management. If this principle is disregarded by a medical professional because he/she believes another decision would be better for the patient, then it is termed paternalism. An autonomous decision should never be overruled by a medical professional, but not all decisions are autonomous. For patients to have autonomy, they must have the capacity to receive and retain the information that is given to them, provided the information is complete and given to them in a manner that they can understand. Consent is an extension of autonomy and has many types.

When a doctor assumes that certain actions or body language from a patient imply that the patient has consented to the planned action of the doctor, it is implied consent. Oral consent is when a patient has verbally given the doctor permission to proceed with the intended procedure. A written consent is documented evidence that the patient has, usually with signature, given consent to a procedure. Written consent should only be obtained after oral consent. Fully informed consent is the consent given after the patient is provided with all the information about the procedure. When possible, fully informed consent, both written and oral, should be obtained before any procedure, examination, or treatment.

III. Truth-Telling

212. The ethical principle of truth-telling is the process in which a doctor gives the patient all known information about his or her health. It allows the patient to be fully informed and, therefore, allows for the ethical principles of autonomy and consent. A fact to be noted is that some patients do not want the information. Therefore, it is important to ask the patient if he or she wants to know or not. The only other occasion when it is acceptable not to tell the patient the truth is when the patient may come to harm on being told.

IV. Confidentiality

213. Confidentiality, in the medical field, refers to the obligation of professionals who have access to patient records or communication to hold that information in confidence. The principle of confidentiality can be traced back to the fourth century B.C. and the Oath of Hippocrates; this concept is foundational to medical professionals' guidelines for confidentiality.[21] The professional obligation to keep health information confidential is also supported in professional association codes of ethics, as incorporated in Principle I of the American Health Information Management Association Code of Ethics, "Advocate, uphold, and defend the individual's right to privacy and the doctrine of confidentiality in the use and disclosure of information."[22] Dating back to English common law, medical doctors and mental health professionals had a tradition of confidentiality with their patients. It has been well established now that anything said by a patient to a doctor or mental health professional in the course of diagnosis or treatment is privileged and confidential except in certain situations. In the US it has been reinforced and expanded with the advent of the Health Insurance Portability and Accountability Act (HIPAA). This federal law deals with a number of issues and creates a number of legal safeguards to protect the confidentiality of a patient's medical and mental health records. The Act created a number of new, formal requirements about disclosures, ways in which information can be exchanged, and keeping patient information confidential. Those who violate the Act can face significant liability.

The ethical principle of confidentiality ensures that the medical information held about a patient is accessible only to those to whom the patient has given access via autonomous and fully informed consent. In order to achieve trust between medical professionals and their patients, confidentiality must be maintained. Confidentiality may be broken if information shared by the patient refers to a potential danger to public safety or if a court orders it.

V. Preservation of Life

214. The ethical principle of preservation of life is a will on the part of the doctor to treat a patient's illness with the aim of prolonging life. After all, most patients want to live longer as most doctors may have joined the profession to save lives.

21. McWay, 2010, p. 174. Referred by Munaoh, Confidentiality in E-Health (May 2017), available at https://ehealthblogsite.wordpress.com/2017/05/13/confidentiality-in-e-health/.
22. American Health Information Management Association (AHIMA) 2011.

VI. Justice

215. Justice refers to the distribution of things and positions of people within the society. In a medical setting, justice involves the allocation of health care resources in a fair way. This may be an equal distribution called egalitarianism or a maximization of the total or average health welfare measures across the whole society known as utilitarianism.

§2. Clinical Ethics

216. In the course of practicing medicine, a range of issues may arise that lead to consultation with a medical ethicist, a lawyer, and/or a risk manager. Clinical ethics is defined as a discipline or methodology for considering the ethical implications of medical technologies, policies, and treatments with special attention to determine what ought to be done or not done in the delivery of health care. Many health care facilities have in-house or on-call trained ethicists to assist health care practitioners, caregivers, and patients with difficult issues arising in medical care. In the hospital setting, this ethics consultation or review process resulted in the formulation of accreditation requirements that mandated that hospitals establish a "mechanism" to consider clinical ethics issues.

I. Risk Management in Health Care

217. The role of lawyers and risk managers is closely linked in many health care facilities. Indeed, in some hospitals, the administrator with the title "Risk Manager" is an attorney with a clinical background. There are, however, important distinctions between law and risk management. Risk management is guided by legal parameters but has a broader institution-specific mission to reduce liability risks. It is not uncommon for a hospital policy to go beyond the minimum requirements set by a legal standard. When legal and risk management issues arise in the delivery of health care, ethical issues may also exist. Similarly, an issue originally identified as falling within the clinical ethics domain may also raise legal and risk management concerns.

If a health care facility is also a religious facility, it may adhere to religious tenets. In general, however, clinical ethics is predominantly a secular professional analytic approach to clinical issues and choices. Risk management may be derived from law, professional standards, and individual institution's mission and public relations strategies and is expressed through institutional policies and practices.

§3. Ethics and Protection of Prisoners and Detainees

218. Principles of Medical Ethics relevant to the Role of Health Personnel, particularly Physicians, in the Protection of Prisoners and Detainees against Torture and

Other Cruel, Inhuman or Degrading Treatment or Punishment have been adopted by General Assembly Resolution 37/194 of 18 December 1982 which provides as follows:

> As per Principle 1 and 2, health personnel, particularly physicians, charged with the medical care of prisoners and detainees have a duty to provide them with protection of their physical and mental health and treatment of disease of the same quality and standard as is afforded to those who are not imprisoned or detained. It will be a gross contravention of medical ethics to engage, actively or passively, in acts which constitute participation in, complicity in, incitement to or attempts to commit torture or other cruel, inhuman or degrading treatment or punishment. The physicians must not be involved in any professional relationship with prisoners or detainees, the purpose of which is not solely to evaluate, protect or improve their physical and mental health (Principle 3).
>
> As per Principle 4, it is a contravention of medical ethics for health personnel, particularly physicians:
>
> (a) To apply their knowledge and skills in order to assist in the interrogation of prisoners and detainees in a manner that may adversely affect the physical or mental health or condition of such prisoners or detainees and which is not in accordance with the relevant international instruments;
>
> (b) To certify, or to participate in the certification of, the fitness of prisoners or detainees for any form of treatment or punishment that may adversely affect their physical or mental health and which is not in accordance with the relevant international instruments, or to participate in any way in the infliction of any such treatment or punishment which is not in accordance with the relevant international instruments.
>
> The health personnel, particularly physicians should not participate in any procedure for restraining a prisoner or detainee unless such a procedure is determined in accordance with purely medical criteria as being necessary for the protection of the physical or mental health or the safety of the prisoner or detainee himself, of his fellow prisoners or detainees, or of his guardians, and presents no hazard to his physical or mental health (Principle 5). There may be no derogation from the foregoing principles on any ground whatsoever, including public emergency (Principle 6).

§4. European Charter of Medical Ethics (ECME)

219. In European Union, each Member State has its own Code of Medical Ethics, which has been adopted by an authoritative medical association, and in some countries, also by the State. On the one hand, these Codes share very similar purposes and values, but on the other hand, they also reflect, to some extent, the cultural, ethical and legal traditions of each country, especially on fundamental bioethical issues.

In view of specific idea of a European Union and free movement of physicians and patients within the EU, there is a need for harmonization of the Codes of Medical Ethics of the European countries. In furtherance of which the project of a common European Code of Medical Ethics was born. In fact, a European Code of Medical Ethics is intended as a practical instrument able both to safeguard the will and need of the patients and to guide the physician's medical practice at a European level.

220. The ECME includes the principles on which a physician's behavior is based in the practice of their profession. The Charter finds its legitimacy in the work carried out since many years by the European Council of Medical Orders. The principles given in the charter inspire the professional conduct of doctors in their contact with patients, with society and between themselves. It also refers to the specific situation of doctors, upon which good medical practice depends. It recommends that medical professional associations in each Member State of the European Community take such measures to ensure that their national requirements relating to the duties and rights of doctors regarding their patients and society, and in their professional relationships, conform with the principles set out in the Charter, and to take all useful measures so that the legislation in their country allows the efficient implementation of these principles.

I. Updating the Principles of Medical Ethics

221. In 2010, it was decided to update the Principles of European Medical Ethics of 1987 by distinguishing what is of ethics or Deontology etc. At present, the European Council of Medical Orders (ECMO) that gathers 15 Medical Councils of the European Member States and Associated Countries (including France, United Kingdom, Ireland, Germany, Austria, Switzerland, Belgium, Luxembourg, the Netherlands, Italy, Spain, Greece, Cyprus, Romania and Slovenia) is the only European official body working on the harmonization of professional rules of medical practice in the EU, with the final goal to elaborate a common European Code of Medical Ethics. For this purpose, the ECMO has so far released a number of documents that include common European principles of medical ethics like the Charter of the Principles of European Medical Ethics (2011) and the Deontological Guidelines (2013).

II. The Charter of European Medical Ethics (2011)

222. The expansion and developments of the European Community provide the opportunity for physicians to extend their influence, not only on a joint ethical basis but also relative to the principles of behavior to be respected in the practice of their profession. The ECME includes the principles on which physicians' behavior in the practice of their profession is based, no matter what type of practice they have. The European medical community agreed to respect the ECME. The Charter provides as follows:

The physician should defend human physical and mental health and relieve suffering while respecting the life and dignity of the person concerned with no discrimination, of any kind, in peace and in war (Principle 1). The physician agrees to give priority to the interest of the patient's health (Principle 2). The physician gives the patient the most essential and appropriate care, without any discrimination (Principle 3). The physician will take the environment in which the patient lives and works as decisive elements relative to his/her health (Principle 4). The physician is the patient's essential confidant. He betrays this confidence on revealing what he has learned from the patient (Principle 5).

The physician uses his professional knowledge to improve or maintain the health of those confiding in him, at their request; he may not act to their detriment under any circumstances (Principle 6). While respecting personal autonomy, the physician will act in accordance with the principle of treatment efficacy, taking into consideration the equitable use of resources (Principle 8). The physician must never accept acts of torture or any other form of cruel, inhuman or degrading treatment, no matter what the arguments may be, under any circumstances, including those of civil or military conflict (Principle 10).

The physician acting as a simple practitioner toward a patient, or as an expert or member of an institution, must ensure the greatest transparency in what might appear to be a conflict of interest and act in full moral and technical independence (Principle 11). If the moral and technical conditions are such as to prevent the physician from acting in full independence, he must inform the patient. The physician is not required to satisfy requests for treatment which he does not approve. However, medical practice involves respect of the life, moral autonomy and freedom of choice of the patient (Principle 14). The physician exercises his profession with conscience, dignity toward himself and the others and in independence (Principle 15).

Chapter 2. Medical Ethics and Human Rights

223. Human rights give fundamental protections to human beings that try to save them from all types of oppression. They prevent the worst excesses of democracy because no society can vote to take away these rights. When someone has a right, another person or institution has a duty to comply with that right. This may be a moral right, where there is a corresponding moral duty, or a legal right, where there is a legal agreement that the right exists. The term human rights, in the international arena, is used to describe rights that are enshrined in international agreements by which states agree not to be in breach and follow them in their actions.

§1. Historical Background

224. References to some of the basic human rights concepts are found in the Code of Hammurabi (1780 BCE) and Aristotle's *Nichomachean Ethics* (330 B.C.). One of the first legal instruments in the UK covering human rights issues was *Magna Carta* (A.D. 1215). Up to this point the sovereign's word was the law, so justice was, at best, arbitrary. As a consequence of *Magna Carta*, men of property gained some rights against the absolute rule of the king. Renaissance brought forth the idea that all men were equal. Hobbes argued that civil wars are so damaging to all concerned that any form of stable society, however totalitarian, was to be preferred. He described the "State of Nature" in which humans coexisted before the first societies had developed, contrasting this with a situation of anarchy in which life was "nasty, brutish and short." Locke, by contrast, argued that "no one ought to harm another in his life, health, liberty or possessions."

I. Social Justice

225. Jean-Jacques Rousseau said that man exchanged the right to self-protection for more subtle rights. Members of the society are to be treated equally, and resources should be allocated on the basis of need. Thus, there is an agreed concept of social justice. These ideas were advanced by the American Declaration of Independence (1776) and the French Declaration of the Rights of Man and the Citizen (1789). The horrors of World War II compelled us to recognize that rights must be enforceable and that states cannot be relied on to protect the rights of minorities. Thus, a system of international agreements was slowly built up, starting with the Universal Declaration of Human Rights in 1948.

Medical ethics, starting with the Hippocratic School in Ancient Greece, attempted to set itself apart from the other healers by stressing that their pursuits were rational and scientific rather than magical or religious. The code provided rules for both the doctor–patient relationship and professional etiquette. Hippocrates lived in around 460–380 B.C. By the beginning of the Renaissance in the early sixteenth century, the rediscovery of the medical writings of antiquity was complete and was beginning to be challenged by scientific developments.

II. Medicine: An Art Based on Sympathy

226. John Gregory lectured on medical ethics as Professor of Practice of Physics in Edinburgh and published his lectures just before dying in 1773. He redefined medical humanism in the context of the Scottish Enlightenment of philosophers such as his friend David Hume. Hume wrote that man was motivated not only by reason but also by compassion. Thus, we all share a common morality, based both on our emotions and on our rationality. Gregory portrayed medicine as an art based on virtues, especially that of sympathy. Like Hippocrates, he wanted to set doctors apart from untrained healers who were interested only in getting money from patients. This instituted the ideal of the humanistic physician with some ethical standards whose effectiveness derives both from empathy and from medical science.

So, bioethics is a collaboration between philosophers of different theoretical schools. One school, the deontologists, adopted a rule-based theory following principally on the works of Kant. The other main school is the utilitarian which follows from the works of Bentham and judges actions by their consequences. The outcome of these deliberations was ethics based on four principles—autonomy, justice, nonmaleficence, and beneficence. Nonmaleficence goes back to Hippocrates, and the principle of not deliberately harming another person is the cornerstone of certificatory justice. However, beneficence is unique to biomedical ethics.

§2. Differences Between Human Rights and Medical Ethics

227. There are some fundamental differences between human rights and medical ethics. One is that the focus in human rights is on state-level action rather than a person-to-person relationship. The other is the issue of benevolence, which is important in the theory of biomedical ethics but has no place in human rights discourse. Rights do not depend on the empathy of other actors. The conflict between human rights and medical ethics has been in court cases where the rule of law, an essential part of democratic society, requires medical confidentiality to be breached. Patients expect confidentiality to be absolute, otherwise they would not trust doctors with their intimate details, and medical ethics require that this information is protected. Human rights, however, demand that justice takes priority and doctors know that, despite great reluctance, they may be obliged to disclose confidential information to a court.

In psychiatry, many patients are considered to lack competence as a consequence of their medical condition. Thus, formal medical ethics falls back on beneficence to decide how patients should be treated. As society has increasingly rejected paternalism, a model based on human rights is replacing it which encourages patients to be involved in decisions about their care, making use of whatever capacity they have and providing legal frameworks to allow clinical decisions to be reviewed regularly. Human rights place a duty on the state and on health care providers to comply with minimum standards. Medical ethics place a duty on individual doctors to comply with parallel standards. Human rights and medical ethics are complementary, and the use of the two together maximizes the protection available to the vulnerable patient.

§3. Right to Health Care

228. Human rights relate to the individual and put limits on what a state can do to that person. They are independent of the state so even in a democratic state there cannot be a vote to take away anyone's human rights. Some rights are absolute, such as the right not to be held in slavery. Some are qualified, such as the right to liberty, which permits detention on following certain procedural norms. The right to health care is well established, encompassing not only the delivery of basic clinical services but also an environment that allows good health to flourish. A right can entail a negative duty, such as not torturing the person, or a positive duty, such as providing legal representation during a trial.

Part V. Medical Research and Legal Issues

229. Medical research involving human subjects must conform to generally accepted safeguards and scientific principles and must be based on a thorough knowledge of the scientific literature, other relevant sources of information, and on adequate laboratory and animal experimentation. It is the duty of the physician in medical research to protect the life, health, privacy, and dignity of the human subject. Caution has to be exercised in the conduct of research, which may affect the environment, and the welfare of subjects used for research must be ensured.

Chapter 1. Regulation of Medical Research on Human Subjects

230. Medical progress is based on research which rests, in part, on experimentation involving animal and human subjects. In medical research on human subjects, the well-being of the human subject should take precedence over the interests of science and society. The primary purpose of medical research involving human subjects is to improve prophylactic, diagnostic, and therapeutic procedures and pathogenesis of the disease. Even the best proven prophylactic, diagnostic, and therapeutic methods must continuously be challenged through research for their effectiveness, efficiency, and quality. In current medical practice and in medical research, most prophylactic, diagnostic, and therapeutic procedures involve risks and burdens.

231. It may be very difficult to determine what constitutes human subjects research. The definitions of human subject research are intentionally broad to include a wide range of research in the hope of capturing both the biomedical and humanities spectrums. "Research" is defined as a systematic investigation, including research development, testing, and evaluation, designed to develop or contribute to generalizable knowledge. The term "Research" is also defined as any experiment that involves a test article and one or more human subjects and that, either, must meet certain requirements. The other related issue is how to define human subjects. A human subject is defined as a living individual about whom a research investigator obtains data through intervention or interaction with the individual or from individually identifiable information. "Intervention" means both physical procedures by which data are gathered and manipulations of the subject or the subject's environment that are performed for research.

§1. WMA Declaration of Helsinki[23]

232. The WMA has developed the Declaration of Helsinki as a statement of ethical principles to provide guidance to physicians and others in medical research involving human subjects. It is the duty of the physician to promote and safeguard the health of the people. The physician's knowledge and conscience must be dedicated to the fulfillment of this duty. The Declaration of Geneva of the WMA binds the physician with the words, "The health of my patient will be my first consideration," and the International Code of Medical Ethics declares that, "A physician shall act only in the patient's interest when providing medical care which might have the effect of weakening the physical and mental condition of the patient."

23. Ethical Principles for Medical Research Involving Human Subjects Adopted by the 18th WMA General Assembly, Helsinki, Finland, June 1964.

§2. Medical Research and Ethical Standards

233. Medical research is subject to ethical standards that promote respect for all human beings and protect their health and rights. Some research subjects are vulnerable and need special protection. The particular needs of the economically and medically disadvantaged sections of the society must be recognized. Special attention is also required for those who cannot give or refuse consent for themselves, for those who may be subject to giving consent under duress, for those who will not benefit personally from the research, and for those for whom the research is combined with care. Research investigators should be aware of the ethical, legal, and regulatory requirements for research on human subjects in their own countries as well as applicable international requirements. No national ethical, legal, or regulatory requirement should be allowed to reduce or eliminate any of the protections for human subjects set forth in this Declaration.

§3. Basic Principles for All Medical Research

I. Experimental Protocol

234. The design and method of each experimental procedure involving human subjects should be clearly formulated in an experimental protocol. This protocol should be submitted for consideration, comment, guidance, and, where appropriate, approval to a specially appointed ethical review committee, which must be independent of the investigator, the sponsor, or any other kind of undue influence. This independent committee should be in conformity with the laws and regulations of the country in which the experimental research is being conducted. The researcher will be under obligation to provide monitoring information to the committee, especially any serious adverse events. The research protocol should contain a statement of the ethical considerations involved and should indicate that there is compliance with the principles enunciated in the Declaration.

II. Proper Risk Assessment

235. Medical research involving human subjects should be conducted only by scientifically qualified persons and under the supervision of a clinically competent medical person. The responsibility for the human subject must always rest with a medically qualified person and never rest on the subject of the research, even though the subject has given consent. Every medical research project involving human subjects should be preceded by careful assessment of predictable risks and burdens in comparison with foreseeable benefits to the subject or to others. This does not preclude the participation of healthy volunteers in medical research. The design of all studies should be publicly available. Physicians should abstain from engaging in research projects involving human subjects unless they are confident that the risks involved have been adequately assessed and can be satisfactorily managed. Physicians should cease any investigation if the risks are found to outweigh the potential benefits. Medical research involving human subjects should only be conducted if the importance of the objective outweighs the inherent risks and burdens to the subject. This is especially important when the human subjects are healthy volunteers.

III. Transparency

236. Medical research is only justified if there is a reasonable likelihood that the populations in which the research is carried out stand to benefit from the results of the research. The subjects must be volunteers and informed participants in the research project. The right of research subjects to safeguard their integrity must always be respected. Every precaution should be taken to respect the privacy of the subject, the confidentiality of the patient's information, and to minimize the impact of the study on the subject's physical and mental integrity and on the personality of the subject. In any research on human beings, each potential subject must be adequately informed of the aims, methods, sources of funding, any possible conflicts of interest, the anticipated benefits and potential risks of the study, and the discomfort it may entail. The subject should be informed of the right to abstain from participation in the study or to withdraw consent to participate at any time without reprisal. After ensuring that the subject has understood the information, the physician should then obtain the subject's freely given informed consent, preferably in writing. If the consent cannot be obtained in writing, the non-written consent must be formally documented and witnessed.

IV. Informed Consent

237. While obtaining informed consent for the research project the physician should be particularly cautious if the subject is in a dependent relationship with the physician or may consent under duress. In that case the informed consent should be obtained by a well-informed physician who is not engaged in the investigation and who is completely independent of this relationship. For a research subject who is legally incompetent, physically or mentally incapable of giving consent, or is a legally incompetent minor, the investigator must obtain informed consent from the legally authorized representative in accordance with applicable law. These groups should not be included in research unless the research is necessary to promote the health of the population represented and this research cannot instead be performed on legally competent persons. When a subject deemed legally incompetent, such as a minor child, is able to give assent to decisions about participation in research, the investigator must obtain that assent in addition to the consent of the legally authorized representative.

238. Research on individuals from whom it is not possible to obtain consent, including proxy or advance consent, should be done only if the physical/mental condition that prevents obtaining informed consent is a necessary characteristic of the research population. The specific reasons for involving research subjects with a condition that renders them unable to give informed consent should be stated in the experimental protocol for the consideration and approval of the review committee. The protocol should state that consent to remain in the research should be obtained as soon as possible from the individual or a legally authorized surrogate.

V. Publication of Results

239. In the publication of the results of research, the investigators are obliged to preserve the accuracy of the results. Negative as well as positive results should be published or, otherwise, be publicly available. Sources of funding, institutional affiliations, and any possible conflicts of interest should be declared in the publication. Reports of experimentation not in accordance with the principles laid down in this Declaration should not be accepted for publication.

§4. Additional Principles for Medical Research Combined with Medical Care

240. The physician may combine medical research with medical care. When medical research is combined with medical care, additional standards apply to protect the patients who are research subjects. The benefits, risks, burdens, and effectiveness of a new method should be tested against those of the best current prophylactic, diagnostic, and therapeutic methods. This does not exclude the use of placebo, or no treatment, in studies where no proven prophylactic, diagnostic, or therapeutic method exists.

241. At the conclusion of the study, every patient entered into the study should be assured of access to the best proven prophylactic, diagnostic, and therapeutic methods identified by the study. The physician should fully inform the patient which aspects of the care are related to the research. The refusal of a patient to participate in a study must never interfere with the patient–physician relationship. In the treatment of a patient where proven prophylactic, diagnostic, and therapeutic methods do not exist or have been ineffective, the physician, with informed consent from the patient, must be free to use unproven or new prophylactic, diagnostic, and therapeutic measures if, in the physician's judgment, it offers hope of saving life, reestablishing health or alleviating suffering. Where possible, these measures should be made the object of research, designed to evaluate their safety and efficacy. In all cases, new information should be recorded and, where appropriate, published.

§5. Multicenter Trials

242. The globalization of health care research and clinical trials brings challenges, which pharmaceutical companies, central labs and other life sciences companies try to overcome. The areas which pose challenges when running multicenter trials can be broadly divided into: statistical, regulatory, ethical, clinical, operational and recruitment challenges. Statistical issues include the effect that differences between countries will have on the sample size or power estimates for the trial, and differences in randomization processes. Clinical issues may include differences in access to health care between countries, how diseases are defined and indications for treatment. Operational issues may include differences in standard operating procedures, access to drugs, training of investigators and the quality of the data obtained from each site. Regulatory issues may include obtaining approvals from different regulatory bodies and the variation in regulations between different countries. Ethical issues may include ensuring that full informed consent is obtained from participants, ensuring sufficient safety of the participants, privacy of data, and ensuring the trials follow the good clinical practice.

There must be sufficient numbers of participants so that the study has enough statistical power.

I. Differing Regulations and Monitoring

243. Each country has its own drug regulatory body with different policies on the use of medicines. Investigators need to obtain agreements from different health authorities and manage different time frames for review and approval. Several research ethics committees from various countries may be involved in reviewing the trial protocol. Their findings may be conflicting, which could delay the review process and in some cases, approval for the trial could be withheld. Regulatory authorities in different countries also have different standards. This could be addressed by adapting international standards to the country in which the trial is based. There could also be adaptation of local standards to more closely follow international guidelines. The variation in standards for monitoring trials between countries may also lead to differences in the accuracy and validity of trial data, and the safety mechanisms in place for participants. Multinational study groups need to ensure that there are high standards across all sites even though formal monitoring by regulatory bodies may not be consistent.

II. Equipment and Medical Products

244. The International Council for Harmonization of Technical Requirements for Pharmaceuticals for Human Use (ICH) has published guidelines that require sponsors to confirm that facilities and equipment are safe enough to use throughout the trial. This includes documenting certification, accreditation or external quality assessment or quality control. Many clinical trial sites are chosen because they offer the potential to recruit sufficient number of patients, rather than their ability to carry out the trial protocol. As a result, sites may not have the best equipment or expertise to carry out more complex trials. An example of this is where trials involve imaging protocols. If, after a site survey, a trial site is not suitable for the protocol, one option might be to find another facility that does have the required imaging equipment that is near to the trial site. It would be desirable that an experienced equipment supplier is contracted to manage all elements of equipment supply. This will ensure that all trial sites receive equipment compatible according to the country and regional equipment specifications, and that all end of study reporting requirements are met. The different requirements for importing medicinal products and medical devices in different countries must be taken into account while formulating a protocol that includes international trial sites.

§6. Vaccine Development

245. Like any other medicine, COVID-19 vaccines are first tested in the laboratory which consists of studies on their pharmaceutical quality and to check first the effects in laboratory tests and animals. In the next stage of studies, vaccines are tested in human volunteers called clinical trials. These tests help confirm how the vaccines work and their safety and protective efficacy are evaluated. The developer then first makes small batches and performs studies to determine a suitable formulation that can keep vaccine components stable to the end of their shelf life. Then the developer decides whether to continue development and scale up production. To assure that the vaccine meets its intended quality profile and complies with regulatory standards, a suitable and effective quality control strategy is formulated. The vaccine developer conducts more studies in laboratory models, using in vitro studies or animal models (in vivo studies) to show how the vaccine triggers an immune response and works to prevent infection. Finally, the vaccine developer studies the vaccine in three phases of clinical trials, with a large number of volunteers in each phase. For approval, the developer must also show that large-scale commercial manufacturing produces vaccines of the required quality. Scaling up production and adaptations to commercial manufacturing can continue in the post-authorization phase.

246. In view of the critical importance of rapid availability and deployment of effective vaccines against COVID-19, WHO has issued R&D Blueprints, namely "Solidarity Vaccine Trial." This protocol is for a large, international, multisite, individually randomized controlled clinical trial that will enable the concurrent evaluation of the benefits and risks of the vaccine within three to six months of it being made available for the trial. Candidate vaccines may be added to the trial as they become available if they meet prioritization criteria (to be defined via the WHO vaccine prioritization group). The aim is to provide reliable data within three to six months of receiving adequate supplies from the sponsor. The proposed primary outcome will be virologically confirmed COVID-19 disease, regardless of severity. Efficacy follow-up includes weekly contacts and blinded study follow-up for at least one year, although for vaccines found to be substantially protective, vaccine and placebo recipients may be un-blinded sooner.

Part VI. Rights and Responsibilities of Medical Professionals and Patients

247. The physician–patient relationship is a relationship of faith and trust which is very important for the fast recovery of the patient. The importance of this relationship has been recognized from ancient times as physicians were required to take Hippocratic Oath. The Hippocratic Oath is an oath historically taken by physicians and other health care professionals swearing to practice medicine ethically and honestly and for them the interest of the patient shall be paramount in all circumstances. It is believed to have been written by either Hippocrates, often regarded as the father of Western medicine, or by one of his students. Physicians, for their failings, may face professional and personal consequences as well as negligence lawsuits. On the other hand, those who do not understand their legal right to refuse to work in unsafe conditions may face serious injury and even death. Globally, physicians are grappling with similar issues, although the legal implications vary in each country.

248. Physicians must be aware of their legal rights and duties specific to the circumstances in which they work. Physicians can gain insight into their obligations by becoming familiar with general legal doctrines and legislation developed in non-pandemic cases. For example, physicians working during a pandemic may contemplate terminating their relationship with certain patients. However, an abrupt severance of the physician–patient relationship could result in a negligence suit if it causes injury to the patient that would have been foreseeable to a reasonable physician.

Chapter 1. The Rights and Duties of Physicians

249. A physician has an important and dignified function in the society and is considered as the main pillar of the well-being of the community. The Declaration of Geneva of the WMA binds the physician with the words, "the health of my patient will be my first consideration." The International Code of Medical Ethics embodies that a physician shall act in the patient's best interest when providing medical care. However, sometimes doctors and hospitals refuse treatment to patients, which is against the basic tenets of medical ethics with certain exceptions. While there can be many valid grounds on part of doctors to refuse treatment, the ground reality remains that helpless patients in need of urgent medical attention are sometimes sent running from pillar to post, without getting the necessary and timely treatment. Another problem is that the prohibitively exorbitant cost of private medical treatment may be beyond the affordability of a patient.

§1. Legal Rights of Physicians

I. Legal Right to Refuse the Work

250. A physician may refuse to work or do a particular work if he or she believes, on reasonable grounds, that it constitutes a danger to his or her safety or health or to the safety or health of another worker or person. The norms for the right to refuse to work because of unsafe conditions may be slightly different in different areas. During a pandemic, physicians may be faced with conditions they believe are unsafe. The right to refuse to work while unsafe conditions exist depends on the circumstances and the country in which they are practicing. If physicians have a legal right, they may stop working until the unsafe situation has been addressed.

A. Pandemic as a Workplace Hazard and Right to Refuse Work

251. Whether a pandemic virus constitutes a workplace hazard depends on the nature of the virus. An infectious disease might be considered a workplace hazard if the risk of contracting the virus is substantially higher in the workplace than in the community. During a pandemic, certain populations will emerge for whom the virus will pose a grave risk. A physician with a susceptibility to infection may refuse to work or practice only if they reasonably believe that the work environment creates an unacceptable hazard. On the other hand, it is unlikely that physicians will refuse work that is part of their normal working conditions. Normal working conditions can be questioned only when the standard safety equipment is malfunctioning or the existing and established practice in the new circumstance creates an imminent danger or risk.

252. The physicians, who are engaged in public health work, should enlighten the public concerning quarantine regulations and measures for the prevention of an epidemic and communicable diseases. At all times the physician should notify the public health authorities over every case of communicable disease under his care, in accordance with the existing laws, rules, and regulations. A balance has to be drawn between the professional right of discretion of doctors regarding which patients they would like to treat and the obligations that a doctor owes to individuals in need of treatment and the public at large.

II. Right to Refuse Treatment

253. As per normal social expectations, a doctor must exercise his professional rights and obligations responsibly. Under no circumstance should he exercise his discretion in providing medical treatment unreasonably, irresponsibly, or arbitrarily. Religion, nationality, race, party politics, social standing, etc. cannot be a ground of refusing treatment to a patient as this profession is considered to be a service to humanity. Thus, a doctor can refuse to treat a patient only on justified grounds. However, an unreasonably onerous burden of responsibility cannot and should not be placed on doctors if there is lack of resources and only limited infrastructure is available. For instance, if even after reasonable and ordinary clinic timings, there is a queue of patients, he may refuse to provide them a consultation on that day except treatment to a patient requiring emergency medical care, which a doctor should not refuse.

254. In the following situations and circumstances a doctor can refuse to give treatment to a patient:

(i) If the doctor does not have adequate skill or means to treat the patient.
(ii) If referring the patient to another medical practitioner is beneficial for the patient; for example, if the doctor does not have the time or the expertise to attend to the needs of the patient.
(iii) If the doctor does not have the adequate facilities or equipment necessary for the treatment of the patient.

III. Right to Withdraw

255. Once a doctor chooses to serve a patient he has to take utmost care of him, and the responsibilities of doctors extend even in the event of withdrawal of medical treatment. A doctor can withdraw from a case only after having given proper notice to the patient or to his friends or relatives, based on good reasons, ensuring that the patient is in no way adversely affected or prejudiced by the withdrawal of treatment. A doctor cannot deny treatment to an existing patient arbitrarily and cannot deprive a patient of necessary medical care as it will amount to medical negligence.

§2. LEGAL DUTIES OF PHYSICIANS

I. Legal Duty of Care in Emergency

256. Physicians working in emergency care of a hospital or who regularly provide emergency services may be found to owe a duty of care to people who are not their patients because of the reliance placed on these physicians to provide emergency treatment. These physicians may face liability if they turn away people who require emergency care during a pandemic. In assessing liability, the courts will consider what a reasonable physician would have done in those circumstances. A physician serving a rural or isolated community might also be legally precluded from turning away a person who is not his or her patient, at least while the condition is serious and travel to an alternative medical facility is unrealistic. Irrespective of a legal duty of care for someone who is not a patient, if a physician chooses to come to a person's aid during an emergency, he or she may have created a physician–patient relationship and, therefore, assumed the resulting liability.

II. Ethical Duty of Care and Legal Implications

257. As members of a self-regulated profession, physicians have ethical responsibilities to their patients, to society, to the profession, and to themselves. Anyone concerned about a physician breaching the Code of Ethics can lodge a complaint with the appropriate authorities. If a breach has occurred, the physician may be found guilty of professional misconduct and can be fined or have his or her medical license revoked. During a pandemic, physicians may experience tension between their ethical responsibilities and their legal rights and duties. For example, the Code of Ethics requires that physicians have a fundamental ethical responsibility to "consider first the well-being of the patient" but also to "promote and maintain [their] own health and well-being." The issues become more complicated when one considers physicians' legal duty of care and their legal right to refuse to work in unsafe conditions. Physicians need to know that the existence of this separate regulatory regime does not negate their right to refuse to work in unsafe conditions, nor does it shield them from negligence liability for a breach of their legal duty of care.

III. Duty to Treat

258. A physician is not bound to treat each and every person asking for his services; however, he should be ready to respond to the calls of the sick and the injured and should also be mindful of his responsibility. In his treatment, he should not forget that the health and the lives of those entrusted to his care depend on his care, skill, and attention. A physician should endeavor to add to the comfort of the sick by making his visits at the hour indicated to the patients. A physician advising a patient to seek service of another physician is acceptable; however, in case of emergency, a physician must treat the patient. However, for a good reason, when a patient is suffering from an ailment that is not within the range of experience of the treating physician, the physician may refuse treatment and refer the patient to another physician.

259. The physician should neither exaggerate nor minimize the gravity of a patient's condition. He should ensure himself that the patient, his relatives, or his responsible friends have such knowledge of the patient's condition as will serve the best interests of the patient and the family. A physician is free to choose whom he will serve but a patient should not be neglected. Once having undertaken a case, the physician should not neglect the patient, nor should he withdraw from the case without giving adequate notice to the patient and his family. A medical practitioner should not willfully commit an act of negligence that may deprive his patient or patients of necessary medical care. Within the legal framework, the right to emergency medical care has been accepted by the international community.

IV. Duty to Keep Privacy Information Confidential

260. Confidentiality is the basic foundation for the physician–patient relationship. For making proper diagnoses and providing treatment, the physician must have relevant information about the patient's illness or injury. This may require the disclosure of sensitive information, which would be embarrassing or harmful if it were known to other persons. The promise of confidentiality enables the patient to trust that information revealed to the physician will not be further disclosed. The expectation of confidentiality derives from the public oath which the physician has taken and from the accepted code of professional ethics. The physician's duty to maintain confidentiality extends from respect for the patient's autonomy. The private information shared and confidence reposed concerning individual or domestic life entrusted by patients to a physician and defects in the disposition or character of patients observed during medical attendance should never be revealed unless their revelation is required by the law. Sometimes, however, a physician must determine whether his duty to society requires him to employ knowledge, obtained through confidence as a physician, to protect a healthy person against a communicable disease to which he is about to be exposed. In such instance, the physician should act as he would wish another to act toward one of his own family in like circumstances.

261. In case of serious illness and in doubtful or difficult conditions, the physician should request consultation, but under any circumstances, such consultation should be justifiable and in the interest of the patient only and not for any other consideration. Consulting pathologists/radiologists or asking for any other diagnostic lab investigation should be done judiciously and not in a routine manner. All statements to the patient or his representatives should take place in the presence of the consulting physicians, except as otherwise agreed. The disclosure of the opinion to the patient or his relatives or friends shall rest with the medical attendant. Difference of opinion should not be divulged unnecessarily, but when there is an irreconcilable difference of opinion the circumstances should be frankly and impartially explained to the patient or his relatives or friends. It would be open to them to seek further advice as they so desire. No decision should restrain the attending physician from making such subsequent variations in the treatment if any unexpected change occurs, but at the next consultation, reasons for the variations should be discussed and explained. The same privilege, with its obligations, belongs to the consultant when sent for in an emergency during the absence of an attending physician. The attending physician may prescribe medicine at any time for the patient, whereas the consultant may prescribe only in case of emergency or as an expert when called for.

V. Duty to Disclose Information

262. A physician should keep secrecy and respect a patient's dignity. He should give patients the information they request about the diagnosis, treatment, and prognosis. Physicians should provide this information to those with parental responsibility where the patients are less than 18 years old. In principle, the patient has the right to know his diagnosis and has the right to keep his diagnosis confidential, even from his family. However, caution should be exercised in disclosing information that is distressing to the patient. The patient's family should be contacted and the diagnosis discussed with them prior to its disclosure to the patient, unless the patient has asked the physician not to discuss his diagnosis with anybody. The physician should be satisfied that the patient has understood what is proposed and consents to it before treatment is started. The right of the patients to be fully involved in the decisions about their care must be ensured.

263. A physician must not allow his views about a patient's culture, beliefs, race, color, gender, age, social status, or perceived economic worth to influence the treatment given to the patient. Physicians have a responsibility to deal with the complaint constructively and honestly. A physician must not allow a patient's complaint to influence the care or treatment provided to the patient. If a patient under the care of a physician has suffered serious harm, action should immediately be taken to put matters right. The concerned physician should explain to the patient and his family what has happened and the likely effects of the same.

VI. Duty to Maintain Medical Records

264. A medical practitioner has to maintain medical records pertaining to its indoor or outdoor patients for a period of at least three years from the date of commencement of treatment. In case any request is made for medical records, either by the patient/authorized attendant or legal authorities involved, the same may be duly acknowledged and records are be issued within a reasonable period of time. It is the right of every patient to obtain, in writing, about his/her medical illness, investigations, and treatment given on a prescription/discharge sheet. Non-providing of medical records to the patients or attendants may amount to deficiency in service.

Chapter 2. Rights of Patient

265. It is common medical practice that physicians or doctors make decisions for their patients, but this view has gradually been supplanted by one promoting patient autonomy whereby patients and doctors share the decision-making responsibility. Consequently doctor–patient relationships are very different now than they were just a few decades ago. However, conflicts still abound as the medical community and patients try to define their respective rights, duties, and roles.

§1. Right of Patient to Be Asked for Consent

266. The concept of consent is based on the inviolability of one's person. This right implies that doctors do not have the right to touch or treat a patient without the patient's approval because the patient is the one who must live with the consequences and deal with any discomfort caused by treatment. A doctor can be held liable for committing a battery if the doctor touches the patient without obtaining the patient's consent. The shift in doctor–patient relationships seems inevitable as in one early consent case, a doctor told a woman he would only be repairing some cervical and rectal tears; instead, he performed a hysterectomy. In another case, a patient permitted her doctors to examine her under anesthesia but insisted that they not operate; the doctors removed a fibroid tumor during the procedure. In yet another case, a doctor assured a man that a proposed operation was simple and without risk; the patient's left hand was paralyzed as a result of the surgery.

I. Informed Consent

267. Simply consenting to treatment is not enough. A patient must give informed consent, which means that before a doctor can treat or touch a patient, the patient must be given some basic information about what the doctor proposes to do and its likely consequences or impact. Informed consent is the most important legal doctrine with respect to the right of a patient. The informed consent requires more detailed disclosure so that the patient understands clearly the implications. Informed consent is required not only in life-or-death situations but also in clinic and outpatient settings as well. A health care provider must first present information regarding risks, alternatives, and success rates. The information must be presented in a language understandable to the patient and should include the following:

(a) a description of the recommended treatment or procedure;
(b) a description of the risks and benefits—particularly exploring the risk of serious bodily disability or death;
(c) a description of alternative treatments and the risks and benefits of alternatives;
(d) the probable results if no treatment is undertaken;
(e) the probability of success and explanation of what the doctor means by success;
(f) length and challenges of recuperation; and

(g) any other information generally provided to patients in this situation by other qualified physicians.

268. Informed consent may not, legally, be required to be in writing, but this does provide evidence that consent was, in fact, obtained. The more specific the consent, the less likely it will be construed against a doctor or a hospital in a court of law. Conversely, blanket consent forms cover almost everything a doctor or hospital might do to a patient without mentioning anything specific and are easily construed against a doctor or hospital. However, blanket forms are frequently used upon admission to a hospital to provide proof of consent to noninvasive routine hospital procedures, such as taking blood pressure. A consent form may not contain a clause waiving a patient's right to sue unless the law provides for binding arbitration upon mutual agreement. Moreover, consent can be predicated upon a certain surgeon doing a surgery. It can also be withdrawn at any time, subject to practical limitations.

II. Material Risk

269. A material risk which is required to be disclosed is one that might cause a reasonable patient to decide not to undergo a recommended treatment. For example, plastic surgery and vasectomies illustrate areas where the probability of success and the meaning of success should be explicitly delineated. For example, a man successfully sued his doctor after the doctor assured him that a vasectomy would be 100% effective as birth control; the man's wife later became pregnant. The purpose of having the procedure was complete sterilization; a careful explanation of probability of success was essential which was not done.

III. Emergency Situation

270. In an emergency situation, where immediate treatment is needed to preserve a patient's health or life, a physician may be justified in failing to provide full and complete information to a patient. Moreover, where the risks are minor and well-known to the average person, a physician may dispense with full disclosure. In addition, some patients explicitly ask not to be informed of specific risks. In this situation, a doctor must only ascertain that the patient understands that there are unspecified risks of death and serious bodily disabilities. The doctor might ask the patient to sign a waiver of informed consent. Finally, informed consent may be bypassed in rare cases in which a physician has objective evidence that informing a patient would render the patient unable to make a rational decision. Under these circumstances, a physician must disclose the information to another person designated by the patient.

A. Right to Treatment

271. Emergency is a situation, which is likely to cause death, serious injury, or disability, if not attended to promptly. In an emergency situation, a patient has a right to treatment, regardless of his ability to pay. Cardiac arrest, heavy bleeding, profound shock, severe head injuries, and acute psychotic states are some examples of emergencies. Some other situations can also be emergencies, like broken bones, fever, and cuts requiring stitches may also require immediate treatment. Both public and private hospitals have a duty to administer medical care to a person experiencing an emergency. If a hospital has emergency facilities, it is legally required to provide appropriate treatment to a person experiencing an emergency. If the hospital is unable to provide emergency services, it must provide a referral for appropriate treatment. Hospitals cannot refuse to treat prospective patients on the basis of race, religion, or national origin or refuse to treat someone with HIV or AIDS.

§2. Privacy and Confidentiality

272. Keeping privacy and confidentiality of the information received by a doctor from a patient is a right of the patient widely understood and practiced in the medical field. Confidentiality between a doctor and patient means that a doctor has the express or implied duty not to disclose information received from the patient or he has, pertaining to patient health condition and health records, to anyone not directly involved with the patient's care. Confidentiality is considered by law as privileged communication between two parties in a professional relationship, such as with a patient and a physician, a nurse, or other clinical professionals. As a patient, one is to expect confidential communication in these relationships. While application in legal proceedings is subject to evidentiary rules and consideration of the public need for information, support of privileged communication can be seen in case law. An example is the landmark decision in *Jaffee v. Redmond* where the US Supreme Court upheld a therapist's refusal to disclose sensitive client information during trial (Beyer, 2000). In writing the majority opinion, Justice Stevens said:

> "Effective psychotherapy ... depends upon an atmosphere of confidence and trust in which the patient is willing to make a frank and complete disclosure ... The psychotherapist privilege serves the public interest by facilitating the provision of appropriate treatment for individuals suffering the effects of a mental or emotional problem." When considering sensitive health information requiring special layers of confidentiality, such as with mental health treatment, state statutes provide guidance for health information management professionals.

I. Patient Feel Safe to Communicate

273. Confidentiality is important so that doctors and health care providers have knowledge of all facts, regardless of how personal or embarrassing, that might have a bearing on a diagnosis and ultimately on patient's health. Patients must feel free that it is safe to communicate such information. Although this theory drives doctor–patient confidentiality, the reality is that many people have routine and legitimate access to a patient's records. A hospital patient might have several doctors, nurses, and support personnel on every shift, and a patient might also see a therapist, nutritionist, pharmacologist, etc. State law may require some confidential information to be reported to authorities. For example, birth and death certificates must be filed; child abuse cases must be reported; and infectious, contagious, or communicable diseases must be reported. In addition, confidential information may also be required to be disclosed pursuant to a judicial proceeding or to notify a person to whom a patient may pose a danger.

274. The patients legitimately demand and expect confidentiality in many areas of their treatment, and they must be asked to consent before being photographed or having others, like medical students, allowed to observe a medical procedure. The patient has a right to refuse to see anyone not connected to a hospital. During physical examination a patient has the right to have a person of the patient's own sex present during a physical examination conducted by a member of the opposite sex. A patient may refuse to see persons connected with the hospital who are not directly involved in the patient's care and treatment. Details of the condition of patients are also protected and cannot be made public.

A patient owns the information contained in medical records, but the owner of the paper on which they are written is usually considered the actual owner of the records. The patient's legal interest in the records generally means that the patient has a right to see the records and is entitled to a complete copy of them. The patient's rights are subject to reasonable restrictions, like inspection and copying to be done on the doctor's premises during working hours.

II. Privacy

275. Privacy, as distinct from confidentiality, is viewed as the right of the patient to be let alone and to make decisions about how personal information is shared. The US Supreme Court's holding in *Whalen v. Roe* addressed the notion of balanced interest seen in the later HIPAA Privacy Rule as follows; "… disclosures of private medical information to doctors, to hospital personnel, to insurance companies, and to public health agencies are often an essential part of modern medical practice," the court did not give individuals absolute control over sharing of their own health information. The *Whalen* decision noted growing concerns with collection of private information in electronic format and the role of regulatory guidelines as follows:

> We are not unaware of the threat to privacy implicit in the accumulation of vast amounts of personal information in computerized data banks … The right to collect and use such data for public purposes is typically accompanied by a concomitant statutory or regulatory duty to avoid unwarranted disclosures.

276. Security refers directly to protection and, specifically, to the means used to protect the privacy of health information and support professionals in holding that information in confidence. The concept of security has long been applied to health records in paper form. As the use of electronic health record systems grew and transmission of health data to support billing became the norm, the need was felt for regulatory guidelines specific to electronic health information. Managing electronic health information presents unique challenges for legal and regulatory compliance, for ethical considerations, and, ultimately, for quality of care. All who work with health information, for example, health informatics and health information management professionals, clinicians, researchers, business administrators, and others, have a clear responsibility to respect the information in their control. At the same time, patients have privacy rights with regard to their own health information and an expectation that information be held in confidence and protected and not be disclosed to the public.

§3. Patient's Right Against Dumping

277. "Patient dumping" is the act of transferring or referring patients to another facility on one pretext or the other and in certain circumstances, like nonavailability of a facility or treatment in the hospital. The law requires hospitals to provide a screening to determine if an emergency condition exists, provide stabilizing treatment to any emergency patient or to any woman in active labor before transfer, and continue treatment until a patient can be discharged or transferred without harm. It also delineates strict guidelines for the transfer of a patient who cannot be stabilized. A hospital that negligently or knowingly and willfully violates any of these provisions can be penalized by terminating or suspending its license. The doctor, the hospital, or both can also be penalized if violation of the law has taken place.

A doctor transferred a woman in active labor to a hospital 170 miles away. The woman delivered a healthy baby during the trip, but the doctor was fined USD 20,000 for the improper transfer of the woman. No doubt, there is no universal right to be admitted to a hospital in a nonemergency situation. In nonemergency cases, admission rights depend largely on the specific hospital, but basing admission on the ability to pay is severely limited by statutes, regulations, and judicial decisions. For example, most hospitals obtain land at cheaper rates or get financial assistance from the government for the construction of the hospital, so they are under duty to provide care in emergency situations. Such hospitals are required to provide a reasonable volume of services to the downtrodden who are unable to pay.

278. Once a patient has been admitted to a hospital, she or he has a right to leave if she or he so wants, otherwise the hospital could be liable for false imprisonment. This is so even if the patient has not paid the bill or if the patient wants to leave against all medical advice. In rare cases, such as contagious disease cases, public health authorities may ask statutory or regulatory authorities to quarantine a patient. In addition, state laws governing involuntary commitment of the mentally ill may be used to prevent a person of unsound mind from leaving the hospital if a qualified psychiatrist determines that the person is a danger to himself or herself or to the lives of others.

§4. Discharging a Patient

279. A doctor familiar with a patient's condition determines when a patient is to be discharged and a written order to that effect is required. If the patient disagrees with a decision to discharge, she or he has the right to demand a consultation with a different physician before the order is carried out. The decision to discharge must be based solely on the patient's medical condition and not on non-payment of medical bills. In the mid-1990s, concerns over maternity patients being discharged just a few hours after giving birth prompted legislation in the US at both the state and federal levels. The law ensured a forty-eight-hour hospital stay for a woman who gives birth vaginally and a ninety-six-hour stay for a woman who has a cesarean section unless the patient and the doctor agreed to an earlier discharge.

280. With the rise of managed care and Health Maintenance Organizations (HMOs), patients faced new issues involving the right to treatment. HMOs may deny authorization for expensive or experimental treatments or for treatments provided outside the network of approved physicians. HMOs contend that they must control costs and make decisions that benefit the largest number of members. In response, state legislatures have enacted HMO regulations that seek to give patients a process for appealing the denial of benefits. The HMOs have opposed these measures and have vigorously defended their denial of benefits in court.

281. In *Moran v. Rush Prudential HMO, Inc.*,[24] the US Supreme Court in a 5–4 decision upheld an Illinois law that required HMOs to provide an independent review of disputes between the primary care physician and the HMO. The law mandated that the HMO must pay for services deemed medically necessary by the independent reviewer. Most importantly, the court ruled that the federal Employee Retirement Income Security Act (ERISA) did not pre-empt the Illinois law. ERISA is an extremely complex and technical set of provisions that seek to protect employee benefit programs. The decision was important because it empowered other states to enact similar laws that give patients more rights in obtaining treatment.

§5. Right Against Medical Experimentation

282. Medical experimentation is necessary for the progress of the medical field, so they have always gone hand in hand. In the process, patients' rights have sometimes been ignored or compromised. Sometimes patients are completely unaware of the experimentation which might have taken place in settings in which individuals

24. 536 U.S. 355, 122 S.Ct. 2151, 153 L.Ed.2d 375 (2002).

may have extreme difficulty asserting their rights, such as in prisons, mental institutions, the military, and residences for the mentally disabled. Legitimate experimentation requires informed consent that may be withdrawn at any time. Some of the notorious and shameful instances of human experimentation in the US in the twentieth century include a 1963 study in which terminally ill hospital patients were injected with live cancer cells to test their immune response; the Tuskegee Syphilis Study, begun before World War II and continued for forty years, in which effective treatment was withheld from poor black males suffering from syphilis so that medical personnel could study the natural course of the disease; and a study where developmentally disabled children were deliberately infected with hepatitis to test potential vaccines.

283. Failure to obtain informed consent can arise even when consent has ostensibly been obtained. The California Supreme Court ruled in 1990 that a physician must disclose pre-existing research and potential economic interests that may affect the doctor's medical judgment.[25] The case involved excision of a patient's cells pursuant to surgery and other procedures to which the patient had consented. The surgery itself was not experimental and the experimentation took place after the surgery and other procedures. The cells were used in medical research that proved lucrative to the doctor and medical center.

284. Patients in hospitals attached to medical colleges are frequently asked to participate in research. Participants do not surrender legal rights simply by agreeing to cooperate, and validly obtained consent cannot protect a researcher from negligence. In hospitals, human experimentation is typically monitored by an Institutional Review Board (IRB). These boards review a proposed research before patients are asked to participate and approve written consent forms. IRBs are meant to ensure that risks are minimized, the risks are reasonable in relation to anticipated benefits, the selection of subjects is equitable, and informed consent is obtained and properly documented.

§6. Advance Medical Directives by Patient

285. Advance medical directives are documents that are made at a time when a person is in his senses and has full decision-making capabilities and are used to direct medical care in the future and in a situation when this capacity is lost. The statutes related to this aspect are narrowly drawn and specify that they apply only to illnesses when death is imminent rather than illnesses requiring long-term life support, such as in end-stage lung, heart, or kidney failure; multiple sclerosis; paraplegia; and persistent vegetative state. Patients sometimes use living wills to direct future medical care. Most commonly, living wills specify steps a patient does not want to be taken in cases of life-threatening or debilitating illness, but they may also be used to specify that a patient wants aggressive resuscitation measures used.

25. *Moore v. Regents of the University of California*, 51 Cal. 3d 120, 793 P. 2d 479.

286. Another way individuals attempt to direct medical care is through a durable power of attorney. A durable power of attorney, or proxy decision maker, is a written document wherein a person (the principal) designates another person to perform certain acts or make certain decisions on the principal's behalf. It is called durable because the power continues to be effective even after the principal becomes incompetent or it may only take effect after the principal becomes incompetent. As with a living will, such a document has little power to compel a doctor to follow a patient's desires, but in the very least it serves as valuable evidence of a person's wishes if the matter is brought into court. A durable power of attorney may be used by itself or in conjunction with a living will.

287. The advance medical directives function as intended and are honored by physicians; they free family members from making extremely difficult decisions. Standard medical care typically requires that a doctor provides maximum care. In essence, a living will change the standard of care upon which a physician will be judged and may protect a physician from legal or professional repercussions for withholding or withdrawing care.

§7. Patient Right to Die

288. Under certain circumstances a person may have a right to refuse life-sustaining medical treatment or to have life-sustaining treatment withdrawn. On the one side, in these cases, is the patient's interest in autonomy, privacy, and bodily integrity and on the other side are the traditional interests of the state in the preservation of life, prevention of suicide, protection of dependents, and the protection of the integrity of the medical profession.

Part VII. Global Implications of Medical Criminal Activities

289. Medical criminal activities with global implications include crimes like intentional abortion, human trafficking, organ sale, violation of professional secrecy, disclosure of confidential information, issuance of false certificates, deceiving the clients, and refusal to help the injured which can be subject to public prosecution in criminal courts. Some instances of medical disciplinary transgressions are deeds contrary to the medical code of conduct and imposition of unnecessary costs on clients. Different authorities address crimes, disciplinary transgressions, and restitution claims.

Chapter 1. Disciplinary Transgression

290. There are different syndicates and disciplinary bodies for professionals of the same occupation so as to protect their interests and also prescribe norms for the professionals. These entities have regulations so that professionals can perform their job in a healthy and honorable way and preserve their existence and professional dignity. Therefore, if any professional commits a prohibited act related to their professional and administrative status, they may be liable to disciplinary action by the very syndicate. In medical profession, the disciplinary transgressions may include: not performing legal duties; disclosure of clients' confidential information and type of disease; deeds contrary to medical codes of conduct; imposition of unnecessary costs on clients; alarming the client through unreal explanations of disease seriousness; prescription of addictive and psychotropic substances in unnecessary situations, etc. The disciplinary bylaws, which address professional transgressions of medical and related practitioners, may also be applicable to physicians, dentists, pharmacists, specialists, and doctors of laboratory sciences, medical diagnostics, gynecologist, and other related branches of medical sciences.

§1. Crime and Disciplinary Transgression

291. Disciplinary transgression is an act that is related to the committer's professional and administrative status and results in disciplinary action and punishment. Contrary to punishable crimes, which are specified by the legislator, disciplinary transgressions are also determined through organizational and administrative bylaws and syndicate regulations. Furthermore, any conduct that jeopardizes the dignity of a syndicate or organization can result in disciplinary sentence and punishment, even if it has not been mentioned in the respective bylaws or regulations.

292. Crime is defined as the behavior of a person which is sometimes realized as an unlawful act and sometimes as an omission, and the presence of punishment is a condition for its realization. The principle of the legality of punishments emphasizes criminalization of prohibited conduct and prescription of punishments for transgressors and offenders by the legislator. The logical relationship between crime and disciplinary transgression is also that of generality and peculiarity. For example, crimes such as abortion, issuance of false certificates, and disclosure of client's confidential information are considered disciplinary transgressions as well, while crimes such as theft or breach of trust are not considered disciplinary transgression. Moreover, disciplinary transgressions, such as committing deeds contrary to the medical code of conduct, nonobservance of basic features of the prescription form and sign, and failure to inform the medical body about the address of the medical practice, may not have been and are not considered as criminal aspects.

A sentence issued in a disciplinary action does not affect criminal or civil action but it may be possible that a conduct is simultaneously the origin of disciplinary, criminal, and civil actions, such as a physician's inadvertence in performing the legal duties leading to infliction of damages on the client or prescription of medicine without scientific justification. In such cases, if the client suffers damages, in addition to disciplinary action, the physician will have criminal and civil liabilities as well.

Chapter 2. Trafficking in Humans

293. Every year, thousands of men, women, and children fall into the hands of traffickers, in their own countries and abroad. Almost every country in the world is affected by trafficking, whether as a country of origin, transit, or destination for victims. Trafficking in persons is a serious crime and a grave violation of human rights. Human trafficking exploits women, children, and men for numerous purposes, including illegal removal of organs, forced labor, and sex. According to the United Nations Office on Drugs and Crime (UNODC) Global Report on Trafficking in Persons, almost a third of all human trafficking victims worldwide are children.

§1. Efforts of the UN General Assembly

294. In 2010, the UN General Assembly adopted the Global Plan of Action to Combat Trafficking in Persons, calling governments worldwide to take coordinated and consistent measures to defeat this scourge. The Plan calls for integrating the fight against human trafficking into the UN's programs in order to boost development and strengthen security worldwide. The Plan establishes a UN Voluntary Trust Fund for victims of trafficking, especially women and children. The Trust Fund facilitates effective assistance and protection to victims of trafficking, through grants to specialized NGOs. It aims to prioritize victims coming from areas of armed conflict and those identified among large refugee and migration flows and focuses its assistance on victims trafficked for the purpose of sexual exploitation, organ removal, forced begging, and emerging exploitative purposes (e.g., skin removal, online pornography).

295. In 2013, the General Assembly held a high-level meeting to appraise the Global Plan of Action on trafficking. Member States adopted a resolution[26] and designated July 30 as the "World Day against Trafficking in Persons." The resolution declared that such a day was necessary to "raise awareness of the situation of victims of human trafficking and for the promotion and protection of their rights." In September 2015, the world adopted the 2030 Sustainable Development Agenda and embraced goals and targets on trafficking in persons. These goals call for an end to trafficking and violence against children, as well as the need for measures against human trafficking, and strive for the elimination of all forms of violence and exploitation of women and girls. Another significant development was the UN Summit for Refugees and Migrants, which produced the New York Declaration. Of the nineteen commitments adopted by countries in the Declaration, three are dedicated to concrete action against the crimes of human trafficking and migrant smuggling.

26. No. A/RES/68/192.

§2. Protecting and Assisting Trafficked Persons

296. UNODC, as guardian of the United Nations Convention against Transnational Organized Crime (UNTOC) and the Protocols thereto, assists states in their efforts to implement the Protocol to Prevent, Suppress and Punish Trafficking in Persons (Trafficking in Persons Protocol). The UNODC was established in 1997 as part of the United Nations reform combining the UN Drug Control Programme and the Centre for International Crime Prevention. The mandate is enshrined in UN conventions, like the three UN Conventions on Drugs, the UN Convention against Transnational Organized Crime, and its three Protocols on Trafficking in Persons, on Smuggling of Migrants by Land, Sea, and Air, and on Illicit Manufacturing of and Trafficking in Firearms, the UN Convention against Corruption, the universal instruments against terrorism, and the UN standards and norms in crime prevention and criminal justice. With the help of these instruments, the UNODC helps Member States address the issues of illicit drugs, crime, and terrorism.

I. Trafficking Defined

297. Article 3, paragraph (a) of the Protocol to Prevent, Suppress and Punish Trafficking in Persons defines "Trafficking in Persons" as the recruitment, transportation, transfer, harboring, or receipt of persons, by means of the threat or use of force or other forms of coercion, of abduction, of fraud, of deception, of the abuse of power or of a position of vulnerability, or of the giving or receiving of payments or benefits to achieve the consent of a person having control over another person, for the purpose of exploitation.

II. Elements of Human Trafficking

298. To ascertain whether a particular circumstance constitutes trafficking in persons, one has to consider the definition of trafficking in the Trafficking in Persons Protocol (TPP) and the constituent elements of the offense, as defined by relevant domestic legislation. The definition contained in Article 3 of the TPP is meant to provide consistency and consensus around the world on the phenomenon of trafficking in persons. Article 5 requires that the conduct set out in Article 3 be criminalized in domestic legislation. Domestic legislation may not follow the language of the TPP precisely but should be adapted in accordance with domestic legal systems to give effect to the basic concepts contained in the Protocol. The legislative definition should be dynamic and flexible so as to empower the legislative framework to respond effectively to trafficking as per circumstances.

§3. UNODC's Response to Human Trafficking

299. The UNODC provides practical help to states by assisting to draft laws and creating comprehensive national anti-trafficking strategies and providing resources to implement them. States receive assistance, including the development of local capacity and expertise as well as practical tools to encourage cross-border cooperation in investigations and prosecutions of offenses. The adoption, in 2000, by the UN General Assembly, of the Protocol to Prevent, Suppress and Punish Trafficking in Persons, Especially against Women and Children marked a significant milestone. As the guardian of the Protocol, the UNODC addresses human trafficking issues through its Global Programme against Trafficking in Persons. The majority of states have signed and ratified the Protocol.

§4. Protection of Victims of Human Trafficking

300. The UNODC has issued a comprehensive strategy setting out the complementary nature of UNODC's work in preventing and combating both human trafficking and migrant smuggling, defining the immediate priorities for UNODC's future action and engagement on these crimes. The new strategy complements UNODC's Thematic Programme against Transnational Organized Crime and Illicit Trafficking (2011–2013). As the guardian of the Organized Crime Convention and its Protocols on Trafficking in Persons and Smuggling of Migrants, the UNODC plays an important and leading role in strengthening and coordinating the criminal justice response to both human trafficking and smuggling of migrants.

Chapter 3. Trade in Human Organs

301. A number of international norms have been developed, creating a comprehensive ethical and legal framework, consisting of guidelines and binding legal instruments, which deal with trading in human organs. These norms not only prohibit commercialization of human body parts but also combat and prevent trafficking in human beings (THB), including the removal of organs, and protect and assist victims of trafficking. The organizations, namely the UN General Assembly, the WHO, the WMA, as well as The Transplantation Society and the International Society of Nephrology (ISN), all have made important steps to help curb the growing problem of human trafficking for the removal of organs. Similarly, European organizations, such as the EU, the Council of Europe, etc., also have taken up this task.

§1. Ethical and Legal Framework Against Organ Commercialism

302. The success and growth of organ and tissue transplantation worldwide developed the awareness that organ shortage would remain a universal problem which prevents many patients from receiving the benefits of transplantation. A serious consequence of this shortage is that many patients do not have access to the waiting lists for transplantation and, worse still, that a considerable number of patients on the waiting list will die every year without ever getting transplanted. Thus, the desperation of patients waiting for transplants leads to different forms of organ commercialism, whereby organs and tissues are bought and sold, which leads even to the THB for the purpose of removing their organs. Because of huge economic disparity in different countries, this has led to a tragic inequity in the access to transplantation procedures and medicine. This, in turn, has given rise to global organ commercialism where poor and vulnerable individuals and populations are exploited to the benefit of the more wealthy citizens.

§2. Role of International Institutions

303. There are international organizations which are practically involved in preventing and taking action against trafficking in human organs, like the WHO, the WMA, etc.

I. Role of the WHO

304. The WHO and its WHA set ethical standards in the field of human organ and tissue donation and transplantation. In 1991 the first version of the Guiding Principles on Human Organ Transplantation was adopted. It focused on issues of free and voluntary informed consent and noncommercialization of human organ and tissues. These Guiding Principles were updated in 2008, elaborating the prohibition of sale or purchase of organs and emphasizing the relationship between organ sales and human trafficking. In 2010 a revised version of the Guiding Principles was published, which adopted the "measures to protect the poorest and vulnerable groups from transplant tourism and the sale of organs and tissues." The revised Guidelines called for special attention to the international trafficking in human organs and tissues. The WHO standards and principles provide guidance to countries' health authorities and health professionals, even though not legally binding in character.

II. Role of the WMA

305. As early as 1985 the WMA issued a Statement on Live Organ Trade, stating the WMA "condemns the purchase and sale of human organs for transplantation, and calls on governments to take effective steps to prevent the commercial use of human organs." In October 2000 the WMA adopted the Statement on Human Organ Donation and Transplantation. It promoted a policy based on ethical principles to give guidance to medical associations, physicians, and other health care providers in issues relating to organ donation and transplantation. One of the key topics was the universal principle of noncommercialization of human organs. Paragraph 30 of the WMA Statement said, "Payment for organs must be prohibited. A financial incentive compromises the voluntariness of the choice for organ donation. Furthermore, access to needed medical treatment based on the ability to pay is inconsistent with the principles of justice. Organs suspected to have been obtained through commercial transaction must not be accepted for transplantation. In addition, the advertisement of organs in exchange for money should be prohibited." In October 2006, the WMA General Assembly revised its statement and reiterated its prohibition of commercialism. The WMA Statement aims to provide guidance to all health professionals, both individually and as members of medical associations, but has no legally binding character.

§3. The Declaration of Istanbul and the DICG

306. The Declaration of Istanbul (DOI) provides a set of moral principles to govern organ donation and transplantation, in general, as well as for combating, curbing, and preventing human organ trafficking. It derives its authority through the voluntary adherence by professional medical and governmental bodies to its principles. In this respect it has been likened to the Declaration of Helsinki on research involving human beings that was adopted by the WMA in 1964. The cause for establishing the DOI in 2008 was the growing awareness that human organ trafficking had become a global phenomenon that threatened to defile the public and professional image of transplant medicine. And indeed, organ trafficking had changed from a hidden illicit activity into a widespread visible activity that involved thousands of illegal transplants annually, using organs from poor, vulnerable, and poorly compensated "donors."

307. As from January 1, 2015, the DOI has been endorsed by 111 organizations, including the Ministries of Health of Ecuador, Malaysia, and South Africa, the

Council of Europe European Committee on organ transplantation (CD-P-TO), and the United Network for Organ Sharing of the United States (UNOS). The Declaration of Istanbul Custodian Group (DICG) was established to foster transparency in transplant practice, promote education on organ donation and transplantation, and encourage all endorsing organizations to adhere to the DOI principles. DICG will also withhold academic recognition from transplant professionals who do not adhere to the DOI principles.

§4. The Legal and Policy Framework and Trafficking Through Removal of Organs

308. From a moral perspective, THB is universally recognized as an infringement of the fundamental rights and dignity of the individual. At the same time, from a legal perspective, it also represents a serious form of transnational organized crime. Taken together, this explains why the act of THB is widely criminalized, both on the basis of international legal instruments and in domestic legislation. It is, therefore, not surprising that the original UN Convention against Transnational Organized Crime Palermo 2000 was accompanied by an Additional Protocol which focused on THB. This Additional Protocol was the first multilateral treaty that explicitly and specifically recognized human trafficking for organ removal as a practice to be criminalized and punished.

I. United Nations Palermo Protocol

309. The United Nations Palermo Protocol is an addition to the UN Convention against Transnational Organized Crime of May 2006 with the full title: "Protocol to Prevent, Suppress and Punish Trafficking in Persons especially Women and Children," which makes it clear that it is focused on THB. The Protocol gives a comprehensive definition of THB in Article 3(a) and includes trafficking for the removal of organs as a form of exploitation of persons. The key element of this protocol is that in order for "trafficking in human beings" to be recognized as organized crime, it must entail the following elements:

(i) an action (recruitment, transport);
(ii) the means used to achieve that action (deception, fraud, coercion); and
(iii) the purpose (exploitation in case of organ removal).[27]

Because of its wide definition and scope of what constitutes "trafficking in human beings," this Protocol has been adopted by other international and European organizations as law enforcement measure against human traffickers. The Palermo Protocol has served as a good instrument to define the concept of trafficking of human

27. United Nations Convention against Transnational Organized Crime and the Protocols thereto, Vienna 2004, Policy Department, Directorate-General for External Policies.

beings for the purpose of organ removal (THBOR) in law enforcement. The Protocol was established primarily to respond to the threat posed by transnational organized crime networks dealing in human trafficking. However, from the perspective of illicit organ removal and transplantation, it is not always clear that suspected commercial transplants comply with the notion of "trafficking" and that these acts fulfill the above three criteria. For instance, in cases of transplant tourism involving Filipino organ sellers, it may be difficult to prove that these sellers were actually trafficked (e.g., use of force); therefore, these organ sales (although illegal) will not easily be classified as THBOR and charged as a trafficking offense under the terms of the Palermo Protocol or national anti-trafficking legislation.

§5. Legal Challenges in the Prosecution of Organ Traffickers

310. In some cases the national legislation on organ transplants is not updated to include trafficking in persons for organ removal (THBOR) as a form of organized crime. In the *Netcare* case the prosecution was hampered by the lack of suitable legislation and they had to resort to charges of fraud, unlawful acquisition and use of human tissues, as well as unlawful payments. This led to relatively light sentences. Further, due to the transnational nature of trafficking in organs, the key players in such operations can easily switch their base from one country to another, making it difficult for prosecutors to investigate cases and arrest perpetrators.

§6. International Police and Judicial Cooperation

311. THBOR involves criminal networks operating on a transnational scale which presents additional challenges to law enforcement agencies. Once the network has been uncovered, the investigation may spread over several countries and even continents. The usual situation is that the country where the transplants have taken place takes the lead in the investigation and prosecution. In the *Moldova* case it was the country where the majority of organ suppliers came from, while the transplants took place in Turkey. If the investigation and prosecution are taken up in a developing country or a country with an unstable political situation and low resources, the capacity and chances for a large-scale investigation may not be present. To tackle this, the prosecution may request legal assistance from other countries when a link with that country in the trafficking network has been established. This procedure is very time-consuming and complex, and some countries may not cooperate or even respond to such a request.

312. Another hurdle is the fact that a transnational crime network means that the law enforcers are confronted with different national jurisdictions so that prosecution and investigation run up against the limits of their legal authority. This is particularly the case when there is the need for extradition of members of the trafficking network hiding in another country. However, extradition is only possible on the basis of mutual agreements between countries, and in the absence of such extradition treaty it is difficult to get hold of offenders. If extradition is not possible, it may result in fugitive offenders being released on bail or the case dropped because the other country has no reason to detain them because of lack of evidence. This has been the case in the *Medicus* case, where the Turkish and Israeli defendants could not be brought to trial in Kosovo.

313. Thus, in transnational trafficking cases, there is a dire need for international policing and legal cooperation among different countries. If such cooperation is not established from the start of the investigation and prosecution process, there is a risk that the case may fail because of a fragmented approach. The problems with respect to cooperation and support can arise when the concerned country is the home country of some of the recipients or suppliers. However, there are cases where international cooperation has been quite successful.[28] There is also an important role for international cooperation, for instance through Europol and Interpol. International arrest warrants issued in some cases have been successful in apprehending some of the key perpetrators.[29]

§7. Information Sharing

314. An important element in international cooperation is information sharing. By collecting and sharing information on the modus operandi of organ traffickers, names of criminal collaborators, and trafficking routes, among others, networks already in operation may be detected and new trafficking networks prevented. The NGOs Organs Watch and DICG are all active in collecting and sharing such information around the world. Europol and Interpol are involved in the development of "indicators of human trafficking" to help local police, immigration officers, and border control officers recognize and detect illicit trafficking operations.

28. Refer to *Rosenbaum*, *Costa Rica*, *Medicus*, *Shalimov Institute*, and *Netcare*.
29. Refer Broker Amit Kumar in the Gurgaon case, and Brazil recruiter Gedaliah Taub in *Netcare*.

Chapter 4. Drug Trafficking

315. Drug trafficking is a global illicit trade involving the cultivation, manufacture, distribution, and sale of substances which are subject to drug prohibition laws. In the Declaration on the Rule of Law, Member States recognized the importance of strengthened international cooperation in countering the world drug problem. The General Assembly has also recognized that "despite continuing increased efforts by States, relevant organizations, civil societies, and non-governmental organizations, the world drug problem … undermines socio-economic and political stability and sustainable development."[30]

316. The UN work in countering the world drug problem is based on international drug control treaties which are mutually supportive and complimentary, namely the Single Convention on Narcotic Drugs of 1961 (as amended in 1972), the Convention on Psychotropic Substances of 1971, and the United Nations Convention against Illicit Traffic in Narcotic Drugs and Psychotropic Substances of 1988. These three conventions attribute important functions to the Commission on Narcotic Drugs and the International Narcotics Control Board (INCB). The United Nations, through the United Nations System Task Force on Transnational Organized Crime and Drug Trafficking, advocates a rebalancing of the international policy on drugs to increase the focus on public health, prevention, treatment and care, economic, social, and cultural measures.

§1. Conventions and Treaties

317. The following are the conventions and treaties on control of drug trafficking:

(i) Single Convention on Narcotic Drugs of 1961 (as amended in 1972).
(ii) Convention on Psychotropic Substances of 1971.
(iii) United Nations Convention against Illicit Traffic in Narcotic Drugs and Psychotropic Substances of 1988.
(iv) The Commission on Narcotic Drugs.
(v) INCB.
(vi) Thematic Debate of the 66th session of the United Nations General Assembly.

The first two treaties codify internationally applicable control measures in order to ensure the availability of narcotic drugs and psychotropic substances for medical and scientific purposes and to prevent their diversion into illicit channels. They also include general provisions on illicit drug trafficking and drug abuse. The 1988 United Nations Convention against Illicit Traffic in Narcotic Drugs and Psychotropic Substances extends the control regime and focuses on establishing measures to

30. International cooperation against the world drug problem, A/Res/66/183.

combat illicit drug trafficking and related money laundering as well as strengthening the framework of international cooperation in criminal matters, including extradition and mutual legal assistance.

I. The Single Convention on Narcotic Drugs of 1961

318. This Convention prohibits production and supply of specific narcotic drugs and of drugs with similar effects except under license for specific purposes, such as medical treatment and research. The Convention has updated the Paris Convention of July 13, 1931, and included a large number of synthetic opioids invented in the intervening thirty years and a mechanism for including new ones. From 1931 to 1961, most of the families of synthetic opioids had been developed, including drugs in whatever way related to methadone, pethidine, morphine, and dextromoramide and any related drugs.

319. Earlier treaties had only controlled opium, coca, and derivatives such as morphine, heroin, and cocaine. The Single Convention consolidated those treaties and broadened their scope to include cannabis and drugs the effects of which are similar to those of the drugs specified. The Commission on Narcotic Drugs and the WHO were empowered to add, remove, and transfer drugs among the treaty's four schedules of controlled substances. This treaty has since been supplemented by the Convention on Psychotropic Substances, which controls Lysergic Acid Diethylamide (LSD), Ecstasy, and other psychoactive pharmaceuticals and the United Nations Convention against Illicit Traffic in Narcotic Drugs and Psychotropic Substances, which strengthens provisions against money laundering and other drug-related offenses. Since the Single Convention is not self-executing, the concerned countries have to pass laws to carry out its provisions.

§2. Commission on Narcotic Drugs

320. The Commission on Narcotic Drugs, composed of fifty-three Member States elected by the ECOSOC for a four-year term, is the central policy-making body with regard to drug-related matters, including the monitoring of the global trends of illicit drug trafficking and abuse. The Commission of the ECOSOC adopts and recommends, for adoption by the Council or to the General Assembly through the Council, resolutions on new concerted measures or agreed policies to better address the drug phenomenon. It decides whether new substances should be included in one of the schedules of the conventions and if changes or deletions in the schedules are required.

§3. International Narcotic Control Board

321. The INCB is a permanent body consisting of thirteen members who are elected for a five-year term by the ECOSOC on the basis of their competence and they serve in their personal capacity. The INCB has controls on drug production, international trade, and dispensation. The UNODC looks after the INCB's day-to-day work of monitoring the situation in each country and working with national authorities to ensure compliance with the Single Convention. The INCB monitors the implementation of the conventions and may make recommendations to states. It gathers information on illicit trafficking and submits an annual report on developments to the Commission on Narcotic Drugs and to the ECOSOC. The UNODC has an important role in assisting these bodies in performing their treaty-based functions, and in assisting States Parties in the implementation of their obligations under the international drug control treaties. The UNODC works with countries' legislatures to ensure compliance.

§4. Interpol and World Customs Organization

322. Drug trafficking accounts for half of all transnational organized crime proceeds according to the UN, providing a constant source of funding for other criminal activities and even threats such as terrorism. While governments are taking action to cope with the COVID-19 pandemic and mitigate its impacts, there is evidence that organized crime syndicates have seized the opportunity to multiply their illicit activities. INTERPOL and the World Customs Organization (WCO) are working to align police and customs efforts in the fight against illicit drug trafficking. The police have had to shoulder the task of adapting to shifting drug trafficking patterns while playing a central role to halt the spread of the virus. Fighting against illicit trafficking of drugs is a key component of the customs community's efforts to make this world a better place. Since the onset of the pandemic, INTERPOL works closely with law enforcement in its 194 member countries to monitor changing drug trafficking patterns and share intelligence. Under the WCO's Drugs and Precursors Programme, which aims at countering global illegal trade covering the cultivation, manufacturing, distribution and sale of substances subject to drug restriction and prohibition laws, a number of initiatives have been developed, often in cooperation with other law enforcement agencies.

These include Project AIRCOP with its Joint Airport Interdiction Taskforces established to strengthen airport controls and the newly established WCO Project COLIBRI. This is a multidisciplinary initiative funded by the European Union with the aim to monitor and control General Aviation through an ambitious capacity building program and technological innovation.

§5. State Drugs Control Laws

323. The drug offenses of criminal nature have been enacted into law in most of the states around the world. These offenses include "supply" offenses, such as the agricultural production, manufacture, and traffic of drugs, and "demand" offenses, such as the use and possession of drugs. National laws criminalize these particular actions in regard to drugs which are specifically identified as harmful. The particular structure of these laws varies from state to state, but these national laws conform to basic frameworks agreed to by those states in multilateral drug conventions adopted for this purpose.

324. Three key elements in the drug conventions determine the scope of national drug offenses: (i) the foundational provision in the drug conventions is Article 4(c) of the 1961 Single Convention on Narcotic Drugs,[31] in terms of which states' parties agree "to limit exclusively to medical and scientific purposes the production, manufacture, export, import, distribution of, trade in, use and possession of drugs;" (ii) the scope of this limitation comprises those drugs listed in the schedules to conventions;[32] (iii) further provisions contained in Article 36 of the 1961 Single Convention, Article 22 of the 1971 Psychotropic Substances Convention, and Article 3 of the 1988 UN Drug Trafficking Convention provide for precise obligations to criminalize specific forms of drug-related conduct. These three elements function together to proscribe the supply and use of drugs throughout the world and are intended to circumscribe the way states are permitted to respond to nonmedical and scientific supply of, and demand for, listed substances and to lead indirectly to the penalization of individuals who engage in these activities. They are the foundations of global drug prohibition, a product of cooperation among states.

§6. Fake, Counterfeit or Fraudulent Medicines

325. Counterfeit or fake medicines are manufactured with the wrong dose or no dose of medicine, or with toxic or harmful ingredients which make them unsafe as well. They are packaged to look like the real thing and it is hard to spot counterfeit drugs. The only way to know if a drug is counterfeit is through chemical analysis done in a laboratory. Sometimes, counterfeit drugs differ in size, shape, or color or are sold in poor-quality packaging, but they often appear identical to the real thing. There are a large number of drug companies involved in the manufacturing of fake medicine and they commit fraud on innocent consumers. Fraudulent or fake medicines pose a considerable public health threat as they can fail to cure, may harm, and even kill patients. The supply chain for medicines operates at a global level.

326. The 20th session of the Commission on Crime Prevention and Criminal Justice (CCPCJ) adopted Resolution 20/6 on fraudulent medicines, otherwise referred to as falsified medicines due to concern about the involvement of organized crime in the trafficking in fraudulent medicines. Resolution 20/6 also highlights the potential utility of the UNTOC, for which the UNODC is the guardian, in reinforcing international cooperation in the fight against trafficking. Resolution 20/6 contains nine action points among which paragraph nine requests that the UNODC,

31. Article 5 of the 1971 Psychotropic Convention in similar terms.
32. The conventions do not spell out the criteria for initial listing but do spell out criteria for adding substances, criteria applied by the Commission on Narcotic Drugs acting on the advice of a WHO Expert Committee on Drug Dependence.

in cooperation with other UN bodies and international organizations, such as the INCB, the WHO, the World Customs Organization (WCO), and the International Criminal Police Organization (ICPO/INTERPOL), as well as relevant regional organizations and mechanisms, national regulatory agencies for medicines and, where appropriate, the private sector, civil society organizations, and professional associations assist Member States in building capacity to disrupt and dismantle the organized criminal networks engaged in all stages of the illicit supply chain, in particular, distribution and trafficking, to better utilize the resources of each organization and to create synergies with interested partners.

I. State Mechanism for Counterfeit Medicines

327. The State Mechanism for Counterfeit Medicines is a global platform where countries can convene, coordinate, decide and organize actions to address substandard and falsified medical products. It was established in order to protect public health and promote access to affordable, safe, and quality medical products, through effective collaboration between Member States and WHO to prevent and control substandard and falsified medical products and associated activities.

II. WHO Surveillance and Monitoring System (SMS)

328. In 2013, WHO launched SMS to encourage countries to report incidents of substandard and falsified medical products in a structured and systematic format, so as to develop a more accurate and validated assessment of the problem. The system provides technical support in emergencies, links incidents between countries and regions, and issues WHO medical product alerts, and gathers a validated body of evidence to demonstrate the scope, scale and harm caused by substandard and falsified medical products. WHO has trained a global network of regulatory staff in Member States to report substandard and falsified medical products to the WHO Global Surveillance and Monitoring System. The structured reporting system allows for a fast response to emergencies and the issue of alerts in the most serious cases. It also facilitates in-depth analyses of the medical products most at risk, the vulnerabilities and weaknesses in health systems, the harm caused to public health and the need for training and stronger regulations and standards.

III. MEDICRIME Convention

329. In October 2020, the Council of Europe invited countries to become signatories of the MEDICRIME Convention, the first international treaty to establish counterfeit medicines as a criminal threat. In 2011, US policymakers made a similar move, introducing the Counterfeit Drug Penalty Enhancement Act, which distinguished fake drugs from other sham goods and increased the prison sentences and fines associated with prosecution for their manufacture and trade. The WHO has proposed a mechanism for harmonizing global enforcement in May 2020, at the

World Health Assembly in Geneva, Switzerland. The scheme excludes trade and intellectual-property considerations and focuses solely on counterfeits as a humanitarian crime. To improve enforcement, researchers have developed new methods to detect fakes. For example, the pharmaceutical company Merck, based in Germany, has sponsored the Global Pharma Health Fund Minilab, which can assess the quality of 57 different compounds.

IV. Prevalence of Counterfeit Medicines

330. In an investigation into counterfeit medicines in South East Asia, it was found that nearly half of the antimalarials seized were fakes and many of the packs presumed to contain life-*saving* medicines were tainted with safrole, a carcinogenic compound used to make the illicit party drug ecstasy. The presence of safrole showed the link between bogus pharmaceuticals and criminal syndicates, which flourish in a grey zone that rewards counterfeiters with high profits at low risk. For a criminal interested in making money, it is less dangerous to deal in counterfeits than to in illegal drugs because the manufacture of counterfeits is classified not as criminal activity but as patent infringement. The global counterfeit drug economy has been valued at USD 75 billion a year, and is projected to grow by up to 13% annually.

V. Problem in Poor and Developing Countries

331. Counterfeit medicine and health products are sold worldwide but are more commonly *found* in low- and middle-income countries where regulations are not strictly imposed, and it may be difficult to enforce drug quality standards. Studies show about 9%–41% of medicines sold in low- and middle-income countries are counterfeit. In contrast, in high-income countries, such as the United States, less than 1% of medicines sold are counterfeit. In developed countries, border agencies intercept most illicit trade before it reaches markets, but poor nations lack equivalent protection. WHO reports that in developing economies, nearly one-third of drugs are either fakes or substandard. As a matter of fact, regulating drug quality requires political will, scientific expertise and sufficient data which are scarce in countries afflicted by poverty and infectious diseases. But the most formidable barrier has been the lack of consensus on how to classify counterfeits. Efforts to establish a universal definition are caught in the controversy regarding safeguarding public health and protecting intellectual property. According to some the prevailing definitions prioritize private interests at the expense of health by treating fake drugs mainly as an intellectual-property issue. The medical community insists that counterfeit medicines should not be placed in the same penal class as other imitation goods.

Part VIII. Biotechnology and Law

332. Biotechnology is a fast-growing area, creating new opportunities and solutions for many health problems but at the same time, posing potential risks to the international community. International law on biotechnology is an example of how the international community creates regulatory responses to problems and challenges arising from scientific innovation and technological change.

The growth of this field raises some of the most fundamental issues currently facing the international community and makes it necessary that there is a common definition at the international level to establish the legal framework and rules for biotechnology.

Chapter 1. Biotechnology and Medical Law

333. The international agreements on biotechnology have adopted a set of principles, rules, guidelines, code of conduct, and resolutions in response to the challenges brought about by rapid development in the field. They also provide a system combining legislative, administrative, and judicial functions for the implementation of these agreements. In totality, they have established an international regime for the governance of biotechnology-related legal issues. The international biotechnology agreements have been designed and adopted not only to balance competing interests but also to pursue sustainable development. Accordingly, they focus on human health, environmental protection, biodiversity and biosafety, scientific innovation, agricultural development, etc.

§1. Biotechnology Defined

334. The word "biotechnology" is made up of the prefix bio-, meaning biological and technology. Karl Ereky, a Hungarian scientist, first devised the term "biotechnology" in 1919. Since its inception, the notion of biotechnology has been variously defined. The Oxford English Dictionary defines biotechnology as "the exploitation of biological processes for industrial and other purposes like genetic manipulation of micro-organisms for the production of antibiotics, hormones, etc."

In 1982, an expert group proposed a common definition of biotechnology for OECD member countries in which it was taken as "the application of scientific and engineering principles to the processing of materials by biological agents to provide goods and services." In 2005, members of the "OECD's Ad hoc Biotechnology Statistics Group" developed a single, list-based definition of biotechnology. The single definition is: the application of science and technology to living organisms, as well as parts, products, and models thereof, to alter living or nonliving materials for the production of knowledge, goods, and services. This list-based definition of biotechnology includes Deoxyribonucleic Acid (DNA)/RNA, proteins and other molecules, cell and tissue culture and engineering, process biotechnology techniques, gene and RNA vectors, bioinformatics and nanobiotechnology, etc.

335. As per Article 2 of the 1992 United Nations Convention on Biological Diversity, biotechnology is defined as "any technological application that uses biological systems, living organisms, or derivatives thereof, to make or modify products or processes for specific use." Article 3 of the Cartagena Protocol on Biosafety defines biotechnology as "the application of: (a) in vitro nucleic and techniques, including recombinant deoxyribonucleic acid (DNA) and direct injection of nucleic acid into cells or organelles, or (b) fusion of cells beyond the taxonomic family, that overcome natural physiological reproductive or recombinant barriers and that are not techniques used in traditional breeding and selection." In the absence of a more specific internationally agreed upon legal definition, the Convention on Biological Diversity is an important reference.

§2. Legal Challenge of Biotechnology

336. The growth of biotechnology and scientific discoveries have opened up new applications in health care and hold the promise of meeting the fundamental food and health needs of the population of the world. Many international organizations have undertaken the task of setting standards while dealing with the impacts of biotechnology on health and the environment. These organizations include the Codex Alimentarius, the WHO, the United Nations Food and Agriculture Organization (FAO), the United Nations Environmental Programme (UNEP), the United Nations Educational, Scientific and Cultural Organization (UNESCO), the United Nations Industrial Development Organization (UNIDO), etc.

337. Great diversity exists between countries with respect to their capacity to develop, apply, and regulate the new biotech products and services. These differences have become a source of tension in international economic relations. Thus, biotechnology presents a new challenge for international law. The fact is that at the international level, there is no single comprehensive legal instrument covering all aspects of biotechnology or biotech products. However, a number of existing international agreements are relevant to different aspects of biotechnology. The development of international agreement and standard and rulemaking relating to biotechnology are of immense assistance to many countries, in particular, developing countries, in establishing appropriate biotech laws while, at the same time, promoting harmonization of national biotech regulations at the international level.

§3. Genetically Modified Organisms

338. Research on genetically modified organisms (GMOs) began in the 1970s. This technology indicated the possibility of realizing significant benefits, like adding nutritional value to foods, and environmental benefits, like reductions in the use of pesticides. The first GMO was created in 1973, and the first GMO plant was produced in 1983. In terms of volume, the first generation GMOs remain the most common. Herbicide and insecticide-resistant crops were developed through the use of biotechnology.

I. Issues Relating to GMO

339. The genetic modification techniques provide significant benefits and also pose potential risks for the continuity of the human race, in present form, and the environment. Possible harmful effects on humans have been identified as arising from GMOs, including toxicity, horizontal gene transfer, antibiotic resistance, etc. The harmful effects on the environment include invasiveness and development resistance, biodiversity risk, etc. Besides, there is significant scientific uncertainty over the long-term effects of the GMOs on human rights and the environment. Biotechnology also raises a number of ethical questions as well, including in relation to the need to ensure food security, conservation and sustainable use of natural resources, the protection of human rights, and sharing the benefits of biotechnology in an equitable manner. International law is one of the ways in which such concerns can be taken care of and operationalized beyond the national level. Early regulations focused on safety standards to be respected in laboratory research and on conditions for field trials.

§4. Regulatory Approaches

340. Different kinds of regulatory approaches have been adopted by the countries on biotechnology. The US has adopted an approach similar to a laissez-faire model. The Food and Drug Administration (FDA) policy statement of 1992 recognized that biotech products were generally considered to be as safe as conventional food products. A large number of countries have adopted some form of regulation on biotechnology and biotech products. The core elements for regulation on biotechnology include laboratory control, risk analysis, and socioeconomic considerations for premarketing authorization. The activity of labeling, traceability, and other monitoring measures for postapproval surveillance are also subject to regulation. Risk analysis covers risk assessment, risk management, and risk communication. Precautionary action is also provided for in the risk analysis and regulatory systems of most countries. These measures provide a fair level of protection of human health, the environment, and the ecosystem.

§5. International Agreements and Rules on Biotechnology

341. The potential of biotechnology to contribute to the alleviation of problems associated with the development and the environment was recognized by the 1992 UN Conference on Environment and Development (the "Earth Summit") which contained Chapter 16 of Agenda 21 on "Environmentally sound management of biotechnology." In addition to providing the basis for future negotiation of a specific protocol on biosafety, the Convention on Biological Diversity required Contracting Parties to establish specific means to regulate risks associated with GMOs. There are many international agreements relating to biotechnology which are legally binding or have strong political consensus, including, *inter alia*, the UN Convention on the Law of the Sea (UNCLOS, 1982), the Convention on Biological Diversity (1992), the WTO Agreement on the Application of Sanitary and Phytosanitary Measures (SPS Agreement, 1994), the WTO Agreement on Technical Barriers to Trade (TBT Agreement, 1994), the International Plant Protection Convention (1997), the UNESCO Universal Declaration on Human Genome and Human Rights (1997), the Aarhus Convention (1998), the Biosafety Protocol (2000), the UNESCO International Declaration on Human Genetic Data (2003), and the UNESCO Universal Declaration on Bioethics and Human Rights (2005).

Chapter 2. Biosafety and Biosecurity

342. The issue of biosafety, biosecurity, and biocontainment has been in the spotlight internationally. There have also been increased international efforts to improve awareness of new practices and concerns with regard to the safe pursuit of life science research, which has decreased, the risk of terrorists acquiring deadly pathogens, or the accidental release of a biological agent. The WHO has revised the IHR (2005)), the Biological Weapons Convention (BWC), and the United Nations Security Council Resolution (UNSCR) 1540 which overlap in their requirements with regard to biosafety and biosecurity in order to improve the understanding of practitioners and policymakers.

343. Biosafety is complementary to biosecurity and refers to the implementation of laboratory practices and procedures, specific construction features of laboratory facilities, safety equipment, and appropriate occupational health programs when working with potentially infectious microorganisms and other biological hazards. These measures are designed to reduce the exposure of laboratory personnel, the public, agriculture, and the environment to potentially infectious agents and other biological hazards. Laboratory-acquired Infections (LAIs) have received more attention in recent years. LAIs may occur in research labs, clinical labs, or animal facilities and, sometimes, it is difficult to determine whether the infection was acquired in the lab or from the community. There is also a strong public health concern related to LAIs, as an infected laboratory worker may transmit the infectious disease to his colleagues, family, or to the community at large. Poor personnel training increases the risk of LAIs or other biological accidents in the laboratory and may also contribute to improper pathogen accounting, storage, and transportation, which could contribute to the illicit acquisition of biological agents by terrorists or bio-criminals.

§1. The Biosafety Protocol

344. The Biosafety Protocol is the first international, legally binding agreement on the trade of GMOs. The Protocol entered into force on September 11, 2003, and a large number of countries and the EU have ratified or acceded to the Protocol. The objective of the Protocol is to ensure, in accordance with the precautionary approach contained in Principle 15 of the Rio Declaration, adequate protection in the field for the safe transfer, handling, and use of LMOs resulting from modern biotechnology that may have adverse effects on the conservation and sustainable use of biological diversity. The parties to the Protocol should ensure that the development, handling, transport, use, transfer, and release of any LMOs are undertaken in a manner that prevents or reduces the risks to biological diversity and risks to human health.

I. Provisions of the Protocol

345. The Protocol contains provisions regarding: the precautionary principle; advance informed agreement ("AIA"); information sharing; a compliance mechanism; public participation; liability and redress; financial resources for developing countries, etc. With regard to the precautionary principle, Article 1 of the Protocol envisages that the objective of the Protocol is to be pursued in accordance with the precautionary approach contained in Principle 15 of the Rio Declaration on Environment and Development. Article 10(6) states that "lack of scientific certainty due to insufficient relevant scientific information and knowledge regarding the extent of the potential adverse effects of a LMO on the conservation and sustainable use of biological diversity in the Party of import, taking also into account risks to human health, shall not prevent a party from taking a decision, as appropriate, with regard to the import of the living modified organism in question."

346. Articles 7 and 8 contain the AIA procedure. Article 7(1) states that the AIA procedure shall apply prior to the first intentional trans-boundary movement of LMOs intended to be introduced into the environment of the importing party. Article 8 requires exporting parties to notify, or to require the exporter to notify, the competent national authority of the importing party. Notification must contain the information specified in Annex I of the Protocol, including risk assessment. In accordance with Articles 11 and 20, a Biosafety Clearing-House is established in order to deal with the significant trade in LMOs which serves as a multilateral information exchange mechanism.

347. The Protocol provides measures for explicit public participation (Article 23). Contracting parties shall: (a) promote and facilitate public awareness, education, and participation concerning safe transfer, handling and use of LMOs in relation to biodiversity conservation and sustainable use; (b) ensure public awareness and education encompass access to information on LMOs identified by the Protocol that may be imported; (c) consult the public in the decision-making process regarding LMOs and shall make decisions available to public while respecting confidential information; and (d) each party is to endeavor to inform its public about access to information on Biosafety Clearing-House. Article 26 allows parties to take socio-economic considerations into account in reaching a decision on the import of LMOs, consistent with their international obligations, insofar as these concerns arise from the impact of LMOs on the conservation and sustainable use of biodiversity. The parties are encouraged to cooperate on research and information exchange on any socioeconomic impacts of LMOs, especially on indigenous and local communities.

348. Thus, the Biosafety Protocol contains most of the core elements relating to regulatory approaches on biotechnology. Prior to the Protocol, there was no global legally binding instrument to address the transfer, safe handling, and use of LMOs resulting from biotechnology in the context of adverse effects on biodiversity. The Protocol is the most comprehensive and important international agreement on biotechnology.

§2. Biosecurity

349. Achieving effective, comprehensive biosecurity to prevent unauthorized possession, theft, misuse, diversion, or intentional release of biological agents and toxins is a shared responsibility of the international community since infectious disease knows no borders. Any outbreaks of disease could pose challenges to global security by undermining national economies, international trade and travel, public health, and safety. The global biological threat to the environment is compounded by the possibility of irresponsible states and/or terrorists using biological agents as weapons of war or terrorism. Any such use of a biological agent can have devastating consequences on public health or the environment. Since there is no single technology or process that could be applied to deter the use of biological agents as weapons, the implementation of international instruments for nonproliferation (such as the BWC and UNSCR 1540) and public health, as well as the establishment of regional and international partnerships in countering biological threat, are critical factors in achieving global health security.

§3. Application of the IHR (2005)

350. The IHR, the legally binding international agreement designed to prevent the spread of disease, were revised and adopted by the 58th WHA on May 23, 2005. The purpose and scope of the IHR (2005) are "to prevent, protect against, control and provide a public health response to the international spread of disease in ways that are commensurate with and restricted to public health risks, and which avoid unnecessary interference with international traffic and trade." The revised IHR apply to diseases irrespective of origin or source, that present significant harm to humans, and offer the international community new opportunities to strengthen the public health capacities and collaborate with other countries and with the WHO.

§4. IHR (2005) Checklist of Indicators for Annual Reporting to WHA[33]

351. Building laboratory capacity to support a public health system cannot be achieved effectively without a strong focus on biosafety. The WHA had highlighted this issue in several resolutions. WHA resolutions on biosafety state as follows:

> A national health security strategy intended to protect the population against public health emergencies must consider a diverse spectrum of threats, including endemic diseases, natural outbreaks, accidents involving biological agent release, bioterrorism attacks, and biological warfare, all of them having a range of consequences. Whether preparing for a natural or a deliberate event, the common denominator is the need for a robust and timely response, and adaptive public health system that can provide early warning and an effective medical response. Implementation of the consistent policies, operating procedures

33. Biosafety and biosecurity are included under indicator 13.

and the operational and technical capacity required by the IHR (2005) help ensure early warning and efficient international management of a biological incident, whether naturally occurring or deliberate in nature, thereby promoting national health security. Laboratory-based surveillance and outbreak detection are essential to the prevention and mitigation of biological threats, and quality laboratory services are dependent on the implementation of biosafety and biosecurity best practices supported by an appropriate legal and regulatory framework.

§5. Biosafety and Biosecurity under the BWC

352. The BWC,[34] formally known as the "Convention on the Prohibition of the Development, Production and Stockpiling of Bacteriological (Biological) and Toxin Weapons and on Their Destruction (the Biological and Toxin Weapons Convention)," was the first multilateral disarmament treaty that banned the production and use of an entire category of weapons. The State Parties of BWC hold Review Conferences every five years. Between these Review Conferences, States Parties have pursued various activities and initiatives to strengthen the effectiveness and improve the implementation of the Convention.

In order to ensure that the tenets of the BWC are adhered to, States Parties are encouraged to implement national legislation to enforce the provisions of the BWC to prohibit and prevent the development, production, stockpiling, acquisition, retention, transfer, or use of biological weapons under their jurisdiction, as well as parallel measures to prohibit and prevent encouraging, inciting, or assisting others in any of these acts. Based on the understandings and agreements reached historically at the Review Conferences, national implementation of BWC includes legislative, administrative, and other measures to enhance domestic compliance with the BWC; national export control systems; education and awareness-raising measures; disease surveillance, detection, and containment; as well as biosafety and biosecurity provisions.

§6. UNSCR 1540

353. On April 28, 2004, the UN Security Council adopted UNSCR 1540 to address the risk that terrorists and illicit networks will acquire Weapons of Mass Destruction (WMD). UNSCR 1540 established, for the first time, legally binding obligations on all UN Member States to develop and enforce measures against the proliferation of nuclear, chemical, and biological WMD, their means of delivery, and related materials. While national implementation efforts under the BWC, Chemical Weapons Convention (CWC), and the Treaty on the Non-Proliferation of Nuclear Weapons (NPT) are intended to accomplish a similar goal, the sole intention of UNSCR 1540 was to create binding obligations regarding all three weapon types and avoid the negotiation processes and voluntary commitments under these

34. Opened for signature on Apr. 10, 1972, and entered into force on Mar. 26, 1975.

treaties. Moreover, it is applicable to all UN Member States, regardless of their membership in multilateral agreements. The resolution calls for the establishment of a national legal framework that should include the following elements:

(i) a system to account for and secure items in production, use, storage or transport;
(ii) effective physical protection measures;
(iii) effective border controls and law enforcement measures; and
(iv) effective national export and transshipment controls.

354. UNSCR 1540 also emphasizes that the international legal framework facilitate a strategy of "prevention" based upon each individual Member State accepting "responsibility" for implementing measures against the proliferation of materials and weapons. It also requires all Member States to report on their national implementation measures to the 1540 Committee established under the Resolution. The 1540 Committee acts as a clearinghouse for information on the issue of assistance through formal and informal contact and dialog with all Member States, especially those expressing interest in offering and receiving assistance. In response to UNSCR 1810 (2008), the 1540 Committee conducted, in the Fall of 2009, a Comprehensive Review as a forum for all Member States and relevant intergovernmental bodies to share experiences and express their views on various aspects of UNSCR 1540 implementation. Based on the findings of the Comprehensive Review, the 1540 Committee prepared an outcome document with recommendations to the Council regarding the implementation of Resolution 1540.

355. The international instruments are part of the system of prevention designed to address the security and health challenges of the present-day world. The countries are working toward building a culture of security and responsibility at the national and international level by involving civic, scientific, and government capacities in its outreach to facilitate a common understanding of the WMD threat and encourage participation in and compliance with international nonproliferation efforts, enhance global efforts to protect and defend against biological threats, and improve disease containment and response in case of an outbreak.

Chapter 3. Biogenetics

356. The use of genetic engineering for therapeutic purposes has held out great promise and inspired studies but has also led to problems. Germ line engineering has the potential of preventing genetic diseases, especially monogenetic diseases, such as hemophilia, Franconi's anemia, and amyotrophic lateral sclerosis. Genetic engineering can also be used for purposes of enhancing human traits. While it is not clear at present how far it could be accomplished, if successful, it may result in creating inequalities about changes in the human nature itself. There is an argument that humans have a human right to their own genetic identity and cloning and inheritable genetic alterations can be seen as crimes against humanity. The European Parliament has adopted a resolution which provides that people have a human right to their own genetic identity.[35]

357. Regulations for biogenetic development are needed but what form they take is a matter of concern. It would be a serious mistake to adopt human rights treaties prohibiting all germ line engineering or all genetic engineering for purposes of human enhancement on the ground that such genetic alterations may violate human rights. However, it may be a mistake to use human rights treaties to ban human reproductive cloning. International treaties regulating human genetic engineering may be desirable, but any prohibition should be viewed as a temporary regulation based on risk assessment and cultural values that can change with the passage of time in light of new developments.

§1. Human Rights Treaties and Proposals

358. The prohibitions of germ line and nontherapeutic genetic engineering are found in the Council of Europe's "Convention for the Protection of Human Rights and Dignity of the Human Being with regard to the Application of Biology and Medicine and Convention on Human Rights and Biomedicine." Article 13 of the Convention states that "An intervention seeking to modify the human genome may only be undertaken for preventive, diagnostic or therapeutic purposes and only if its aim is not to introduce any modification in the genome of any descendants."[36]

§2. Reproductive Cloning of Human Beings

359. Article 1 of the Additional Protocol envisages that reproductive cloning of humans is prohibited (Council of Europe 1998, Article 1). Article 11 of UNESCO's Universal Declaration on the Human Genome and Human Rights also prohibits human reproductive cloning, and Article 12(b) rules out genetic engineering for purposes of enhancement.[37] Article 12(b) states that the applications of research,

35. European Parliament, 1998, Art. 1.
36. Council of Europe, 1997.
37. UNESCO, 1997.

including applications in biology, genetics, and medicine, concerning the human genome, shall seek to offer relief from suffering and improve the health of individuals and humankind as a whole.[38] Article 2(A) of UNESCO's Universal Declaration on the Human Genome and Human Rights states, in part that, "everyone has a right to respect for their dignity."[39]

I. Action by UN General Assembly

360. In December 2001, the General Assembly established an ad hoc working group of the Sixth Committee to consider an international instrument to ban the reproductive cloning of human beings. This initiative was motivated by the public announcements by certain laboratories of impending attempts to begin reproductive cloning of humans. The committee met in two sessions, from 2001 to 2002, to elaborate a mandate for the proposed treaty, but controversy swelled before the end of the first session. The majority of state delegations supported the original proposal, which limited the treaty's subject matter to the reproductive cloning of human beings. However, some states, led by the US, supported extending the proposed prohibition to therapeutic cloning and embryonic stem cell research. Ultimately, the negotiations for the treaty failed and, in 2005, the UN General Assembly adopted a resolution calling upon Member States to prohibit all forms of human cloning "in so far as they are incompatible with human dignity and the protection of human life."[40] The problem is that codifying an international treaty on reproductive cloning is not on the priority agenda of most countries and particularly in poor states. At the time of the cloning treaty negotiations, only thirty states had legislation on human cloning. Nevertheless, consistent with the contemporary process for initiating multilateral negotiations, a select few states were able to initiate negotiations.

II. Cloning and Cultural Values

361. It is considered that reproductive cloning is simply too dangerous to tolerate and is repugnant and that we should pay attention to our feelings of repugnance.[41] Along the same lines, it is sometimes argued that reproductive cloning would violate cultural understandings and basis, such as assumptions about family relationships and expectations. If a human right prohibiting cloning is grounded in current values or concerns about dangers, then there may come a time in the future when these conditions change. Similarly, if human right is grounded in current cultural understandings, then there may come a time when these values may change.

38. *Id.*
39. *Id.*
40. UN General Assembly, 2005.
41. L. Kass, *The Wisdom of Repugnance: Why We Should Ban Cloning*, 32(2) Valparaiso Univ. L Rev. 679–705 (1998) and M. Midgley, *Biotechnology and Monstrosity: Why We Should Pay Attention to the "Yuck Factor."* 30(5) Hastings Center Report 7–15 (2000).

Some have also argued that reproductive cloning is a violation of a more general human right to genetic identity or dignity. This is the position, for example, of the Council of Europe and UNESCO.

III. Risk Involved in Genetic Cloning

362. Germ line and nontherapeutic genetic engineering, including reproductive cloning, pose risks of adverse effects, and they can also be used for immoral purposes. In many cases, the regulations should take the form of national statutes. Individual nations have the ability to make statutes that reflect the current local perceptions and conditions. These regulations can be passed, amended, or repealed as the changing situation warrants. Treating human rights in this way would weaken them by reducing them to the status of mere regulations so international treaties may be an appropriate medium. This is true in cases where science has not progressed to the point where genetic engineering can be carried out with reasonable safety. At this stage of the science of genetic engineering, it is not clear what advances will be made in the science, and it is not clear how the culture will change in light of those advances or otherwise. The potential for benefit, as well as harm, along with current uncertainties favor taking small regulatory steps rather than sweeping prohibitions based on human rights.

§3. Genetics and Human Rights

363. There is a strong view that principles constituting human rights treaties not be stated in terms of specific forms of technology or on the basis of current scientific assumptions that might change. Just as scientific theory will change over time in light of continuing research, cultural attitudes may also change over time. Activities that people find repulsive at one time may come to be accepted at another time and vice versa. For example, when in vitro fertilization (IVF) techniques were first developed many felt revulsion and spoke of "test tube babies." At the present time, IVF is widely accepted, both emotionally and morally. Human rights treaties, in the face of advancing science and changing cultural values, cannot effectively apply human rights to future generations. Therefore, prohibitions on genetic engineering must not be regarded in themselves as human rights.

I. Prohibitions on Genetic Engineering

364. Germ line genetic engineering, reproductive cloning, and genetic engineering for purposes of enhancement may pose dangers to the society, making them unjustified at a particular point of time. On the other hand, the time may come when genetic engineering can safely be used to prevent diseases, such as Tay–Sachs or Huntington's. If human rights are used to prohibit germ line engineering in such cases, serious problems may arise. Suppose that germ line engineering is prohibited because there is a human right not to be subjected to such engineering; in cases such as Tay–Sachs Disease, this would be a right that no reasonable person would want to claim or have exercised on his or her behalf. In order to avoid such absurdity, the right would have to be regarded as weak and capable of being overridden or specific exceptions would have to be carved out from time to time as science advances.

II. Genetic Enhancement

365. Similar considerations may also arise regarding genetic enhancements. While attempts to genetically enhance people may be dangerous to allow, there may come a time when such enhancements could be done safely in a manner that would not be objectionable. Creating blanket prohibitions of germ line genetic engineering on the grounds that there is a human right not to be subjected to such engineering poses a problem for future development. If there is a human right not to be genetically enhanced, then the right must apply to humans generally. It must apply in the present and the future, as well as in all cultures. The problem is that what counts as an enhancement will vary depending on various cultural and technological considerations and time zones. Such considerations have troubling implications for human rights treaties that allow genetic engineering for purposes of therapy but not enhancement. Genetic techniques that are prohibited as enhancements in one society may be permitted as treatments in another society. Moreover, what is permitted or prohibited will change from time to time within a society. Thus, the use of human rights in this context appears to be farfetched.

§4. Human Right to Dignity and Genetic Identity

366. A right to one's genetic identity makes sense when interpreted as a right to genetic privacy and dignity. One has a right to keep one's genetic information confidential within certain limits. But it cannot be interpreted so as to prevent germ line engineering. If genetic identity is regarded such that any change in one's genetic structure is a change in one's identity, then beneficial therapies are ruled out. If, however, genetic identity is construed so that there is a core genetic identity, a sort of essence of the individual, then germ line engineering may proceed without affecting that identity. Germ line engineering that prevents a disease, for example, does not threaten the identity of the individual because having a particular disease need not be part of the individual's identity.

367. The issues of individual identity and authenticity are important. but individual identity should not be reduced to genetic identity (Rovane, 2002). After all, identical twins are not harmed merely by the fact that they are identical twins (Hayry, 2004, 10). If dignity requires respect for a core set of personality traits, then genetic engineering that does not undermine those traits is not prohibited. This can include germ line genetic engineering and even genetic engineering for purposes of enhancement. If, on the other hand, it simply means that the human genome is inviolable, then obviously beneficial therapies are ruled out. In this respect, prohibitions on germ line genetic engineering and genetic enhancement look a lot more like regulations that follow from human rights than human rights themselves.

§5. GENETIC TESTING

368. In gene tests, scientists scan a patient's DNA sample for mutated sequences. A DNA sample is obtained from any tissue, including blood. For some types of gene tests, researchers design short pieces of DNA, called probes, whose sequences are complementary to the mutated sequences. These probes seek their complement among the three billion base pairs of an individual's genome. If the mutated sequence is present in the patient's genome, the probe will bind to it and flag the mutation. Another type of DNA testing involves comparing the sequence of DNA bases in a patient's gene to a normal version of the gene.

369. Gene tests or DNA-based tests are the most sophisticated of the techniques used to test for genetic disorders and involve direct examination of the DNA molecule itself. Other genetic tests include biochemical tests for such gene products as enzymes and other proteins and for microscopic examination of stained or fluorescent chromosomes. Genetic tests are used for several reasons, including: carrier screening, which involves identifying unaffected individuals who carry one copy of a gene for a disease that requires two copies for the disease to be expressed. Before Preimplantation Genetic Diagnosis (PGD), couples with higher risks for conceiving a child with a particular disorder would have to initiate the pregnancy and then undergo chorionic villus sampling in the first trimester or amniocentesis in the second trimester to test the fetus for the presence of disease. If the fetus tested positive for the disorder, the couple would be faced with the dilemma of whether or not to terminate the pregnancy. With PGD, couples are much more likely to have healthy babies. Although PGD has been practiced for years, only a few specialized centers worldwide offer this procedure.

I. Pros and Cons of Gene Testing

370. Gene testing has improved the lives of persons suffering from genetic disorders. Some tests are used to clarify a diagnosis and direct a physician toward appropriate treatments while others allow families to avoid having children with diseases or identify people at high risk for conditions that may be preventable. Aggressive monitoring for and removal of colon growths in those inheriting a gene for familial adenomatous polyposis, for example, has saved many lives. Commercialized gene tests for adult-onset disorders, such as Alzheimer's disease, and some cancers are the subject of most of the debate over gene testing. These tests are targeted at healthy people who are identified as being at high risk because of a strong family medical history for the disorder. The tests give only a probability for developing the disorder. One of the most serious limitations of these susceptibility tests is the difficulty in interpreting a positive result because some people who carry a disease-associated mutation never develop the disease. Scientists believe that these mutations may work together with other, unknown mutations or with environmental factors to cause disease.

II. Genetic Test and Insurance

371. The economics of health insurance make it unlikely that insurers will rely on genetic test information. Employers provide most health insurance and the premiums for those plans are based on the experience of the insured group, not on the characteristics of any one member. Life insurers, however, could have an incentive to use genetic test information because their customers buy their policies individually and tend to keep the same insurer their whole lives. Furthermore, even if life or health insurers were to find it practical to base underwriting decisions on genetic test results, the practice is unlikely to produce one class of genetically blessed and another class of genetically cursed individuals. Nearly all diseases with a genetic component can be prevented or treated with early detection, so widespread genetic testing is far more likely to result in improved health outcomes for most genetic diseases.

372. It is not even correct to assume that those genetically predisposed to some disease will have worse health outcomes when compared to the general population. In many cases, those with the knowledge that they are genetically predisposed to a given disease might well change their behavior and control their environments sufficiently to gain a statistical edge over those not so genetically predisposed but who do not similarly alter their behavior. That could result in lower health or life insurance premiums. However, forbidding insurers from using genetic test results or other types of relevant information could restrict efficient underwriting and force all consumers to pay higher costs.

III. Preimplantation Genetic Diagnosis

373. Genetic diseases can be diagnosed prior to a child being born. The most common way is to diagnose if there is a problem in the unborn child is by doing a chorion biopsy at eight to nine weeks or amniocentesis at around the fourth to the fifth month of pregnancy (prenatal diagnosis). In case a baby is found to be abnormal, it can be aborted. However, this is a traumatic process. Instead of undergoing this trauma, PGD can be done. In this, a standard Intracytoplasmic Sperm Injection (ICSI) cycle is carried out and a lot of embryos are produced. A small piece of the embryo is then removed and examined for any genetic or chromosomal defects. The defective embryos are discarded and the normal embryos are put back in the womb. Thus, with the help of PGD, one can have normal babies without undergoing the trauma of amniocentesis and abortion. The detection of genetic disease in the human embryo before implantation gives parents a chance to start a pregnancy, knowing that the baby will be free of an inherited disorder that is prevalent in their family.

Chapter 4. Bioethics, Health Law and Human Rights

374. Bioethics refers to the ethical implications and applications of the health-related life sciences. Dilemmas can arise for the scientist as to moral limits on their work. In clinical trials involving human subjects, a set of challenges arises, from ensuring informed consent, to protecting vulnerable research participants to guarantee their participation is voluntary and informed. The added costs of new therapies inevitably strain available resources, forcing hard choices about how to fairly serve the needs of all, especially those already underserved by the health care system.

Ethical questions in medicine and the life sciences are the subject of two academic fields: "bioethics" and "health and human rights." The growth of these fields has drawn attention to important moral questions in medicine and biology. "Bioethics" can be understood in a broader or narrower way. Following the broader concept, bioethics includes not only philosophical study of the ethics of medicine but also medical law, medical anthropology, medical sociology, health politics, health economics, and even some areas of medicine itself. From the narrower angle, bioethics, although it may draw other disciplines, is itself only an area of philosophical inquiry. More specifically, bioethics is one branch of practical or applied ethics, which is one branch of ethics and which in turn is one branch of philosophy. If bioethics construed in the narrow way, it is not denying the importance of the sciences, social sciences, and law to bioethics. These disciplines are clearly indispensable to practical ethics.

375. There is a parallel problem for those who work in the area of practical ethics because this area requires knowledge of science, social science, and, sometimes, law as practical philosophers have to familiarize themselves with scholarly discussions in these disciplines. This is unavoidable and is not troubling as long as the philosopher does not purport to be doing science, social science, or law but only reporting its findings.

§1. Disciplinary Slip

376. The problem of "disciplinary slip," where one departs from working in one's own discipline, in which one is trained, to working in another, in which one is not, is more acute in some cases than in others. For example, there are fewer obstacles to health care workers or scientists slipping into doing moral philosophy than there are obstacles to philosophers slipping into medicine or science. This is partly because of the obviously special knowledge and training required to become a health care professional or a scientist. But it is also partly because of the widespread but mistaken assumption that doing philosophy may not really require any training or aptitude. Indeed, it is this attitude that underlies the common confidence to pronounce about moral and other philosophical matters without any sense of the complexity of these matters. The expertise and skills of philosophers are often underrated. There are somewhat lesser obstacles to philosophers drifting into the softer sciences that are to be found under the umbrella of bioethics, but even these obstacles are greater than the obstacles in the reverse direction. Social scientists can slip into doing moral philosophy more readily than philosophers can slip into doing social science.

377. A second reason why there are fewer obstacles to medical professionals and scientists slipping into bioethics is the fact that bioethics is making greater inroads into academic medical contexts than medicine and medical science are making into academic philosophy. Thus, articles on bioethics are now quite commonly published in medical journals, and so-called "bioethicists" are invited to speak to groups of medical practitioners. It is much rarer for doctors and scientists to be published in philosophy journals or for doctors to be giving academic talks to philosophers. A parallel problem can occur when scientists do publish science in a bioethics journal. These problems of disciplinary quality are exacerbated by a number of factors. First, because the discipline of bioethics is currently understood in the broader way, it is filled with people who have slipped from their area of medical, scientific, or other nonphilosophical expertise into moral philosophy. Given that the discipline is so populated with such people, many of them do not see that many of the rest are not doing moral philosophy very well.

378. In ultimate analyses where there are disciplinary standards in most disciplines, there are no such standards in bioethics. Indeed, much of what goes on in bioethics is undisciplined. Some think that the absence of disciplinary standards is acceptable in bioethics because it is a "field" rather than a "discipline." Others seek some consolation in the claim that bioethics is a new field which has yet to find its feet and establish standards.

§2. Broader Concept of Bioethics

379. Defenders of the broader conception of bioethics may say that because answering bioethics questions involves answering both philosophical and nonphilosophical questions, the field of bioethics must incorporate both. To bolster their point, they might want to claim that what unites these two kinds of questions and marks out the field is a distinctive kind of bioethics reasoning. But this suggestion is implausible on at least two counts. First, it is unlikely that bioethics reasoning differs (in anything other than content) from other forms of practical ethics reasoning. Second, although answering practical ethics questions does require both philosophical and nonphilosophical reasoning, there is no overarching distinct form of reasoning that unites these two. As the scientific, social scientific, and legal questions that are integral to bioethics can also be asked and answered quite independently of any ethical interest, they are not distinctively ethical. They are scientific, social scientific, and legal questions and must be answered by those best equipped to answer them, employing the tools of the relevant discipline.

§3. The Universal Declaration on Bioethics and Human Rights, 2005

380. The Universal Declaration on Bioethics and Human Rights 2005 (UNBHR) defines the universally acceptable norms, principles and procedures in the field of bioethics, in conformity with *human* rights as enshrined in international law. The UDBHR presents 15 principles, including respect for human dignity, human rights and fundamental freedoms, and the priority of individual interests and welfare over the interests of science and society. The UDBHR commits governments to establish ethics committees and to promote bioethics education. The inclusion of social responsibility, including access to health care and essential medicines, takes care of the needs of developing countries.

§4. Health and Human Rights

381. Some of those engaged in academic work on moral problems in medicine identify their field as "health and human rights," which they see as distinct from bioethics. According to the health and human rights view, the moral defects of medical practice and human life are to be rectified through the promotion of human rights. Those advocates of health and human rights who think that the relevant rights are legal ones, either national or international, face an obvious difficulty. Law and morality are neither the same things nor are they coextensive. The law can be morally defective, and moral rights can fail to be incorporated into law or be incorporated only inadequately. The upshot of this is that legal rights, like law, in general, are inadequate to the task of resolving moral dilemmas or rectifying the moral defects of medical practice.

382. One of the distinctive features of rights is that they have correlative duties. To ascribe a right is also to ascribe the correlative duty. There simply could not be a right without its correlative duty. For example, my right not to be killed is correlated with the duty of others not to kill me. I could not have a right not to be killed if others were under no duty not to kill me. A second distinctive feature of rights is that they have unusual moral strength. They are said to have "trumping" power. That is to say, they can defeat other moral considerations.

383. Human rights are rights someone has in virtue of being human. In other words, a human right is a kind of natural right—a right that somebody has on account of his (human) nature. Not all rights that humans have are human rights. Some rights are possessed not on account of the bearer's nature but rather because of some other consideration. For example, if you lend me GBP 100, you acquire a right to receive GBP 100 from me. This is not a human right but rather a right arising from the loan. Thus, human rights are but one kind of right. However, even the expanded class of rights obviously does not exhaust the range of moral concepts that can be employed to understand and evaluate an ethical issue.

384. A health and human rights approach is unable to consider a nonnatural right, such as a right arising from a promise or from membership in a medical insurance scheme. Even if the notion of "human rights" were extended to include not only natural rights possessed by humans but also nonnatural rights possessed by humans, the human rights approach would still be unable, adequately, to approach important issues in medicine. For example, it could not take account of the interests of those animals on which medical experimentation is conducted. Even those who think that such experimentation is morally justifiable must agree that reaching that conclusion via an ethical approach that considers only the rights of a human, and nothing else, is highly questionable.

385. Discussion about (moral) rights is part of what ethics or bioethics involves with, but these disciplines need not restrict themselves to this one moral concept. Unlike the human rights approach, those who do bioethics need not commit the error of mistaking the part for the whole. Rights are part of ethics, but they are not all there is to ethics. Thus, those doing ethics or bioethics can and do employ whatever moral concepts are relevant to some issue. One suggestion could be that the human rights approach to ethical problems in health and health care is an activist approach. It aims at bringing about positive change. The objection here is that bioethics is too much of an academic exercise and too little a mechanism for social change.

Part IX. Armed Conflict and Medical Professionals

386. Wars draw civilian medical personnel to work with large numbers of ill or desperate people from unfamiliar cultures in settings of considerable danger in war-ravaged areas. Epidemic disease may affect war-torn societies that cannot possibly pay for the cures available in normal times. Despite the fact that genocide can be, and is, committed with weapons as simple as machetes, much scientific effort and tremendous resources are being spent on designing new ways to wage war or combat terrorism on a massive scale. Since the end of World War II, rules and standards have been developed to deal with the civilian population, dead, and wounded. The rules and standards of medical care during wartime have been and will continue to be modified as we learn more about our capacities and acquire more complex technology.

Chapter 1. Role of Medical Personnel in Armed Conflict

387. The Geneva Conventions of 1949, formed by combining the three previous conventions of 1864, 1906, 1929, binds nation-state signatories to a tight set of obligations regarding the care of the wounded, treatment of servicemen, management of prisoners of war, and protection of civilians. In addition, the Hague Convention of 1899, a pivotal document in a long series, seeks to limit methods of war and prohibit certain weapons. These two bodies of law, of Geneva and of The Hague, form the cornerstone of international humanitarian law dealing with the conduct of individuals and nations in wartime. The Universal Declaration of Human Rights establishes a set of principles regarding the state's relationship to individuals and communities, for example, that no one should be held in slavery and that everyone has a right to social security and education. It has served as the basis for the growing number of legally binding covenants, such as the Covenant on Civil and Political Rights that contribute to that body of international law that is thought to apply to states in times of peace. However, international humanitarian law and human rights provide the functioning norms for those who try to deliver medical and emergency relief in war zones.

§1. International Law Relating to Conduct of Medical Personnel

388. The main principles of international humanitarian law of relevance to physicians are neutrality, nonpartisanship, independence, and humanitarianism. Physicians and other health care workers are protected from hostile action to the extent that they understand these principles and abide by the rules that flow from them. The physicians must practice both competently and according to the highest principles of medical ethics during wartime. Thus, to be protected in war, a physician must first be deemed competent to practice in peace. The major points of law of The Hague relate to an appreciation of the concepts of superfluous injury and unnecessary suffering and how to assess the design or use of weapons from that perspective.

Violations of human rights often have serious medical consequences and physicians can be particularly helpful. They can use their clinical skills or deploy the analytical frame of epidemiology and public health to document the nature and impact of injuries created by human rights abuses, supply expert testimony, and advocate on behalf of those who have suffered. Further, doctors should recognize the range of torture and repression in state systems.

389. The discourses of international humanitarian law and human rights, once thought to be entirely separate—one for war and the other for peace—are also now seen to overlap. Current legal analyses of war and conflict allow for applying core human rights law, as well as international humanitarian law, so that important human rights for refugees, for example, the right not to be forced back across a border into a hostile country of origin or for children, for example, the right not to be forced into slave labor or into the army, are considered inviolate in settings of active hostilities.

I. Geneva Convention

390. As per Rule 25 of the Geneva Convention, the medical personnel exclusively assigned to medical duties must be respected and protected in all circumstances. They lose their protection if they commit, outside their humanitarian function, acts harmful to the enemy. State practice establishes this rule as a norm of customary international law applicable in both international and non-international armed conflicts. Rule 25 has its roots in 1864 Geneva Convention and was repeated in the subsequent Geneva Conventions of 1906 and 1929.[42] It, now, found its place in the First, Second, and Fourth Geneva Conventions of 1949.[43] Its scope was expanded in Article 15 of Additional Protocol I to cover civilian medical personnel in addition to military medical personnel in all circumstances.[44] This extension is widely supported in state practice, which generally refers to medical personnel without distinguishing between military or civilian medical personnel. It is also supported by states not, or not at the time, party to Additional Protocol I.

A. *War Crimes*

391. Under the Statute of the ICC, "intentionally directing attacks against … personnel using the distinctive emblems of the Geneva Conventions in conformity with international law" constitutes a war crime in international armed conflicts.[45] This war crime is relevant to medical personnel because they are entitled to use the distinctive emblems of the Geneva Conventions. Numerous military manuals contain the obligation to respect and protect medical personnel. Under the legislation of many states, it is a war crime to violate this rule. Furthermore, the rule is supported by official statements and reported practice of the warring parties.

B. *Care for Wounded and Sick*

392. Article 3 of the 1949 Geneva Conventions requires that the wounded and sick be collected and cared for because the protection of medical personnel is a subsidiary form of protection granted to ensure that the wounded and sick receive medical care. The rule that medical personnel must be respected and protected is explicitly stated in Additional Protocol II.[46] Respect for and protection of medical personnel are also included in military manuals which are applicable in or have been applied in non-international armed conflicts. It is an offense under the law of a number of states to violate this rule in any armed conflict. This rule has also been invoked in official statements relating to non-international armed conflicts.

---

42. 1864 Geneva Convention, Art. 2; 1906 Geneva Convention, Arts. 9–10); 1929 Geneva Convention, Arts. 9–10).
43. First Geneva Convention, Arts. 24–26; Second Geneva Convention, Art. 36; Fourth Geneva Convention, Art. 20.
44. Additional Protocol I, Art. 15 (adopted by consensus).
45. ICC Statute, Art. 8(2)(b)(xxiv).
46. Additional Protocol II, Art. 9(1).

§2. Definition of Medical Personnel

393. The term "medical personnel," in the context of war, refers to personnel assigned, temporarily or permanently by a party to the conflict, exclusively to the search for, collection, transportation, diagnosis or treatment, including first aid treatment, of the wounded, sick and shipwrecked, and the prevention of disease, to the administration of medical units or to the operation or administration of medical transports. The definition of medical personnel is also set out in Article 8(c) of Additional Protocol I and is widely used in state practice. The essence of the definition is that medical personnel have to be exclusively assigned to medical duties in order to enjoy the specific protection to which they are entitled. If the medical assignment is permanent, respect and protection are due at all times. If the medical assignment is only temporary, respect and protection are due only during the time of that assignment. Only medical personnel specifically assigned to medical duties by a party to the conflict enjoy protected status. Other persons performing medical duties enjoy protection against attack as civilians as long as they do not take a direct part in hostilities (Rule 6). Such persons are not medical personnel and, as a result, they have no right to display the distinctive emblems. On the other hand the term "military medical personnel" refers to medical personnel who are members of the armed forces. The term "civilian medical personnel" refers to medical personnel who are not members of the armed forces but who have been assigned by a party to the conflict exclusively to medical tasks.

394. Additional Protocol II does not contain a definition of medical personnel and the term medical personnel, as used in non-international armed conflicts, and may be understood in the same sense as that defined in Additional Protocol I. It can be understood that "medical personnel" means those persons assigned, by a party to the conflict, exclusively to the search for, collection, transportation, diagnosis or treatment, including first aid treatment, of the wounded, sick and shipwrecked, and the prevention of disease, to the administration of medical units or to the operation or administration of medical transports. Such assignments may be either permanent or temporary. The term medical personnel includes:

(i) medical personnel of a party to the conflict, whether military or civilian, including those assigned to medical tasks of civil defense;
(ii) medical personnel of Red Cross or Red Crescent organizations recognized and authorized by a party to the conflict;
(iii) medical personnel of other aid societies recognized and authorized by a party to the conflict and located within the territory of the State where the armed conflict is taking place.

§3. Respect for and Protection of Medical Personnel

395. According to the UK Military Manual and US Field Manual, the term "respect and protection" means that medical personnel "must not knowingly be attacked, fired upon, or unnecessarily prevented from discharging their proper functions." Military manuals of Germany and Switzerland contain a similar understanding. The military manuals of Croatia, Madagascar, Nigeria, and Togo state that medical personnel may not be attacked and must be allowed to carry out their tasks as long as the tactical situation permits. Spain's manual states that protection includes the duty to defend, assist, and support medical personnel when needed. Additional Protocol I also requires that "if needed, all available help should be afforded to civilian medical personnel in an area where civilian medical services are disrupted by reason of combat activity."[47] Additional Protocol II requires that medical personnel "be granted all available help for the performance of their duties."[48]

§4. Loss of Protection of Medical Personnel

396. In case a medical personnel engages in a hostile act, they lose the specific entitled protection. This exception is linked to the requirement that such personnel be exclusively assigned to medical duties for them to be accorded respect and protection. Further, under the protection regime, which is a corollary to the duty of care for the wounded and sick, specific protection is due because the wounded and sick are being cared for. Spain's manual explains that the protection of medical personnel is not a personal privilege but rather a corollary of the respect and protection due to the wounded and sick who must be treated humanely in all circumstances, and medical personnel will lose the special protection if they commit acts of hostility. The First Geneva Convention and Additional Protocol I provide for the loss of protection of medical units and transports in case they are used to commit "outside their humanitarian function, acts harmful to the enemy." Further, Additional Protocol II provides for the loss of protection in case they are used to commit "hostile acts, outside their humanitarian function."

397. So, taking a direct part in hostilities, in violation of the principle of strict neutrality and outside the humanitarian function of medical personnel, is considered as an act harmful to the enemy. Thus, in case medical teams are incorporated into combat units and their medical personnel bear arms and take a direct part in hostilities, they are not entitled to protection. However, neither the mere caring for enemy wounded and sick military personnel nor the sole wearing of enemy military uniforms or bearing of its insignia can be considered a hostile act. The equipment of medical personnel with small arms to defend themselves or their patients and the use of such arms for this purpose may not lead to loss of protection. Furthermore, in analogous application of the similar rule applying to medical units, it is not to be considered a hostile act if medical personnel are escorted by military personnel or such personnel are present or if the medical personnel are in possession of small arms and ammunition taken from their patients and not yet handed over to the proper authorities.

47. Additional Protocol I, Art. 15(2), adopted by consensus.
48. Additional Protocol II, Art. 9(1), adopted by consensus.

§5. Equipment of Medical Personnel

398. State practice indicates that the protected status of medical personnel does not cease if they are equipped with light individual weapons solely to defend their patients or themselves against acts of violence, for example, against marauders. If they use such weapons in combat against enemy forces acting in conformity with the law of war, notably to resist capture, they forfeit their protection. This interpretation was first set out in the 1906 Geneva Convention and repeated in the 1929 Geneva Convention. It is now codified in the First Geneva Convention and Additional Protocol I.

399. The military manuals specify that the carrying of light individual weapons does not deprive medical personnel of their protected status. According to Germany's military manual, such "individual weapons" are pistols, submachine guns, and rifles. The military manual of the Netherlands provides the same interpretation of the term and adds that it excludes machine guns or other weapons that have to be handled by more than one person, weapons intended for use against objects, such as missile launchers and other anti-tank weapons, and fragmentation hand grenades and the like.

§6. Hold Perpetrators to Account

400. Starting from 1980, human rights organizations documented human rights and international humanitarian law violations against patients, health workers, and health facilities in war and political conflict. In 2011, the Security Council decided to include the names of parties that attack schools and hospitals in the annexure of persistent perpetrators of grave violations in the annual report of the Secretary General's Special Representative on Children and Armed Conflict. The following year, the World Health Assembly directed the WHO to begin collecting and disseminating data on attacks on health care in emergencies. In 2013, the UN Special Rapporteur on the Right to the Highest Attainable Standard of Physical and Mental Health explicated the scope and application of the right to health in conflict, including protection from violence. Ultimately in 2015, the General Assembly passed a resolution demanding compliance with protection mandates. In 2016, the Security Council adopted Resolution 2286, condemning attacks and committing to prevent them and holding perpetrators to account domestically and internationally. Although it made no new law, the resolution represented a political breakthrough. It reinforced the requirements of the Additional Protocols to the Geneva Conventions not to punish health workers for conduct consistent with medical ethics. It called upon states to reform domestic laws, adopt measures to protect heath care in military operations, and strengthen domestic and international investigations and procedures so that perpetrators can be held to account.

401. There is evidence of acts that sabotaged the purposes of the resolution but U.N. succumbed to pressure from powerful states to omit their names from the list of perpetrators of grave violations against schools and hospitals in armed conflict.

Security Council referral of Syria to the International Criminal Court was stymied by repeated Russian vetoes. The United States and the UK found excuses to sell massive amounts of arms to Saudi Arabia despite evidence that its conduct in the war in Yemen may have amounted to war crimes. The WHO's surveillance system declined to name perpetrators of attacks. For safeguarding health services in conflict zone, the Secretary General has appointed a Special Representative on violence against health care. The representative will advise and consult with states on implementation, but also to report publicly what they have and have not done to implement Resolution 2286 as a means of holding them to account for fulfilling their duty.

402. Expert groups and investigative bodies appointed by the Human Rights Council and the General Assembly, along with human rights organizations and the High Commissioner for Human Rights, have laid ample groundwork for criminal investigations and prosecutions. Germany has launched prosecutions under principles of universal jurisdiction for war crimes in Syria. The UN established a special criminal court in the Central African Republic. Resolution 2286 retains its potential importance. States should not be let off the hook in observing their commitments to human rights and international humanitarian law and must instead be judged by whether they act to protect and respect health care.

Part X. Law Relating to Disability and Mental Health

403. Until the nineteenth century, the care of the insane was largely a community and family responsibility rather than a medical one. The vast majority of the mentally ill were treated in domestic contexts with only the most unmanageable or burdensome were likely to be confined in homes or mental hospitals. This situation was transformed radically from the late eighteenth century as a newfound optimism emerged in the curability of insanity within the asylum setting. Therefore, lunacy was perceived less as a physiological condition than as a mental and moral one to which the correct response was persuasion, aimed at inculcating internal restraint rather than external coercion. This new development, referred to as moral treatment, was epitomized in French physician Philippe Pinel's unchaining of the lunatics in a hospital in Paris and realized in an institutional setting with the foundation in 1796 of the York Retreat in England. The Quaker-run York Retreat gained international prominence as a center for moral treatment and a model of asylum reform following the publication of Samuel Tuke's Description of the Retreat (1813).

Chapter 1. Disability and Mental Health

404. In many countries lower income groups do not have access to basic mental health care and the treatment they require. In others, the community-based mental health care is not available. So, the only care available is in psychiatric institutions and hospitals which are associated with gross human rights and other legal violations including inhuman and degrading treatment and bad living conditions. The patients are also excluded from community life and denied basic rights, such as shelter, food, and clothing, and are discriminated against in *employment*, education, and housing due to their mental disability. Many are denied the right to vote, marry, and to have children. A number of people with mental disabilities live in extreme poverty which affects their ability to gain access to appropriate care, to recover and to integrate into society.

405. Mental patients are exposed to human rights violations as well, which occur inside institutions, through inadequate and harmful care and treatment, and also outside, with people experiencing limitation to the exercise of civil liberties and rights to employment, education, and housing. These violations are often motivated by the stigma, myths, and misconceptions associated with mental illnesses which can, in turn, also impact their ability to gain access to appropriate care and reintegrate into the community.

§1. UN Convention and Work of the WHO

406. In 2008, the UN Convention on the Rights of Persons with Disabilities (CRPD) came into force providing protection to disabled or persons with different ability, which also includes mental disability. The Convention sets out a wide range of rights including, among others, civil and political rights, the right to live in the community, participation and inclusion, education, health, employment, and social protection. The Convention is a major milestone in efforts to promote, protect, and ensure the full and equal enjoyment of all human rights of persons with disabilities. The WHO, working under the Convention of the Rights of Persons with Disabilities, creates awareness and advocates for the rights of people with mental disabilities and collaborates with international organizations to disseminate norms of international human rights. India has enacted legislation namely Right of Persons with Disabilities Act, 2016. At the state level, mental health policies and laws are absent or inadequate in most countries of the world.

The WHO's work in supporting countries to develop human rights oriented mental health policies and plans and creates mechanisms to assess and improve human rights conditions. Many people with mental disabilities are assumed to have no capacity to make decisions for themselves and are, therefore, being detained and treated in psychiatric institutions and hospitals unjustifiably and against their will where they, sometimes, are being treated appallingly and inhumanely. The WHO Quality Rights Project works to unite and empower people to improve the quality of care and promote human rights in mental health facilities and social care homes.

§2. PROTECTION UNDER INTERNATIONAL INSTRUMENTS

407. International human rights instruments are important in the context of mental health because they are the only source of law that legitimizes international scrutiny of mental health policies and practices within a sovereign country. These instruments also provide fundamental protections that cannot be taken away by the ordinary political process. Mental health and human rights are inextricably linked and are complementary approaches to the betterment of human beings. Human rights are indispensable for mental health as they provide security from harm or restraint and the freedom to form and express beliefs that are essential to mental well-being. Therefore, international and regional systems have addressed the human rights of persons with mental illnesses through treaties, declarations, and resolutions. Countries which have ratified or adhered to international human rights conventions are obliged to respect, protect, and fulfill the rights enshrined in them. The international human rights law requires the state to safeguard the human rights of all people, including individuals with mental illnesses.

I. Relevant Instruments

408. The instruments dealing with international human rights include the UN Declaration of Human Rights (1948), the International Covenant on Civil and Political Rights (ICCPR) (1966), and the International Covenant on Economic, Social and Cultural Rights (ICESCR) (1966). The Universal Declaration of Human Rights, in itself, is not a legally binding instrument; it establishes a fundamental set of human rights that apply to all nations. Article 1 of the Declaration provides that "all people are free and equal in rights and dignity," which establishes that people with mental illnesses are protected by human rights law by virtue of their basic *humanity*. The Universal Declaration was followed by the two main UN human rights conventions established in 1966. These international covenants, although not specifically designed for the protection of persons with mental illnesses, provide legally enforceable protection of human rights.

409. The important international instruments dealing with disability and mental health are Equalization of Opportunities for Persons with Disabilities (1993; the Declaration of Madrid (1996) and other standards, such as WHO's Mental Health Care Law: ten basic principles and WHO Guidelines for the Promotion of Human Rights of Persons with Mental Disorders (1996). These *standards* serve as interpretative guides to countries so as to meet international treaty obligations. International human rights instruments create a number of broad protections that provide important rights to people with mental illnesses, such as: the right to the highest attainable standard of physical and mental health; protections against discrimination; protections against torture, inhuman, or degrading treatment; and protection against arbitrary detention.

II. Right to Health and Mental Health

410. The ICESCR, in its Article 12, provides steps for the realization of the right to health. To clarify and operationalize this provision, the UN Committee on Economic, Social and Cultural Rights adopted, among other provisions, General Comment 5 in 1996 and General Comment 14 in 2000. In General Comment 5, the Committee recognized the application of ICESCR with regard to people with mental and physical disabilities. The General Comment 14 affirmed that the right to health extends not only to timely and appropriate health care but also to the underlying determinants of health.

The right to health has undergone an evolution and resulted in the appointment by the UN of a Special Rapporteur on the right to health, whose mandate includes the right to mental health as well. However, in spite of these developments, the lack of language that pertains specifically to people with mental illnesses in the International Bill of Rights and other mainstream conventions has impaired the application of these instruments to people with mental illnesses.

III. Conventions and Declarations

A. *Vienna Declaration, 1993*

411. The Vienna Declaration emphasized the fact that people with mental and physical disabilities are to be protected by international human rights law and that governments must establish domestic legislation to realize these rights.[49] The ICCPR requires governments an obligation of result, as State Parties, must ensure the enforcement of human rights under the Covenant. Therefore, it creates immediate obligations on governments to begin planning to bring about the full enforcement of the rights recognized under the Covenant. The World Conference on Human Rights declared in Vienna in 1993 that, "all rights are universal, indivisible, interdependent and interrelated."[50]

B. *General Comments*

412. General Comments are important sources of interpretation of human rights conventions formulated by human rights oversight bodies to guide governments in the preparation of their official reports. These are non-binding but represent the official view as the proper interpretation of the convention by the human right oversight body. General Comment 14 confirms that the right to health is not a right to

49. UN, 1993—Vienna Declaration.
50. WHO, The Role of International Human Rights.

be healthy. It is a right to facilities, goods, services, and conditions that are conducive to the realization of the highest attainable standards of physical and mental health.[51]

C. The Human Right Commission

413. The UN Human Rights Commission, with the UN General Assembly and international human rights oversight bodies, has taken a stand on the need for all governments to enforce human rights conventions with respect to people with disabilities. In April 2000, the UN Human Rights Commission adopted Resolution 2000/51 urging governments to cover the issue of the human rights of persons with disabilities. As a result, the UN General Assembly, in 2006, adopted the CRPD, intended to protect the rights of persons with disabilities, including the ones with mental disabilities. The Convention gives substance to the complex nature of the right to health by adopting a social, rather than a medical, model of disability. The social model of disability addresses environmental constraints that limit people with disabilities to engage in community life, emphasizing the relationship between stigma, discrimination, structural inequalities, inadequate service provision, and deficits in health.

414. The CRPD provides a framework for ensuring that mental health laws fully recognize the rights of people with mental illness. There are also agreed international standards of good practice which are not legally binding but still applied. These include: the UN Declaration on the Rights of Mentally Retarded Persons (197); the Principles for the Protection of Persons with Mental Illness and for the Improvement of Mental Health Care (1991); the Standard Rules for WHO—The Role of International Human Rights.

The preamble of the CRPD recognizes that "disability is an evolving concept and that disability results from the interaction between persons with impairments and attitudinal and environmental barriers that hinders their full and effective participation in society on an equal basis with others." In addition, Article 1 states that "persons with disabilities include those who have long-term physical, mental, intellectual or sensory impairments."[52]

D. Mental Disability

415. "Mental disabilities" includes people with disabilities caused by a mental illness (such as people with a diagnosis of mental illness or with intellectual or

51. Paul Hunt & Judith. Mesquita, *Mental Disabilities and the Human Right to the Highest Attainable Standard of Health*, 28(2) Human Rights Quarterly 332–356 (2006). http://www.jstor.org/stable/20072740.
52. P. Weller, *Human Rights and Social Justice: The Convention on the Rights of Persons with Disabilities and the Quiet Revolution in International Law*, J. L. & Soc. Just. (Public Space v. 4). Available at https://doi.org/10.5130/psjlsj.v4i0.1167.

developmental disabilities). The Declaration affirms that persons with intellectual disability have the same rights as other human beings. These rights cannot be restricted without due process that must contain proper legal safeguards against abuse. It protects against the common practice, in some countries, of stripping away a person's rights through a finding of mental incompetence or by placing people with an intellectual disability under guardianship for a lifetime without process.

416. The United Nations Principles for the Protection of Persons with Mental Illness and the Improvement of Mental Health Care are the broadest human rights rules concerning mental health treatment and assistance. Such principles are particularly useful as guidelines for the interpretation of the rights established in human rights treaties. They established minimum standards of practice in the mental health field and have served as models for mental health legislation in many countries. The provisions establish standards for treatment and living conditions in psychiatric institutions and also create protections against arbitrary detention in such facilities.

417. The international and regional human rights documents emphasize that persons with mental illnesses should not need to prove they deserve certain rights or that they can be trusted to exercise them in socially and culturally acceptable ways. However, several of these instruments do not establish monitoring and accountability mechanisms, making it hard to achieve the realization of these rights. Also, as much as the right to health means more than access to treatment, the great majority of nonbinding instruments, approved mainly by the UN and WHO, focus on guidelines and minimal standards which can be used in providing treatment to people with mental illness. Besides, mental health legislation is more than care and treatment legislation that is narrowly limited to the provision of treatment in institution-based health services. Rather, it must set minimal standards for therapeutic environment and prevention of neglect and abuse of patients, establishing the role of governments, as well as health professionals, in the process of assuring the human rights of people with mental illnesses.

E. Freedoms and Entitlements

418. The Declaration of Madrid was approved by the General Assembly of the World Psychiatric Association in 1996, emphasizing ethical standards for psychiatric practice. The "Ten Basic Principles" and the "Guidelines" represent a further interpretation of the 1991 Principles and are used as a tool to evaluate human rights conditions in institutions and to draft mental health legislation (WHO, 1996). The right to health and the right to mental health contain both freedoms and entitlements. The freedoms include the right to control one's health and body and the right to be free from interference, such as the right to be free from torture, nonconsensual treatment, and experimentation. The entitlements consist of the right to a system of health protection, which provides equality of opportunity for people to enjoy the highest attainable level of health. It includes the right of access to rehabilitation services and individualized treatment, the right to informed consent and to refuse treatment, protection of human dignity, nondiscrimination, rule of proportionality, and due process protections.

§3. International Instruments and Domestic Governments

419. The human rights instruments have left domestic governments with a wide range of discretion in relation to the rights and freedoms of people with mental illness. However, International mental health legislation provides a general legal framework for addressing critical issues such as the community integration of persons with mental disorders, the provision of high-quality care, the improvement of access to care, the protection of civil rights. Human rights are a matter of international law enforceable against the state on behalf of persons living within or under the control of the state. This renders each country's mental health laws, policies, and practices subject to international human rights standards and amenable to international monitoring and control. Without a basic government obligation to satisfy basic health needs, including mental health, other rights are meaningless, and people with mental illnesses become more vulnerable to economic and social marginalization.

I. African Charter

420. The African Charter on Human and People's Rights was adopted on June 27, 1981 and entered into force on October 21, 1986. In addition to the general protections under the convention, the African Charter is the only one of the three regional conventions that explicitly creates special protections for people with disabilities. The European and inter-American regional systems have the most developed mechanisms for implementation.

II. American Declaration

421. In the American continent, a combination of instruments affords protection of human rights to all persons, including those with mental illness. These instruments include the American Declaration of the Rights and Duties of Man (1948), the American Convention on Human Rights (1969), the Additional Protocol to the American Convention on Human Rights in the area of Economic, Social and Cultural Rights (1988), and the Inter-American Convention on the Elimination of All Forms of Discrimination Against Persons with Disabilities (1999). The American Declaration of the Rights and Duties of Man is a nonbinding instrument that covers the protection of civil, political, economic, social, and cultural rights. The American Convention on Human Rights explicitly states that every person has the right to physical, mental, and moral integrity, that no one shall be subject to cruel, inhuman, or degrading punishment and treatment, and that all persons deprived of their liberty shall be treated with the inherent dignity of the human person.

422. The Additional Protocol to the American Convention on Human Rights provides further protection for people with mental illnesses, stating that, in order to achieve the full exercise of the right to education, programs of special education should be established so as to provide special instruction and training for persons with physical disabilities or mental deficiencies. It also establishes that all persons affected by a diminution of their physical or mental capacities are entitled to receive special attention to help them to achieve the greatest possible development of their personality and that everyone has the right to social security to protect them from the consequences of old age and disability which prevent them, physically or mentally, from securing the means for a dignified and decent existence. In addition, the Inter-American Convention on the Elimination of All Forms of Discrimination against Persons with Disabilities was adopted in 1999 and entered into force in 2001, calling on governments to facilitate the full integration of persons with disabilities into society through legislation, social initiatives, and educational programs.

III. Caracas Declaration

423. A nonbinding regional instrument, the Declaration of Caracas, was adopted in 1990 by the Regional Conference on Restructuring Psychiatric Care in Latin America and is an example of regional collaboration for the protection of the rights of persons with mental illnesses. This Declaration aimed to promote community-based integrated mental health services by restructuring psychiatric care involving services provided in mental hospitals. It further states that mental health legislation should safeguard the human rights of persons with mental illnesses and that services should be organized so that these rights can be enforced.

IV. Inter-American Convention

424. The Inter-American Convention on the Elimination of All Forms of Discrimination Against Persons with Disabilities is an international instrument that specifically addresses the issue of people with disabilities and represents a commitment by the Latin American States to ensure that they will enjoy the same rights the rest of the community is endowed with their families and adopted the Montreal Declaration on Intellectual Disability (Montreal Declaration) at an international conference organized by the Pan American Health Organization and the WHO. This Declaration recognizes the human rights of persons with intellectual disabilities, including the right to health. The Montreal Declaration represents an important step in standard-setting rights and obligations surrounding intellectual disabilities.

§4. Lack of Precise Definition

425. The instruments dealing with disability and mental health show the absence of agreement on the most appropriate terminology. Mental retardation, mental illness, mental disorder, mental incapacity, mental disability, and several other terms are all used in different connotations and shades of meanings. These differences have a crucial bearing on how the right to health must be interpreted and implemented to people with mental illnesses. The CRPD does not precisely define disability, in order to make it more comprehensible to different people, considering this an evolving concept. But, on the other hand, the lack of a specific language regarding people with mental illnesses in human rights international instruments makes it difficult to apply the rules to such people. Further, such persons are classified as mental patients, which depict a social category rather than a medical condition. So, once persons are labeled, the label tends to remain with them, even after their successful treatment. Historically, after a certain point, the damage done by the label of "patient with a mental illness" becomes pervasive and permanent, no matter how slight or temporary the actual problem was. Then, it is very difficult to prove and convince the society that someone became "normal" again.

§5. Lack of Monitoring and Accountability Mechanism

426. The instruments dealing with mental disability do not establish monitoring and accountability mechanisms, making it hard to achieve the realization of these rights. Also, as much as the right to health means more than access to treatment, the great majority of nonbinding instruments, approved mainly by the UN and WHO, focused on guidelines and minimal standards which should be used in providing treatment to people with mental illness.

Chapter 2. Psychology, Psychiatry, and Medical Law

427. Psychology is the application of psychological principles to the practice of medicine, primarily drug-oriented, for both physical and mental disorders. The American Society for the Advancement of Pharmacotherapy defines medical psychology as "that branch of psychology integrating somatic and psychotherapeutic modalities into the management of mental illness and emotional, cognitive, behavioral and substance use disorders."

428. Medical psychologists apply psychological theories, scientific psychological findings, and techniques of psychotherapy, behavior modification, cognitive, interpersonal, family, and lifestyle therapy to improve the psychological and physical health of the patient. Psychologists with postdoctoral specialty training as medical psychologists are practitioners with refined skills in clinical psychology, health psychology, behavioral medicine, and medical science. Highly qualified and postgraduate specialized doctors are trained for service in primary care centers, hospitals, residential care centers, and long-term care facilities and in multidisciplinary collaboration and team treatment.

429. A medical psychologist who holds prescriptive authority for specific psychiatric medications and other pharmaceutical drugs must first obtain specific qualifications in psychopharmacology. A trained medical psychologist who has prescriptive authority is equated with a mid-level provider who has the authority to prescribe psychotropic medication, such as antidepressants for neurotic disorders. However, a medical psychologist does not automatically equate with a psychologist who has the authority to prescribe medication. In fact, most medical psychologists do not prescribe medication and do not have the authority to do so.

§1. Medical Psychology

430. Medical psychology is defined as specialty training at the postdoctoral level and designed to deliver advanced diagnostic and clinical interventions in medical and health care facilities utilizing the knowledge and skills of clinical psychology, health psychology, behavioral medicine, psychopharmacology, and basic medical science. A distinction is made between the "psychopharmacologist," who is a psychologist with advanced training in psychopharmacology and may prescribe medicine or consult with physician or nurse practitioner prescribers to diagnose mental illness and select and recommend appropriate psychoactive medicines, and the "medical psychologists," who are prepared to do the psychopharmacology consulting or prescribing but also must have training which prepares them for functioning with behavioral and lifestyle components of physical disease and functioning in or in consultation with multidisciplinary health care teams.

431. The field of medical psychology may include pre-doctoral training of the disciplines of health psychology, rehabilitation psychology, pediatric psychology, neuropsychology, and clinical psychopharmacology, as well as subspecialties in pain management, primary care psychology, and hospital-based psychology as the foundation psychological training to qualify for proceeding to required postdoctoral specialty training to qualify to become a specialist in medical psychology. The term "medical psychologists" is not an umbrella term, and many other specialties in psychology, such as health care psychology, embracing the biopsychosocial paradigm (Engel, 1977) of mental/physical health and extending that paradigm to clinical practice through research and the application of evidence-based diagnostic and treatment procedures, are akin to the specialty and are prepared to practice in Integrated and Primary Care Settings.

432. Adopting the biopsychosocial paradigm, the field of medical psychology has recognized that the Cartesian assumption that the body and mind are separate entities is inadequate, representing as it does an arbitrary dichotomy that works to the detriment of health care. The biopsychosocial approach reflects the concept that the psychology of an individual cannot be understood without reference to that individual's social environment. For the medical psychologist, the medical model of disease cannot, in itself, explain complex health concerns any more than a strict psychosocial (LeVine & Orabona Foster, 2010) explanation of mental and physical health can in itself be comprehensive.

§2. Duties of Psychologists

433. Medical psychologists are trained and equipped to modify physical disease states and functioning of the central nervous and related systems using psychological and pharmacological techniques and to provide prevention for the progression of disease having to do with poor personal and lifestyle choices and conceptualization, behavioral patterns, and chronic exposure to the effects of negative thinking, attitudes, and negative contexts. The specialty of medical psychology includes training in psychopharmacology and, in states providing statutory authority, may prescribe psychoactive substances as one technique in a larger treatment plan which includes psychological interventions.

The medical psychologists who serve in states that have not yet modernized their psychology-prescribing laws may evaluate patients and recommend appropriate psychopharmacological techniques in collaboration with a state-authorized prescriber. Medical psychologists strive to integrate the major components of an individual's psychological, biological, and social functioning and are designed to contribute to that person's well-being in a way that respects the natural interface among these components. The whole is greater than the sum of its parts when it comes to providing comprehensive and sensible behavioral health care, and the medical psychologist is uniquely qualified to collaborate with physicians that are treating the patients' physical illnesses.

§3. Psychosurgical Interventions

434. Psychosurgery, also called Neurosurgery for Mental Disorder (NMD), is the neurosurgical treatment of a mental disorder. Psychosurgery has always been a controversial medical field. The modern history of psychosurgery began in the 1880s under the Swiss psychiatrist Gottlieb Burckhardt. The first significant foray into psychosurgery in the twentieth century was conducted by the Portuguese neurologist Egas Moniz who, during the mid-1930s, developed the operation known as leucotomy. The practice was enthusiastically taken up in the US by the neuropsychiatrist Walter Freeman and the neurosurgeon James W. Watts who devised what became the standard prefrontal procedure and named their operative technique lobotomy, although the operation was called leucotomy in the UK. In spite of the award of the Nobel Prize to Moniz in 1949, the use of psychosurgery declined during the 1950s. By the 1970s the standard Freeman-Watts type of operation was very rare, but other forms of psychosurgery, although used on a much smaller scale, survived. Some countries have abandoned psychosurgery altogether; in others, for example, the US and the UK, it is only used in a few centers on small numbers of people with depression or obsessive-compulsive disorder (OCD); in others, it is also used in the treatment of schizophrenia and other disorders.

435. Psychosurgery is the collaboration between psychiatrists and neurosurgeons. During the operation, which is carried out under a general anesthetic and using stereotactic methods, a small piece of the brain is destroyed or removed. Lesions are made by radiation, thermocoagulation, freezing, or cutting. About a third of patients show significant improvement in their symptoms after operation. Advances in surgical technique have greatly reduced the incidence of death and serious damage from psychosurgery; the remaining risks include seizures, incontinence, decreased drive and initiative, weight gain, etc. Currently, interest in the neurosurgical treatment of mental illness is shifting from ablative psychosurgery (where the aim is to destroy brain tissue) to deep brain stimulation (DBS) where the aim is to stimulate areas of the brain with implanted electrodes.

§4. Role of Psychiatric Drugs

436. In the 1950s new psychiatric drugs, notably the antipsychotic chlorpromazine, were developed in laboratories and slowly came into use. Although often accepted as an advance in some ways, there was some opposition due to serious adverse effects. Patients often opposed psychiatry and refused or stopped taking the drugs when not subject to psychiatric control. There was also increasing opposition to the use of psychiatric hospitals and attempts to move people back into the community on a collaborative user-led group approach ("therapeutic communities") not controlled by psychiatry. Lobotomy was used until the 1970s to treat schizophrenia.

I. Psychiatric Conceptualization

437. From the early nineteenth century, as lunacy reform movements gained in influence, ever more governments in the West extended their authority and responsibility for the mentally ill. Small-scale asylums, conceived as instruments to reshape both the mind and behavior of the disturbed, emerged across these regions. By the 1830s, moral treatment, together with the asylum itself, became increasingly musicalized and asylum doctors began to establish a distinct medical identity with the establishment in the 1840s of associations for their members in France, Germany, the UK, and the US. Processes of long-term institutional segregation, allowing for the psychiatric conceptualization of the natural course of mental illness, supported the perspective that the insane were a distinct population, subject to mental pathologies stemming from specific medical causes. From the mid-nineteenth century, heredity started to be seen as the central causal element in chronic mental illness, and, with national asylum systems overcrowded and insanity apparently undergoing a rise, the focus shifted from a concern with treating the individual to maintaining the racial and biological health of national populations.

II. Shell Shock

438. Emil Kraepelin (1856–1926) introduced new medical categories of mental illness. Shell shock, among frontline soldiers exposed to heavy artillery bombardment, was first diagnosed by British Army doctors in 1915. By 1916, similar symptoms were also noted in soldiers not exposed to explosive shocks, leading to questions as to whether the disorder was physical or psychiatric. In the 1930s several controversial medical practices were introduced including inducing seizures (by electroshock, insulin, or other drugs) or cutting parts of the brain apart (leucotomy or lobotomy).

Chapter 3. Transgender

439. The term "transgender or transgender people" is generally used to describe those who transgress social gender norms. Transgender is often used as an umbrella term to signify individuals who defy rigid, binary gender constructions, and who express or present a breaking and/or blurring of culturally prevalent stereotypical gender roles. Transgender people may live full- or part-time in the gender role "opposite" to their biological sex. At present "transgender" has become an umbrella term that is used to describe a wide range of identities and experiences, including but not limited to: preoperative, postoperative and nonoperative transsexual people (who strongly identify with the gender opposite to their biological sex); male and female "cross-dressers."

§1. Historical Background

440. There is a long and old history of the existence of gender-variant males—who in present times would have been labeled as "transgender women." Ancient Indian text *Kama Sutra* provides detailed description of the sexual lives of people with "third nature" (*Tritiya Prakriti*). In India, people with a wide range of transgender-related identities, cultures, or experiences exist which in the local language called *Hijras, Aravanis, Kothis, Jogtas/Jogappas, Shiv-Shakthis*, etc. Often these people have been part of the broader culture and treated with great respect, at least in the past, although some are still accorded particular respect.

§2. Trans Men and Trans Women

441. Transsexual people may refer to themselves as trans men or trans women but often desire to establish a permanent gender role as a member of the gender with which they identify. Some transsexual people pursue medical interventions as part of the process of expressing their gender. These medically based physical alterations are collectively referred to as sex reassignment therapy and may include female-to-male or male-to-female hormone replacement therapy or through surgery. Surgeries may include genital surgery, such as orchiectomy or sex reassignment surgery; chest surgery, such as top surgery or breast augmentation; or, in the case of trans women, facial surgery. The entire process of switching from one physical sex and social gender presentation to another is referred to as transition and usually takes several years. But not all transsexual people undergo a physical transition. Some find reasons not to, for example, the expense of surgery, the risk of medical complications, medical conditions which make the use of hormones or surgery dangerous.

442. Some transsexual people live heterosexual lifestyles and gender roles while some as gay, lesbian, or bisexual. Many trans people find that a shift occurs in their sexual orientation as they undergo transition. Many transsexual people choose the language of how they refer to their sexual orientation based on their gender identity, not their morphological sex, though some transsexual people still find identification with their community.

§3. Transgender and HIV

443. HIV programs included transgender women under the epidemiological and behavioral term—"men who have sex with men" (MSM), although many transgender people did not want to be included under that term. In addition to respecting the preferred term to be used by the transgender women, it is recognized that transgender people have unique needs and concerns and that it is better to view them as a separate group. Even the umbrella term "transgender" may hide the complexity and diversity of the various subgroups of gender-variant people and may hinder the development of subgroup-specific HIV prevention and care interventions and policies.

§4. U.N. Resolution and Other State Laws

444. The United Nations has passed resolutions recognizing that transgender persons should be guaranteed the right to recognition with the full range of rights and freedoms by the State. They are likely to suffer aggravated forms of violence and are targets of extra-judicial killings because of their gender identity and require special protections against torture. However, these resolutions and principles remain declarations and statements of a commitment to addressing LGBTQI+ rights in general but holding little statutory or authoritative value. The international human rights conventions do create obligations for States but make no explicit mention of LGBTQI+ persons. These persons have been subsequently interpreted by the UNHRC through General Comments. While this increases the scope of protections offered by the Conventions, the evolution of jurisprudence is extremely slow and creates only limited, specific obligations.

445. Article 26 of the ICCPR prohibits discrimination and gives equal protection to all persons before the law, has been interpreted to include transgender persons under the category of "sex." As per interpretations of Article 9 of the ICCPR, the right to liberty is available to "everyone" which includes all persons of LGBTQ identity as well. Article 12 of the ICESCR recognizes the right to health of transgender persons as a vulnerable group that requires positive State protections. Similarly, the Committee on the Anti-Torture Convention requires special measures to protect transgender persons from torture under Article 2, as well as provide effective redressal mechanisms for transgender victims of torture under Article 14 of the Convention. Most of these interpretations were made in response to petitions under the (optional) Individual Complaint Mechanism of the respective human rights treaties or a voluntary reference to trans issues. But these obligations are not broad enough to cover the systematic discrimination faced by transgender persons in access to justice, health care, employment, housing, travel, and education or offer comprehensive protection from gender-based violence, police abuse or physical and psychological torture.

446. In 2017, the Office of the United Nations High Commissioner for Human Rights (OHCHR) released a statement insisting that LGBTQI+ persons are protected under the UN Charter, Universal Declaration on Human Rights and did not require the creation of new specific obligations. Nevertheless, putting the fate of LGBTQI+ rights at the mercy of a notoriously inaccessible and slow treaty interpretation system denies sexual and gender minorities recognition of their rights and dignity. It consequently robs them of their voice in the international law-making process.

447. In the absence of concrete universal standards, States are free to formulate laws that grant limited or arbitrary rights to transgender persons. India's recent 2019 Transgender Persons Act denies transgender persons the right to declare their self-perceived gender identity without undergoing sex reassignment surgery, and reservations in jobs and educational institutions. The act has also been criticized for imposing less punishment for crimes against transgender people. In Nepal, trans persons may only register under the "Others" category regardless of what gender the person identifies with.

Part XI. Manufacture and Marketing of Medicines

Chapter 1. Regulation of Manufacturing of Medicines

448. The manufacturing of medicine is a very important aspect of medical care and law and requires persons of integrity in this business. But, nowadays, spurious and adulterated drugs proliferate, and licensing, accreditation, and regulatory systems are subverted. In India sometimes pharmacists sell their licenses to unqualified persons to run chemist shops. Even in the big cities, quacks practice without registration.[53] Sex determination tests are performed though they are illegal. Doctors are known to prescribe unnecessary diagnostic tests, hazardous drugs, and inappropriate surgical procedures, all for the kickbacks they receive from the health care industry. The avenues for corruption are endless. Medical establishments work closely with drug manufacturers whose main objective is to maximize their profits. Doctors are the principal salespeople of drug companies and they are rewarded with research grants, lavish perquisites, participation in seminars, and foreign tours. The principal sufferers are the general public.

§1. Intellectual Property Standards in Different Countries

449. The global framework for pharmaceutical regulation has undergone a profound transformation. Implementation of the new global system for regulation of intellectual property standards since the mid-1990s has forced developing countries to establish new institutions to review, approve, and manage the emerging intellectual property rights system. As a result, the pharmaceutical sector and its governance have given rise to conflict over the ownership rights, access, and marketing of pharmaceutical products. The developing countries have been pushed to implement intellectual property standards. The pharmaceutical standards and regulatory systems across the world in many countries are fragile, uneven, and highly dependent on aid and technical support from international donors from rich countries. The weakness of the regulatory apparatus in many pharmaceutical markets was illustrated in a study that looked at least developed countries. Olsson et al. (2010) found

53. A. Tiwari & Farzi Doctor Ne Lee Maasoom Ki Jaan. Chandigarh Bhaskar Newspaper (Chandigarh Ed.). 16:3 (March 2009) (col.1).

that less than half of the least developed countries publically funded their pharmaceutical regulatory agencies. Moreover, many state institutions with the mandate to approve, review, and regulate pharmaceutical products in the survey were found to be highly dependent on financing from international organizations. In one-third of the countries studied by Olsson et al., these activities were entirely financed by one international source: the Global Fund to fight AIDS, Tuberculosis and Malaria. Such studies suggest that quality regulation is tied to a more pervasive lack of local, democratic control of health systems in developing countries.

450. The industrialized nations which are key market players drive international norms related to pharmaceuticals. These countries formulate, establish, and then extend dominant regulatory standards. Firms operating across borders face lower transaction costs when, for example, the EU's European Medicine's Agency and the US's FDA share the same standards for bioequivalency and accept data from the same certified laboratories. Consumers, be they individuals or public procurement entities, may benefit from the lower costs charged by these firms. A generic company based in the UK, in theory, benefits when Brazil has standards equal to those in markets where the firm already has operations because the barrier to market entrance is lowered.

§2. Quality Control Regulations

451. The pharmaceuticals have particularities that distinguish them fundamentally from other economies or products. The political economy of medicine is markedly different, as economist Daniel Carpenter has written, because neither the consumer nor the regulatory agency can be entirely sure of the product's quality. Thus, gatekeeping through governmental premarket review for new products becomes the basic tool. But such review is based in part upon an experimental (non-market) history of the product. Moreover, regulators must guarantee the quality of approved drugs that reach consumers. This makes quality control an essential aspect of pharmaceutical regulation. Gatekeeping of pharmaceutical markets has important political and public health implications. Brazil, for example, has been widely praised for its successful program of ensuring universal access to antiretroviral medicine since the mid-1990s. The public production and distribution in this country have relied not only on patent holding multinationals but also with Indian and Chinese suppliers of active pharmaceutical ingredients in order to manufacture generic production.

452. The global rules governing intellectual property have posed challenges for developing states which are reinforced by the geographic distribution of pharmaceutical production and local institutional and political capacity. Fewer suppliers have increased competitive pressure for the region's public procurement programs and for local producers. At the same time, so-called second tier suppliers have flooded the international pharmaceutical market with products which may not meet quality standards. States face a double-edged regulatory challenge, harmonizing their intellectual property rights norms to global standards and working to upgrade and implement quality standards for local populations.

§3. REGULATORY STRUCTURE

453. Basic regulatory authorities and policies are essential to the implementation and enforcement of pharmaceutical policy. The State Regulatory Infrastructure must take into account the existence of a national medicines policy and a medicines regulatory authority as well as the existence of established good practices in manufacturing, distribution, and retail. In developing countries, ensuring access to quality medicines is complicated by complex and interdependent problems, which are best addressed using a common framework.

A national medicines policy is a first step in identifying and resolving problems within the pharmaceutical sector. Medicine Regulatory Authorities (MRAs), whatever their official names, are a first step toward ensuring a strong regulation of the market and the protection of public health. But without a central authority monitoring, testing, and tracking medicines, as well as licensing and inspecting pharmacists and points of distribution, even the best statutes can become ineffective. The publication of good practices by the government not only provides manufacturers, distributors, and retailers a clear guide for action; it also provides regulators clear guidelines for monitoring the market and for implementing policies that will help develop a well-functioning market for medicines.

I. Control on Manufacturing

454. Access to quality medicines can only be ensured by the presence of a strong regulatory system internationally as well as domestically. Control over the processes and people involved in the production, distribution, and sales of medicines requires a legal framework for licensing, monitoring quality, and pharmacovigilance. Every modern regulatory system requires a legislative framework to permit the implementation and enforcement of policies as well as ensure that relevant actors meet the requirements of quality before participating in the market. Without licensing requirements the quality of medicines cannot be ensured. Licensing, in itself, does not provide proof of quality, but it is an indispensable element. The monitoring and quality control of all segments of the private market plays an important role in safeguarding the quality of medicines. The quality control check requires that the product must contain the right ingredients in the right amounts. It also verifies that products are transported and stored correctly in hot and humid climates. Pharmacovigilance ensures the safety of drugs consumed within the market. Given that adverse drug reactions (ADRs) are common and may cause death, every country should have a system in place to monitor medications for potential side effects. The detection, assessment, understanding, and prevention of ADRs play a critical role in protecting public health.

II. Monitoring the Public Health System

455. In poor countries, the citizens' access to medicines depends on the public health system so it is critical to assess the degree and standards of quality control with the public health system. Following the recommendations of the WHO, the licensing of pharmacists, public pharmacies, and dispensing points is an important part of the regulation. Public pharmacies require routine inspection and sampling of medicines should take place regularly. The quality of medicines distributed depends directly on how it is procured and stored. Testing public products prior to acceptance and prequalifying suppliers play a critical role in ensuring the quality of medicines by reducing corruption within the public health system. A competitive and transparent procurement process can also help safeguard the quality of medicines.

III. Good Practice Guidelines

456. The publication of good practice guidelines usually emerges from the implementation of a national medicines policy and a causal relationship would seem to exist between the two. However, not all countries with a national medicines policy have taken the time or have the ability to develop good practice guidelines. The discrimination scores on the variables associated with the publication of good practice guidelines can be interpreted as the benefit accrued by developing and publishing core criteria for the pharmaceutical market, after establishing a national medicines policy. At the same time, it is little use to have good policies on the books if regulators cannot easily track licenses, registration, medicines, etc. through a modern information management system.

Chapter 2. Marketing of Medicines and Law

457. Pharmaceutical marketing, also called medico-marketing or pharma-marketing is the business of advertising or otherwise promoting the sale of pharmaceutical drugs. The fact is that pharmaceutical company spending on marketing may exceed its research budget. The marketing practices can negatively impact both patients and the health care profession. Marketing to health care providers takes three main forms: activity by pharmaceutical sales representatives, provision of drug samples, and sponsoring continuing medical education (CME). The use of gifts, including pens and coffee mugs embossed with pharmaceutical product names, has been prohibited by PhRMA ethics guidelines since 2008. Doctors doing private practice are easy to approach but those who work in hospitals or health systems are difficult to approach as appointments in case of hospitals have to go through headquarters.

§1. Marketing Strategies and Incentives

458. Various marketing strategies are adopted by the pharma companies for marketing of their products, some of the important practices are described below.

I. Free Samples and CME

459. Free samples have been shown to affect physician prescribing behavior. Physicians with access to free samples are more likely to prescribe brand name medication over equivalent generic medications. Receiving pharmaceutical samples does not reduce prescription costs. Even after receiving samples, sample recipients remain disproportionately burdened by prescription costs. Free samples give immediate access to the medication and the patient can begin treatment right away. Since not all medications work for everyone, and many do not work the same way for each person, free samples allow patients to find which dose and brand of medication works best before spending money on a prescription. Pharmaceutical companies also offer various continuing education and seminars preferably at tourist destinations to attract doctors and sometimes hours spent by physicians in industry-supported CME is more than that from either medical schools or professional societies.

II. Medical Representatives

460. A medical representative often visits doctors and try to meet a given physician every few weeks. Because of the large size of the pharmaceutical sales force, the organization, management, and measurement of the effectiveness of the sales force are significant business challenges. Some pharmaceutical companies have realized that training sales representatives on high science alone is not enough, especially when most products are similar in quality so they are aggressively trained in the marketing of the product. Thus, training sales representatives on relationship selling techniques in addition to medical science and product knowledge can make a difference in sales force effectiveness. Besides, specialist physicians also rely on specialty sales representatives for product information, because they are more knowledgeable than primary care representatives.

461. Marketers decide on the appropriate size of a sales force needed to sell a particular portfolio of drugs to the target market. Factors influencing this decision are the optimal reach and frequency for each individual physician, how many patients suffer from that disease, how many sales representatives to devote to the office and group practice and how many to devote to hospital accounts if needed. The customers are broken down into different classes according to their prescription behavior, patient population, and their business potential. Marketers attempt to identify the set of physicians most likely to prescribe a given drug. This is done by measuring the number of total prescriptions (TRx) and new prescriptions (NRx) per week written by each physician. This information is collected by commercial vendors.

III. Role of Physician

462. Physicians are the most important component and at the center stage in the sale of medicine. They write the prescriptions that determine which drugs will be used by the patient. Influencing the physician is the key to pharmaceutical sales which is accomplished by a large pharmaceutical sales force. Sales representatives call upon physicians regularly, providing clinical information, approved journal articles, and free drug samples. This is still the approach but economic pressures on the industry have forced pharmaceutical companies to rethink the traditional sales process to physicians. The industry has seen a large-scale adoption of Pharma CRM systems that works on laptops and more recently tablets. The new age pharmaceutical representative is armed with key data at his fingertips and tools to maximize the time spent with physicians.

IV. Targeting Key Opinion Leaders

463. The sales representatives generally target key opinion leaders, who are respected individuals, such as prominent medical school faculty and those who can influence physicians through their professional status. Pharmaceutical companies generally engage key opinion leaders early in the drug development process to provide advocacy and key marketing feedback. Some pharmaceutical companies identify key opinion leaders through direct inquiry of physicians. The pharmaceutical companies also use social network analysis to uncover thought leaders and map out the scientific community.

Alternatives to segmenting physicians purely on the basis of prescribing do exist, and marketers can call upon strategic partners who specialize in delineating which characteristics of true opinion leadership, a physician does or does not possess. Physicians acquire information through informal contacts with their colleagues, including social events, professional affiliations, common hospital affiliations, and common medical school affiliations. Some pharmaceutical companies identify influential colleagues through commercially available prescription writing and patient level data. Doctor dinner meetings are an effective way for physicians to acquire educational information from respected peers. These meetings are sponsored by major pharmaceutical companies.

V. Private and Public Insurers

464. Public and private insurers affect the writing of prescriptions by physicians through formularies that restrict the number and types of drugs that the insurer will cover. The insurer affects drug sales by including or excluding a particular drug from a formulary, they can also affect sales by placing bureaucratic hurdles to prescribing certain drugs.

VI. Direct Consumer Advertising

465. Some countries prohibit whereas others may allow direct-to-consumer advertising (DTCA). Since the late 1970s, DTCA of prescription drugs has become important in the US. It takes two main forms: the promotion or creation of a disease out of a non-pathologic physical condition or the promotion of a medication. The objective of DTCA is to directly influence the patient–physician dialog. Many patients will inquire about, or even demand a medication they have seen advertised on television. There has also been an increase in mass media advertisements for pharmaceuticals.

466. In many developed countries, mass marketing to users of pharmaceuticals is banned. Some feel it is better to leave the decision wholly in the hands of medical professionals while others think that users education and participation in health is useful, but users need independent, comparative information about drugs and not promotional information. That is why most countries impose limits on pharmaceutical mass marketing. In some areas it is required that advertisements for drugs include a list of possible side effects so that users are informed of both facets of a medicine. Canada's limitations on pharmaceutical advertising ensure that commercials that mention the name of a product cannot in any way describe what in fact it does. Commercials that mention a medical problem cannot also mention the name of the product for sale. However, they can direct the viewer to a website or telephone number operated by the pharmaceutical company.

VII. Drug Coupons

467. The pharmaceutical companies often provide drug coupons to consumers to help offset the co-payments charged by health insurers for prescription medication. These coupons are used to promote medications that compete with non-preferred products and cheaper, generic alternatives by reducing or eliminating the extra out-of-pocket costs that insurers typically charge a patient for a non-preferred drug product. The pharmaceutical companies make large investments in marketing their products. However, overall promotional spending has been decreasing over the years. Pharmaceutical companies are cutting costs mostly in detailing and sampling while spending on mailings and print advertising has grown.

§2. Regulation of Marketing

468. In the European Union (EU), marketing of pharmaceuticals is regulated by EU Directives.[54] It requires Member States to prohibit off-label marketing and direct-to-consumer marketing of prescription-only medications. In the US, marketing and distribution of pharmaceuticals are regulated by the Federal Food, Drug, and Cosmetic Act and the Prescription Drug Marketing Act respectively. FDA regulations require all prescription drug promotion to be truthful and not misleading, based on "substantial evidence or substantial clinical experience," to provide a "fair balance" between the risks and benefits of the promoted drug and to maintain consistency with labeling approved by the FDA. The FDA Office of Prescription Drug Promotion enforces these requirements.

469. The major international companies selling the drugs like Bristol-Myers Squibb, Eli Lilly, Pfizer, AstraZeneca, and Johnson & Johnson, have either settled government cases, under the False Claims Act, for hundreds of millions of dollars, or are under investigation for possible health care fraud. Following charges of illegal marketing, two of the settlements in 2009 set records for the largest criminal fines ever imposed on corporations. One such claim involved Eli Lilly's antipsychotic Zyprexa and the other involved Bextra. In the *Bextra* case, the government charged Pfizer with illegally marketing another antipsychotic, Geodon. Pfizer settled that part of the claim for USD 301 million, without admitting any wrongdoing. Legal claims against the pharmaceutical industry have varied widely, including Medicare and Medicaid fraud, off-label promotion, and inadequate manufacturing practices.

I. Harmonization of Domestic and International Regulations

470. The regulatory systems among developing countries are being harmonized with international standards through regulation of companies as they register and

54. 92/28/EEC.

introduce their products in national markets. Better regulation is indicated by licensing permission to companies, compliance and pharmacovigilance. For example, whether of inspections conducted on a regular basis, as well as importation only through authorized ports and inspection of imported pharmaceutical products, a port of entry have little discriminatory value. Restricting ports of entry and conducting inspections at the port are an important part of the regulatory arsenal in industrialized countries, indicating that developing countries may be evolving their own regulatory norms.

II. Regulation of Private Market

471. Given the importance of a good legal framework and institutional mandates for the regulation of the pharmaceutical market, a positive relationship may exist between regulatory infrastructure and the regulation of the private market. Unlike the regulation of the private market, now there seems to be a relationship between the rating for public quality control and the quality of a country's regulatory infrastructure. Numerous countries that rated very poorly on the regulation of the private market have a fairly high rating for the public quality control. Public quality control and regulation of the private market have no clear association. The disjuncture between these two indices may stem from various factors. First, countries with large private markets for medicines, especially essential medicines, may find a need to carefully regulate private distributors and retailers, while countries that provide most of their citizen's needs through public sources may feel little need to closely regulate the private market. This would generate a negative relationship between the indicators in some countries. However, many countries have public and private markets for medicines which require regulators to pay attention to both markets. However, guaranteeing the provision of high-quality medicines in the private market is much more difficult. Regulating the private market requires the ability and legal infrastructure necessary to inspect and sanction producers, distributors, and retailers as well as monitor a wide variety of medicines from multiple sources for adverse effects.

III. Prequalification System

472. The WHO has a prequalification system which is an evidence of the diffusion of global standards through norms-making institutions such as an international agency. They also suggest that encouraging and supporting countries in the adoption of prequalification programs have been beneficial to the quality of public systems in small and developing countries. Quality regulation does not have feedback across public and private markets and sometimes is cross-matched. There is no relationship between the adoption of global standards for public pharmaceutical markets and for private markets. The result may be that the states establishing rules for transparency of standards in their private pharmaceutical markets are no more likely to set standards for public purchasing systems and vice versa.

Part XII. Practical Application of Medical Law

Chapter 1. Medical Jurisprudence

473. Medical jurisprudence is the branch of science and medicine involving the study and application of scientific and medical knowledge to legal problems, such as inquests, and in the field of law. The medico-legal cases involving death, rape, paternity, etc. require a medical practitioner to produce evidence and appear as an expert witness, these two fields have traditionally been interdependent. Forensic medicine, which includes forensic pathology, is a narrower field that involves the collection and analysis of medical evidence in the form of samples to produce objective information for use in the legal system. Medical jurisprudence includes areas of the legal and ethical duties of physicians, competence or sanity in civil or criminal proceedings, issues of competence of minors in matters affecting their own health etc. Further, assessment of illness or injuries that may be work-related (relating to workers' compensation or occupational safety and health) or otherwise compensable; assessment of injuries of minors that may relate to neglect or abuse; certification of death or else the assessment of possible causes of death through postmortem also fall under it. Thus, medical jurisprudence covers a broad range of medical, legal, and ethical issues, as well as human rights and the rights of individuals. Physicians have a duty to act in their patient's best interest and can be charged in a court of law on their failure. On the other hand, a physician may be required to act in the interest of third parties if his patient is a danger to others.

§1. Medical Science

474. The main function of medical law is found in forensic medicine, medical jurisprudence, and toxicology. Application of medical science to legal problems is the subject matter of medical jurisprudence. It is typically involved in cases concerning blood relationship, mental illness, injury, or death resulting from violence. Autopsy is often used to determine the cause of death, particularly in cases where foul play is suspected. Postmortem examination can determine not only the immediate agent of death (e.g., gunshot wound, poison) but may also yield important contextual information, such as how long the person has been dead, which can help trace the killing.

475. Forensic medicine plays an important role in solving cases involving crimes. Modern techniques use such specimens as semen, blood, and hair samples of the criminal found in the victim's bodies, which are compared with the genetic makeup of the accused through DNA fingerprinting. This technique is also used to identify the body of a victim. The establishment of serious mental illness by a licensed psychologist can be used in demonstrating incompetence to stand trial, a technique, which may be used in the insanity defense.

I. Autopsy or Postmortem

476. Autopsy is the examination of a dead body for study or for determining the cause of death. Autopsy literally means, "see for yourself." It is a special surgical operation, performed by specially trained physicians, on a dead body. Its purpose is to know the truth about the person's health during life, and how the person died, determine the cause, timing, etc., of death. Autopsies use many methodical procedures to determine the etiology and pathogenesis of diseases, for epidemiologic purposes, for the establishment of genetic causes, and for family counsel. Postmortems may be performed at the request of the authorities in cases of unexplained and suspicious death or where a physician did not attend death. In other circumstances postmortem examination may be performed only with the consent of the deceased's family or with permission granted by the person himself before death.

477. The autopsies nowadays are more frequently being used for the acquiring of organs and tissues for the purpose of transplantation. Besides, useful medical information can be learned from a postmortem examination, which can be applied for the benefit of others. Autopsy is important for many reasons, like to expose mistakes, to delimit new diseases and new patterns of disease, and to guide future studies. Morbidity and mortality statistics acquire accuracy and significance when based on careful autopsies. The autopsy procedure involves a detailed outer and internal examination of the body and each of its part, and through various tests on tissue and viscera in labs. The first step is a general examination of the exterior for any abnormality or trauma and a careful description of the interior of the body and its organs. This is usually followed by further studies, including microscopic examination of cells and tissues.

II. DNA Fingerprinting

478. DNA fingerprinting or DNA profiling or other similar techniques for analyzing and comparing DNA from different sources are used to identify suspects from their hair, blood, semen, or other biological materials found at the scene of a crime or on the body of a victim of crime. It is because, except identical twins, DNA structure of all other individuals differs. The DNA samples of the culprit can be obtained from the scene of crime itself for example, blood samples from a scene of murder or samples of seminal fluids deposited on the clothes or furniture or floor or in the body of the victim in case of rape, are used to acquire a sample of the culprits DNA.

These samples can be compared with those taken from a suspect in the case. DNA evidence, apart from its use in criminal law to determine the killer or the rapist, is also employed for various other purposes like paternity testing, personal identification (of a mutilated body or skeletal remains), study of the evolution of the human population and study of inherited diseases like Alzheimer's disease.

479. A large number of complex criminal cases are solved and the success rates have increased after the discovery and use of DNA evidence technologies. The introduction of DNA evidence in the field of criminal law has particularly facilitated convictions in the matters involving the offense of rape, murder, determining parenthood, etc. Prior to the use of DNA evidence, matters involving the offense of rape could be solved primarily by circumstantial evidence only. It was very difficult for the victim of rape to prove the offense in the absence of either circumstantial evidence or an eyewitness, which was very rare. Since, the introduction of the DNA evidence, this has been greatly simplified. First samples of the seminal fluids found at the scene of the crime by the investigating officer are analyzed. If this is not available, then samples of the seminal fluid are extracted from the victim's body itself. The DNA from this sample is then compared with the DNA sample taken from the accused. If these samples match, then this acts as definite evidence in the court proving rape. Similarly, in case of offense of murder, DNA samples that are collected from the blood, mucous, saliva, skin, hair samples, etc., found on the crime scene are used to extract the DNA sample. These DNA samples are examined and compared with the DNA samples of the accused and this provides for a very effective technique to nail the real culprit.

480. Apart from its use to nail the culprit, Post-conviction DNA testing is also a very effective method to exonerate the innocent. The sophisticated scientific technology makes it possible to obtain conclusive results in cases in which the previous testing had been inconclusive. Post-conviction testing is required not only in cases in which the DNA testing was never done but also in cases in which more refined technology will result in an indisputable definite answer. The remarkable feature of DNA is that individuals leave traces of it in all the places they have visited.

§2. BENEFITS OF MEDICAL JURISPRUDENCE

481. The medical jurisprudence has benefited both the medical and the legal field. A better understanding and cooperation has resulted and has facilitated a smoother working of both disciplines. The cases previously unsolvable are now solved with ease with the development of medical jurisprudence. It covers in its ambit the provision of evidence for a wide range and scope of cases. It can be used to determine the paternity of a child and also be employed in determining the identity of human bodies that have been mutilated beyond recognition in accidents like bomb blasts, factory explosions, etc. In the field of evidence, it can be appropriated to solve cases involving murder, rape, etc. However, despite their vast benefits to the field of law, some medical jurisprudential techniques are not treated as primary evidence.

482. The technical findings, such as results of DNA tests, are considered as expert evidence by courts. When the court has to form an opinion upon a point of science, or art, or as to the identity of handwriting or finger impression, the opinions of experts is sought. But because of misuse, technical manipulation and sometimes lack of adequate knowledge as regards scientific evidence, courts are hesitant in applying these techniques in full measure. In order to determine whether scientific evidence is admissible, the court generally considers:

(i) whether the principle or technique has been or can be reliably tested;
(ii) whether it has been subjected to peer review or publication;
(iii) its known or potential rate of error;
(iv) whether there are standards or organizations controlling the procedures of the technique;
(v) whether it is generally accepted by the community; and
(vi) whether the technique was created or conducted independently of the litigation.

Part XIII. Medical Tourism and Treatment While Travelling

Chapter 1. Medical Tourism

483. Medical tourism and health tourism is becoming a fast-growing industry, with countries in Europe, Asia, and South America offering cheap and/or specialized medical care to people from other countries. Some look for care outside their native home because of cost, while other medical tourists are immigrants who return to their home country for care. Additionally, many of these countries offer not only medical care but other comforts as well, including interesting tourism opportunities and spa-like amenities. Medical tourism refers to people traveling to a country other than their own to obtain medical treatment. In the past this usually referred to those who traveled from less-developed countries to major medical centers in highly developed countries for treatment unavailable at home. However, in recent years it may equally refer to those from developed countries who travel to developing countries for lower-priced medical treatments. The motivation may be also for medical services unavailable or illegal in the home country.

484. Medical tourism generally refers to surgeries (cosmetic or otherwise) or similar treatments, though people also travel for dental tourism or fertility tourism. People with rare conditions may travel to countries where the treatment is better understood. However, almost all types of health care are available, including psychiatry, alternative medicine, convalescent care, and even burial services. Health tourism is a wider term for travel that focuses on medical treatments and the use of health care services. It covers a wide field of health-oriented, tourism ranging from preventive and health-conductive treatment to rehabilitation and curative forms of travel. Wellness tourism is a related field.

§1. Background History

485. The first recorded instance of people traveling for medical treatment dates back thousands of years when Greek pilgrims traveled from the eastern Mediterranean to a small area in the Saronic Gulf called Epidauria. This territory was the sanctuary of the healing god Asklepios. Spa towns and sanitaria were early forms of medical tourism. In eighteenth century Europe patients visited spas because these were places with supposedly health-giving mineral waters, treating diseases from gout to liver disorders and bronchitis. Factors that have led to the increasing popularity of medical travel include the high cost of health care, long wait times for certain procedures, the ease and affordability of international travel, and improvements in both technology and standards of care in many countries. The avoidance of waiting time is the leading factor for medical tourism from the UK, whereas, in the US, the main reason was cheaper prices abroad.

§2. Motive for Medical Travel

486. Many surgical procedures performed in medical tourism destinations cost a fraction of the price they do in other countries. A large draw to medical travel is because of convenience and speed. Countries that operate public health care systems often have long wait times for certain operations, for example, an estimated 782,936 Canadian patients spent an average waiting time of 9.4 weeks on medical waiting lists in 2005. Canada has also set waiting time benchmarks for nonurgent medical procedures, including a twenty-six-week waiting period for a hip replacement and a sixteen-week wait for cataract surgery. Some patients in First World countries are finding that insurance either does not cover orthopedic surgery (such as knee or hip replacement) or limits the choice of the facility, surgeon, or prosthetics to be used.

487. The term "Medical tourism" can also be used to describe medical outsourcing, which is characterized by travel away from one's home region to procure treatment in another. It may take one of two forms: obligatory or elective. The former occurs when necessary treatments are unavailable or illegal in the place of origin. The latter includes elective and medically indicated procedures that, although available at the place of origin, may be delivered more quickly or in a more cost-effective manner in another location. Reproductive outsourcing is a special form of medical tourism that has quickly become an important area of present-day medicine. Legal and policy limitations have created a global environment where, in a rising number of instances, individuals and couples must travel elsewhere to procure fertility procedures that are unavailable in the home country. With low-cost airfares, a growing number of "medical cartographers" have set out to map which places are the "best" in terms of cost, effectiveness and timeliness, for what procedures, and for whom. On the other hand, physicians, legal experts, and policymakers have only begun to shape how government and health care agencies should formally guide or regulate medical tourism. In doing so, a number of factors may challenge the limits of ethics, policy, and legality in this most important trend in modern medicine.

488. Expatriates who are not overseas with a large multinational company often lack the resources of a large company when it comes to supporting health care, so they seek other options. The most common procedures that people undergo on medical tourism trips include cosmetic surgery, dentistry (general, restorative, cosmetic), and heart surgery. Other health care services that register large include orthopedics (joint and spine; sports medicine); cancer; reproductive (fertility, IVF, women's health); weight loss; scans, tests, health screenings, and second opinions.

§3. Popular Medical Tourism Destinations

489. Popular medical travel worldwide destinations include: Canada, Costa Rica, Ecuador, India, Israel, Jordan, Malaysia, Mexico, Singapore, South Korea, Taiwan, Thailand, Turkey, and the US. Popular destinations for cosmetic surgery include: Argentina, Bolivia, Brazil, Colombia, Costa Rica, Cuba, Ecuador, Mexico, Turkey, Thailand, and Ukraine. However, perceptions of medical tourism are not always positive. In places like the US, which has high standards of quality, medical tourism is viewed as risky. In some parts of the world, wider political issues can influence where medical tourists will choose to seek out health care. Some medical/ health travel destinations are being described hereunder.

I. Malaysia

490. With more than half a million medical tourists coming to the country each year, Malaysia ranks as one of the most health care-friendly spots for those looking to find help outside of their home country. Americans are attracted to the country's large English-speaking population and strong infrastructure. Malaysia's medical tourism industry has been beefed up so as to diversify its economy during the Asian financial crisis. Malaysian hospitals are known for being big players IVF at a price that's 20% less than many other Western facilities. Physicals and blood work that might cost upwards of thousands of dollars in the US are also substantially cheaper. Malaysia's hospitals are also known for their sophisticated treatment for burn victims. In fact, Prince Court Medical Center in Kuala Lumpur was ranked as the number one hospital for "patients without borders" by the Medical Travel Quality Alliance.

II. India

491. Medical tourism is a growing sector in India. India is becoming the 2nd medical tourism destination. Chennai is regarded as "India's Health City" as it attracts 45% of health tourists visiting India and 40% of domestic health tourists. As medical treatment costs sharply increase in the developed world—with the US leading the way—more and more Westerners are finding the prospect of international travel for medical care increasingly appealing. Many of them travel to India for low-priced health care procedures every year. Cosmetic surgery, bariatric surgery, knee-cap replacements, liver transplants, and cancer treatments are some of the most sought out medical tourism procedures opted by foreigners.

492. A report from Deloitte forecasts that India's medical tourism market will grow to nearly USD 4 billion, doubling what it was just three years ago. According to Patients Beyond Borders, of the 250,000 international patients, the majority head to cities like Bangalore, Chennai, Hyderabad, Mumbai, and New Delhi. One of the reasons for such a strong growth is that a number of patients are coming from surrounding countries that offer far less-developed health care, such as Pakistan, Bangladesh, and Myanmar. Many people from other regions such as Africa, the Middle East, Canada, and the US are finding big cost savings in India. Popular treatments in India consist of those for fertility, orthopedic, cardiac and oncology problems, and organ transplants.

III. Turkey

493. The beautiful lands of Turkey are welcome spots for American-trained doctors, who have helped the country become one of the favorite destinations of patients from Europe and the US. The top procedures here include cardiac, cancer and orthopedic care. The country has also established itself as one of the leading places in the world for eye treatments—especially laser surgery, which costs approximately USD 1,100 for both eyes. Turkey's Dunyagoz Hospitals Group runs several eye centers in the country and is a popular choice for foreign patients, with nearly 30,000 medical tourists from 100 countries.

IV. Brazil

494. For people looking for a cheap option for cosmetic surgery, Brazil is one of the top destinations in the world. According to Patients Beyond Borders, approximately 200,000 foreign travelers went to Brazil last year for cosmetic procedures. The cost savings is extreme, with prices about 30%–50% below what American doctors would charge for treatment. Brazil has long been known for its Ivo Pitanguy Clinic in Rio de Janeiro, which has performed probably more cosmetic surgery operations than any other place in the world.

V. Thailand

495. Another country known for its cosmetic surgery is Thailand. The Bangkok Bumrungrad International Hospital has been treating foreign patients for the past twenty years. According to Patients Beyond Borders, up to 1.2 million patients came to the clinic last year alone. Bangkok's Bumrungrad International employs more than 900 physicians across 55 specialties and treats more than 1,000 international patients every day. According to The Medical Tourism Research Guide, more than 30,000 Americans visit the country each year for medical treatments.

Thailand has thirty-nine JCI-accredited hospitals. In 1994 The Thai Dental Council was established and is the premier governing body of dental practices in Thailand, and has now formulated uniform competency requirements for dental practitioners, thus directly influencing the medical and dental teaching programs. The Ministry of Public Health plays an important role in developing health care to promote science-based education. In addition, the Thai government has placed a more important role in public health programs for its citizens. Foreigners seeking treatment for everything from open heart surgery to gender reassignment have made Thailand a popular destination for medical tourism, attracting an estimated 2.81 million patients in 2015, up 10.2%. The development of Thailand's sex reassignment surgery has expanded the country's medical tourism industry throughout the years. Through the portrayal of *kathoey*, transgender women, represented in the media, Thailand has become one of the leading countries with a growing number of medical tourism per year.

VI. Israel

496. Israel is a popular destination for medical tourism. Many medical tourists to Israel come from Europe, particularly the former Soviet Union, as well as the US, Australia, Cyprus, and South Africa. Medical tourists come to Israel for a variety of surgical procedures and therapies, including bone marrow transplants, heart surgery and catheterization, oncological and neurological treatments, orthopedic procedures, accident rehabilitation, and IVF. Israel's popularity as a destination for medical tourism stems from its status as a developed country with a high-quality level of medical care, while at the same time having lower medical costs than many other developed countries. Israel is particularly popular as a destination for bone marrow transplants among Cypriots, as the procedure is not available in Cyprus, and for orthopedic procedures among Americans, as the cost of orthopedic procedures in Israel is about half that of in the US. Israel is a particularly popular destination for people seeking IFV treatments. Medical tourists in Israel use both public and private hospitals, and all major Israeli hospitals offer medical tourism packages which typically cost far less than comparable procedures than in facilities elsewhere with a similarly high standard of care. There are reports that these medical tourists obtain preferential treatment, to the detriment of local patients.

VII. Iran

497. In 2012, 30,000 people came to Iran to receive medical treatment. In 2015, It is estimated that between 150,000 and 200,000 health tourists came to Iran, and this figure is expected to rise to 500,000 a year. Iran has low endemicity for Hepatitis B virus and Hepatitis C virus infections and there is a unique experience of control of these infections that can be presented to people in Middle East countries.

VIII. The United Arab Emirates

498. The United Arab Emirates (UAE), especially Dubai, Abu Dhabi, Ras Al Khaimah, is a popular destination for medical tourism. UAE has the distinction of having the maximum number of JCI-accredited hospitals (under various heads). UAE has both inbound medical tourist as well as people going out for medical treatment. The inbound tourism usually is from African countries like Nigeria, Kenya, Uganda, Rwanda etc. The outbound can be categorized into two segments—the local population (citizens of UAE) and the expats. The locals prefer to go to European destinations like the U.K., Germany etc. The expats prefer to go back to their home countries for treatment. Several major medical centers and teaching hospitals offer international patient centers that cater to patients from foreign countries who seek medical treatment in the US. Many of these organizations offer service coordinators to assist international patients with arrangements for medical care, accommodations, finances, and transportation, including air ambulance services.

IX. Health Care in China

499. Ctrip's 2016 Online Medical Tourism Report indicates that the number of travelers who enroll in the overseas medical tourism through its platform increased fivefold over the previous year, and more than 500,000 Chinese visitors are expected to go on medical tourism. Regular health checks made up the majority share of Chinese medical tourism in 2016, representing over 50% of all medical tourism trips for tourists originating in China.

X. Singapore

500. Singapore has a dozen hospitals and health centers with JCI accreditation. In 2013 medical expenditure generated from medical tourists, mostly from more complex medical procedures, such as heart surgery, was SGD 832 million, a decline of 25% from 2012's SGD 1.11 billion, as the hospitals faced more competition from neighboring countries for less complex work. Singapore is the most popular destination for medical tourism due to its expertise in complex surgical procedures, the demand for medical tourism is also surging in other parts of Asia, according to research analyst of Future Market Insights.

XI. Finland

501. On December 9, 2013 the City of Helsinki decided, that all minors under the age of 18 and all pregnant mothers living in Helsinki without a valid visa or residence permit, are granted the right to the same health care and at the same price as other citizens of the city. Volunteer doctors of Global Clinic, a health clinic run by volunteer health care professionals in Helsinki, Turku, Joensuu, Oulu, and Tampere, have tried to help these people, for whom only acute care has been available. This means that the Finnish health care system is open for all people coming from outside of the EU. The service covers special child health care, maternity clinics, specialist medical care, etc. practically for free.

XII. The United Kingdom

502. The National Health Service in the UK is publicly owned. It attracts medical tourism principally to specialist centers in London. Some private hospitals and clinics in the UK are medical tourism destinations. Very few UK private hospitals have gone through independent international accreditation, so they have not as yet measured themselves against the best clinics and hospitals elsewhere in the world.

503. These are just some of the countries that are popular destinations for medical tourism. In addition, Mexico, Jordan, and Colombia are also common for medical tourism as millions of patients travel overseas in search of medical care.

Joint Commission International (JCI) approves, identifies, measures, and shares best practices in quality and patient safety in the world. The Joint Commission launched its international accreditation program in 1999 in response to increased interest in accreditation and quality improvement worldwide. Its standards are based on international consensus standards and set uniform, achievable expectations for structures, processes, and outcomes for hospitals. Health tourism providers have developed as intermediaries which unite potential medical tourists with provider hospitals and other organizations. Companies that focus on medical value travel typically provide nurse case managers to assist patients with pre and post travel medical issues. They also help provide resources for follow-up care upon the patient's return.

§4. Circumvention Health Tourism

504. Circumvention tourism is also an area of medical tourism that has grown. Circumvention tourism is travel in order to access medical services that are legal in the destination country but illegal in the home country. This can include travel for fertility treatments that aren't yet approved in the home country, abortion, and doctor-assisted suicide. Abortion tourism can be found most common in Europe, where travel between countries is simple. Ireland and Poland, two European countries with highly restrictive abortion laws, have the highest rates of circumvention tourism. In Poland especially, it is estimated that each year nearly 7,000 women travel to the UK, where abortion services are free through the National Health Service. Efforts are also being made by independent organizations and doctors, such as with Women on Waves, to help women circumvent draconian laws in order to access medical services. With Women on Waves, the organization uses a mobile clinic aboard a ship to provide medical abortions in international waters, where the law of the country whose flag is flown applies.

§5. International Health Care Accreditation

505. International health care accreditation is the process of certifying a level of quality for health care providers and programs of the different countries. International health care accreditation organizations certify a wide range of health care programs such as hospitals, primary care centers, medical transport, and ambulatory care services. There are a number of accreditation schemes available in different countries around the world. The oldest international accrediting body is Accreditation Canada, formerly known as the Canadian Council on Health Services Accreditation, which accredited the Bermuda Hospital Board as early as 1968. Since then, it has accredited hospitals and health service organizations in many other countries.

I. JCI Gold Seal: International Hospital Standard Accreditation

506. In the US, the accreditation group JCI was formed in 1994 to provide international clients with education and consulting services. Many international hospitals today see obtaining international accreditation as a way to attract American patients. JCI and the Joint Commission in the US are US-style independent private sector not-for-profit organizations that develop nationally and internationally recognized procedures and standards to help improve patient care and safety. They work with hospitals to help them meet Joint Commission standards for patient care and then accredit hospitals which meet the standards.

507. A British scheme, QHA Trent Accreditation, is an active independent holistic accreditation scheme, as well as GCR.org which monitors the success metrics and standards of medical clinics worldwide. The different international health care accreditation schemes vary in quality, size, cost, intent and the skill and intensity of their marketing. They also vary in terms of cost to hospitals and health care institutions which use them. Increasingly, some hospitals are looking toward dual international accreditation, perhaps having both JCI to cover potential US clientele, and Accreditation Canada or QHA Trent. As a result of competition between clinics for American medical tourists, there have been initiatives to rank hospitals based on patient-reported metrics.

§6. General Risks of Medical Tourism

508. Some countries, such as South Africa, or Thailand have very different infectious disease-related epidemiology to Europe and North America. Exposure to diseases without having built up natural immunity can be a hazard for weakened individuals, specifically with respect to gastrointestinal diseases (e.g., Hepatitis A, amoebic dysentery, paratyphoid) which could weaken progress and expose the patient to mosquito-transmitted diseases, influenza, and tuberculosis. However, because in poor tropical nations diseases run the gamut, doctors seem to be more open to the possibility of considering any infectious disease, including HIV, TB, and typhoid, while there are cases in the West where patients were consistently misdiagnosed for years because such diseases are perceived to be "rare" in the West.

The quality of postoperative care can also vary dramatically, depending on the hospital and country, and may be different from US or European standards. Further, traveling long distances soon after surgery can increase the risk of complications. Long flights and decreased mobility associated with window seats can predispose one toward developing deep vein thrombosis and potentially a pulmonary embolism.

509. Differences in health care provider standards around the world have been recognized by the WHO, and in 2004 it launched the World Alliance for Patient Safety. This body assists hospitals and government around the world in setting patient safety policy and practices that can become particularly relevant when providing medical tourism services. If there are complications, the patient may need to stay in the foreign country for longer than planned or if they have returned home, will not have easy access to follow-up care.

§7. Complicated Legal Issues

510. Receiving medical care abroad may subject medical tourists to unfamiliar legal issues. The nature of litigation in various countries is a reason for the accessibility of care overseas. While some countries which present themselves as attractive medical tourism destinations provide some form of legal remedies for medical malpractice, these legal avenues may be unappealing to the medical tourist. Should problems arise, patients might not be covered by adequate personal insurance or might be unable to seek compensation via malpractice lawsuits. Hospitals and/or doctors in some countries may be unable to pay the financial damages awarded by a court to a patient who has sued them, owing to the hospital and/or the doctor not possessing appropriate insurance cover and/or medical indemnity. Issues can also arise for patients who seek and get services that are illegal in their home country. In this case, some countries have the jurisdiction to prosecute their citizen once they have returned home, or in extreme cases extraterritorially arrest and prosecute them. In Ireland, especially in the 1980s and the 1990s, there were cases of young rape victims who were banned from traveling to Europe to get legal abortions. Ultimately, Ireland's Supreme Court overturned the ban following which Ireland and many other countries have created "right to travel" amendments.

511. There can be major ethical issues around medical tourism. For example, the illegal purchase of organs and tissues for transplantation had been methodically documented and studied in countries such as India, China, Colombia, and the Philippines. The DOI distinguishes between ethically problematic "transplant tourism" and "travel for transplantation." Medical tourism may raise broader ethical issues for the countries in which it is promoted. For example, in India, some argue that a "policy of 'medical tourism for the classes and health missions for the masses' will lead to a deepening of the inequities" already embedded in the health care system. The negative side of medical tourism is that doctors in the receiving country may become so busy with foreigners that local or domestic patients may have trouble getting care. Medical tourism centered on new technologies, such as stem cell treatments, is often criticized on grounds of fraud, blatant lack of scientific rationale and patient safety. However, when pioneering advanced technologies, such as providing "unproven" therapies to patients outside of regular clinical trials, it is often challenging to differentiate between acceptable medical innovation and unacceptable patient exploitation.

I. Licensing and Regulation of Facilities and Professionals

512. The local licensing requirements of professionals and facilities rendering the service may be of interest to the patient in medical tourism. In terms of licensure, governing rules may often be local and not national laws, which may govern. For the patient, this means that requirements may differ from region to region of a destination country. Medical tourists, facilitators, and insurers have come to ask whether the destination medical facility is accredited. In the US, foreign health care facility accreditation by the JCI is considered reliable, akin to a facility having Joint Commission (a JCI "sister organization") accreditation in the US. When JCI facility accreditation is present, potential medical tourists, their facilitators, and increasingly, group health benefit plan insurers in the US, begin to look seriously at and compare the costs of performing a surgical procedure in a US facility compared to costs of the same procedure if performed at a JCI-accredited hospital. Where JCI accreditation is present, it helps the traveling patient, their facilitators, family members, local providers, and insurers gain confidence in and choose the medical tourism option, including providing insurance coverage benefits for the patient's out-of-country health care services.

II. Informed Consent of Patient

513. It is generally the duty of the licensed professionals and facilities as a condition of their license to obtain the patient's informed consent before performing medical treatments and procedures, and whereas the governing rules generally arise from the location where the licensed provider or facility are rendering the services, the informed consent rules and laws of the provider's jurisdiction are likely to control in the case of medical tourism services. Informed consent is the process whereby the patient is informed of the risks, benefits and treatment alternatives available so as to allow the patient to make an informed decision electing the care and treatment provided. The informed consent process should be substantially addressed well before funds are invested for travel and procedures are scheduled by the provider, even if the final written consent forms are not presented to the patient until their initial in-country meeting with their surgeon and hospital staff dealing with intake.

III. Surrogate Decision Makers

514. A patient traveling for medical procedures should also inquire and understand whether and how patients have the right to designate a surrogate decision maker if the patient becomes unable to voice his or her care preference at some point in the process. If such rights exist, a medical tourist and their traveling companion should understand under what circumstances do they arise, and what are the limitations on the extent of authority which is given to a surrogate decision maker. The forms and procedures required must be identified to establish such a backup decision maker. In case the destination country has different laws than the patient's home country, the question is as to which laws will control- those of the patient's home country or the laws of the site of the provider. If no local laws exist, will the patient's existing documentation be honored, or can the patient and provider contractually agree to honor and permit the surrogate decision maker to step in if the same conditions exist which would vest authority in the patient's country should arise, such as during the patient's loss of capacity due to heavy anesthesia, unconsciousness, or other conditions.

IV. Transfer of Medical Records

515. Other practical considerations exist with regard to sharing and providing medical records to the out-of-country providers in advance of treatment. Certain portions of the patient's historical medical record may be needed in order to authorize and ultimately deliver care and perform procedures such as diagnostic tests, imaging scans, or history and physical notation of certain diagnostic codes/disease states under the international classification of diseases system. The authorizations which are required by the providers and the patient's governing laws as a condition of releasing records to other providers, to insurers for payment or reimbursement of patient's charges, and to the patients or their advocates.

V. Controversial Treatments and Procedures

516. There can be some controversy regarding the use of stem cell therapies, organ transplant, (organ donation, harvest/and transplantation), fertility and conception-including genetic screening, gene therapy/genetic code splicing, and use of certain pharmaceutical, biological agents, or medical devices which are not approved or legal for use in the medical tourist's home country. Often there are fewer rules and prohibitions when it comes to the most cutting edge of therapies, treatments, and procedures; and opportunities often exist where the medical community is "out front." Although payers often deny payment of innovative or controversial treatments and therapies as being "experimental," it does not mean that the patient does not have the choice to obtain such cutting edge treatments. As a procedure or treatment moves into and becomes "evidence-based medicine," it often also becomes a covered service under payment and insurance benefits, and part of the accepted and ever changing landscape of medical care. Medical tourism has a place at the forefront, given that with the myriad of geographic locations and governments, and cultural and religious diversity around our world, there are always going to be places where a meritorious, innovative treatment or procedure can be obtained by those medical tourists of our time in search of excellence in health care.

VI. Cost of Medical Complications

517. Most hospitals, wherever they are located, will not cover the cost of medical complications. Therefore, it is important to speak to the international medical provider to see their definition of what constitutes a "medical complication" and who will be liable to bear the cost. So both parties must be clear of their rights and liabilities and they should get everything in writing before the procedure is started. Whether insurance will cover the cost of complications will depend on the type of policy. It will also depend on the policy of the hospital chosen. One needs to be extremely careful of the choice of hospital and clinic and therefore it must be made sure that a hospital or clinic is used that is reputable and trustworthy.

VII. Contract for Overseas Medical Treatment

518. A patient may enter into a contract for overseas medical treatment or surgery. Any contract that the patient receives must be read very carefully. It is unwise to sign any contract in circumstances where there is no easy recourse to informed legal advice. It may be that such contracts contain one-sided clauses like exclusive jurisdiction clauses which expressly exclude certain courts from hearing disputes under the contract. In such a situation when errors are made, medical tourists can find legal redress difficult if not impossible to access. Problems can include difficulties identifying the defendant, language barriers in the gathering of evidence, and jurisdictional disputes amongst the parties. A foreign patient seeking legal redress may have limited protection or support in the overseas legal system. There may also be significant differences in the medical complaint dispute resolution procedures. In the case of an adverse event or incidence of medical negligence, patients should be aware that there may not be standard international complaints system. Even where a court in the patient country has jurisdiction over a claim, it is a well-established legal principle that the applicable law is the law of the place of the wrongdoing.

§8. Medical Malpractice

519. The risk of medical malpractice occurring within medical tourism is very high, especially because patients are traveling outside their home country and away from the legal and ethical systems they are used to. Physicians can convince foreign patients to let them perform unethical procedures and can also refuse to grant them legal recourse in the case of a medical error. The numbers, cases, and examples of medical malpractice are endless and are happening on a daily basis.

I. Defining Medical Malpractice

520. Medical malpractice is the act of professional "wrongdoing" by a health care or medical professional catering to the needs of a patient. Malpractice occurs through negligence by act or omission where medical providers stray from the accepted medical practices within their profession that could potentially result in harm or fatalities to the patient. Health care professionals have a responsibility to treat patients to the best of their ability, so when a physician or another medical professional deviates away from standard medical procedures, they have to be accountable to their patient and for their mistake. Medical malpractice causes enough confusion for doctors, lawyers, and patients when it occurs locally. However, when brought into the larger sense of international travel, it can be even more difficult to understand and manage as there are no universal laws that regulate how individual countries handle medical malpractice. Within the realm of medical tourism itself, there is no regulating body to which patients with medical malpractice concerns can report. Without regulations and standardizations, medical tourism has the potential to be a hub of medical malpractices in which unqualified health care professionals treat naive patients. This is why the concept of medical malpractice is so important to address and discuss for individuals involved in the medical tourism industry.

II. Variations in Legal Systems

521. Since there are no universal laws or standards in place dictating medical malpractice, physicians can travel outside their country and consult or even treat foreign patients in a region where they are not licensed to practice. This could be detrimental for patient safety and for the reputation of medical tourism. Since the majority of communication between a patient and physician during medical tourism occurs when both parties are in different countries, there is a great potential for physicians to be unethical. Prior to a patient flying in for treatment, the patient could receive a lot of false information about the procedure in order to lure them into traveling. This is due to a lack of transparency and additionally a lack of regulation. These two issues combined are a great hurdle which must overcome for medical tourism. Further, in case of medical error or an act of negligence in the form of medical malpractice, a patient has the right to duly receive retribution. This retribution usually comes in the form of a monetary reward or by fixing the medical error made. However, when it comes to medical tourism, the variations in the legal systems of different countries could prevent a patient from receiving any legal recourse.

III. Medical Malpractice Claim

522. Any act of wrongdoing in which the results of the malpractice have a negative impact on a person's life, community or country could be considered unethical, regardless of whether or not it meets a patient's expectations. Malpractice and the violation of ethics are more severe when the action is performed intentionally and with the understanding that such practices could be harmful. Intentional acts of medical malpractice all fall under the sphere of unethical practices. The justice system of certain countries has placed great emphasis on legal consequences when an act of medical negligence has occurred. Patients want some sort of retribution when a medical error occurs, and this is often tied to the litigious aspect of it. This may result in patients having the ability to file a medical malpractice claim and sue their health care professional when they feel they have been wronged. Nowadays, physicians practicing in countries with stringent medical malpractice regulations can get sued over any case of medical malpractice to the detriment of their career. Some countries, like the US, take the issue of medical malpractice very seriously, causing doctors to purchase malpractice insurance in order to protect themselves.

IV. Unethical Practices as Medical Malpractice

523. There are several examples of how foreign physicians can use unethical practices with foreign patients. These include: charging higher prices to international patients as compared to locals, covering hospital documents in the local language and refusing to provide translator services, misuse of medical technology (via using technological means to predict or even influence the characteristics of the fetus or through unethical organ transplant procedures) and not providing the patient with enough pre and postoperative information. All these unethical cases also fall into the category of medical malpractice; however, depending on the legal system of the medical tourism destination they might or might not have a legal affiliation.

524. Medical tourism has been in practice for centuries, but due to the recent widespread globalization and ease of travel, the medical tourism industry has been thriving and set to continue growing well into the future. But there are several hurdles that we still have to face in order to keep the reputation of medical tourism strong. One of the greatest issues is the lack of legal regulation for cases of medical malpractice. The fact that no standards are in place or no regulatory body has been created in order to address the very relevant issue of medical malpractice is weakening the industry and all it has to offer. Patients should have a right to retribution if negligence has been done upon them and doctors need to take responsibility for their actions. Additionally, as individuals invest in the medical tourism industry, we need to work together to ensure that patients have the safest medical journey possible and that they have an outlet to voice their cases when medical negligence occurs. A sound support system for practitioners is needed to protect themselves in the case of unfortunate results or complications that have occurred because of unintentional practice.

Chapter 2. Travel and Legal Position of Doctors

525. As more and more people are traveling so medical emergencies while in travel are becoming more common. Some such emergencies require assistance from passenger doctors who act as Good Samaritans. Their liability and the associated medico-legal issues of providing assistance in emergencies while the doctor, as well as the patient, is in travel are not clearly defined and known. The obligations, liability and legal protection of doctors when acting as Good Samaritans in travel emergencies involves questions of jurisdiction, existing legislation, case law etc. However, doctors' liability is unclear and uncertain, legal protection is inadequate and inconsistent and in case of air travel, airlines' liability is also restricted.

§1. Travel by Air

526. Airlines are required to provide first aid training for cabin crew to enable them to recognize common symptoms of distress and to respond with first aid, basic resuscitation techniques and the use of emergency medical oxygen and a defibrillator. The airlines' cabin crew undergoes a refresher course each year which also covers first aid. In many cases both they and any *health* experts who volunteer their services can call for backup from doctors on the ground. MedLink is a specialist medical service that offers continuous multilingual support from doctors who specialize in the remote treatment of passengers who require in-flight emergency medical treatment. MedLink staff discusses with flight crew or physicians and nurses on board through whatever procedures might be necessary to deal with a patient's condition. In extreme cases MedLink might advise a flight diversion to the nearest airport, and alert ground-based medical services on standby, although this decision ultimately rests with the pilot.

527. Since in-flight deaths are rare and space is at a premium, airlines do not have a dedicated area on their aircraft in which to store a dead body. Practices for dealing with a dead body vary from one airline to another but generally the corpse is covered with a blanket and placed out of sight as far as possible, which might be in a vacant row toward the rear of the aircraft, or even in business or first class where screens confer a degree of privacy, and passengers are not exposed to what could be an upsetting spectacle.

§2. Carrying Prescribed Medicines by International Travelers

528. Travelers who need to carry medication should be aware that their medication's legal status in other countries may be different. Legal requirements for carrying personal medicines across international borders are highly variable and often not consistently enforced. This applies to over-the-counter medication as well as prescription drugs. Some countries may not allow the entry of certain types of medicines, and others may have blanket regulations requiring specific permission. The regulations regarding whether a traveler needs to carry a doctor's letter describing the medication also varies widely.

I. Before Travel

529. Travelers who take regular medication should prepare for their trip well in advance of travel. A medical checkup is recommended to discuss fitness to travel, and ensure medication is optimized and sufficient supplies are available (including cover for possible travel delays). Travelers should check the regulations on importing or transporting medicines to their chosen destination by contacting the relevant embassy/high commission or checking the Foreign and Commonwealth Office (FCO) country advice. Check the INCB Guidelines if traveling with medications that are narcotics or psychotropic. Be aware of medications with potential for abuse (e.g., anabolic steroids). Some countries permit taking only a thirty-day supply of certain medicines and require carrying a prescription or an import license certificate. Keep the tablets together with the original packaging and information leaflet. Carry a copy of your prescription, particularly for prescribed medicines that act on the Central Nervous System (CNS). Travelers taking certain "controlled drugs" may be required to obtain an export license prior to transporting set quantities (usually three months' or more supply) into or out of the country. Some examples of controlled drugs include: diamorphine, diazepam, codeine, fentanyl, methadone, morphine, pethidine, Ritalin, and temazepam. Those carrying controlled drugs and other prescription drugs on shorter trips are advised to obtain and carry a letter from the doctor or prescriber detailing the medicines.

530. Travelers should avoid the risk of purchasing counterfeit medication by obtaining all the medication they need prior to travel. Travelers should also be advised to carry medicines (including those bought over the counter) in their correctly labeled container, as issued by the pharmacist, in their hand luggage. Airline regulations should be checked, particularly for injectable medications or liquids as restrictions apply to the quantity that can be carried in hand luggage. Passengers needing to fly with oxygen, insulin or other injectable medicines should contact their airline in advance to make appropriate arrangements. Consider packing a spare supply of medication in the hold luggage in case of loss of hand luggage. Storage requirements for medication must be checked in advance. Arrangements for control of temperature during transit with certain medications may be needed.

II. Carry a Copy of All Prescriptions

531. A letter from the prescriber detailing the medicines with the generic names for the medications can be helpful for border control checks, and in case medicines have to be replaced or medical help is required. Carry a note from the prescribing physician on letterhead stationery for controlled substances and injection medications. Take out an appropriate level of travel health insurance including repatriation and specific cover for any pre-existing illnesses. Carry a letter from a doctor (preferably translated in the language understood at destination) or a traveler clinical record describing the condition and the treatment plan. This will facilitate border crossing and help the attending physician abroad. If one needs syringes, they should get a note from their doctor explaining their use and also find out from the airline or other transportation company about the use of syringes during transit.

III. During Travel

532. Travelers who need to obtain extra medication during travel should be aware of the risks of counterfeit medications. They should carry copies of prescriptions of regular medications and consult a recognized pharmacy or health care provider. Medicines should not be purchased from open markets or street vendors. The International Association for Medical Assistance to Travelers and the International Society of Travel Medicine global clinic directory can provide contact details of medical practitioners overseas.

§3. Counterfeit Medications

533. Counterfeit medications are drugs produced by unauthorized manufacturers, presented to the consumer as authorized products. Very often, both packaging and medication appear virtually identical to the authentic medication. Counterfeit medications may contain inactive substances or toxic ingredients, resulting in treatment failure and/or serious harm. Medications for legitimate health conditions may come under intense scrutiny by foreign officials at border controls. This can result in delays, disruption or medicines being confiscated if the correct paperwork and permissions have not been arranged. On rare occasions, travelers who have been found to have drugs that are illegal at the destination or transit country have been imprisoned.

§4. Searching Out Regulations of Destination Country

534. Searching out the regulations of destination country can be extremely difficult. Country websites that might deal with questions relating to medicine regulations abroad are also quite hard to interpret. There are some countries where regulations are quite strictly applied and the UAE and Japan are the two best-known examples. Despite this seeming confusion there do appear to be very few cases of travelers encountering serious problems. However, a large number of travelers carry medicines for personal use across international borders every day.

§5. Medications Which Can Be a Problem

535. Two classes of medicines—narcotics and psychotropic—are under the purview of international law. This covers any medicine that can have an effect on the CNS and the potential to be abused. The narcotic class mostly relates to analgesic opioids and their derivatives (e.g., morphine and codeine) which tend to be highly regulated. Psychotropics are all those medications likely to be used to treat mental disorders such as anxiety, depression, and psychotic conditions. Some countries will include a range of medications used to treat neurological conditions such as epilepsy and Parkinson's disease to their regulated list. Others would even include sedating antihistamines as a banned substance. The message is, therefore, to be wary of carrying any medicine with the potential to affect the CNS. However, a few countries such as the UAE also include a range of non-CNS items.

536. The international agreements governing the transportation of medications across borders are available on the website of the INCB. An independent and quasi-judicial organization, the INCB is responsible for international drug control. Their site contains statements and broad principles relating to travelers intending to travel with narcotics and psychotropic substances.

The travelers may be allowed to carry small quantities of such substances for personal use, usually for use of up to one month. The travelers should have a letter or prescription from their doctor if traveling with a narcotic substance.

I. Commission on Narcotic Drugs

537. The question of provisions regarding medical preparations containing controlled drugs carried by international travelers was raised during the forty-third session (March 2000) of the Commission on Narcotic Drugs. The Commission noted that relevant provisions were included in the Convention on Psychotropic Substances of 1971, but that a problem existed concerning travelers being treated by means of medical preparations containing narcotic drugs controlled under the Single Convention on Narcotic Drugs of 1961, and that Convention as amended by the 1972 Protocol 3. In its Resolution 43/11, the Commission invited the INCB to examine existing provisions. Pursuant to that resolution, a review of the issue was included in the report of INCB for 2000.[55] The review showed that in most of the States that had transmitted relevant information to INCB, travelers under treatment were permitted to carry small quantities of preparations containing narcotic drugs and/or psychotropic substances for personal use.

II. Guidelines for International Travelers

538. During its forty-fourth session (March 2001), the Commission, in its Resolution 44/15, invited the United Nations International Drug Control Programme

55. Paragraphs 119–127.

(UNDCP), in cooperation with INCB and the WHO, to convene a meeting of experts to develop guidelines for national regulations concerning travelers under treatment with internationally controlled drugs.

Resolution 44/15 indicated that the guidelines should cover the following topics:

(a) The type of drug that people under treatment can carry with them.
(b) The length of treatment involved and the maximum authorized quantities of drugs.
(c) The type of documentation required to demonstrate that the substances were lawfully obtained in the country of origin.

539. In November 2001, a questionnaire was sent to a number of Governments to obtain their views on those specific issues and draft guidelines were prepared by UNDCP, with the cooperation of INCB and WHO, and with the assistance of a consultant, for submission to the meeting of experts convened in Vienna on February 12 to 14, 2002, pursuant to Resolution 44/15. The guidelines have been developed primarily to assist national authorities in introducing a regulatory framework to deal with situations in which patients under treatment with preparations containing internationally controlled drugs are traveling abroad and carrying with them small quantities of such preparations for personal use. Such regulations would enhance the security of patients by making them aware of national requirements in the country they intend to visit.

540. The guidelines present elements of unified procedures that can be implemented by national authorities responsible for the control of narcotic drugs and psychotropic substances. A wide application of those procedures would facilitate both the mutual disclosure of relevant information through INCB and the work of government authorities. However, it should be understood that countries have the latitude to implement the guidelines only partially or with suitable modifications, depending on their legal requirements and practical considerations.

The guidelines are dealing with issues pertaining to medical preparations containing controlled substances that are licensed in the country of departure of the traveler in the dosage form only and not with individually compounded preparations. The provisions of the guidelines do not relate to the carrying of pure active substances (raw materials), such substances being mentioned in the guidelines only for the purpose of calculation of their amounts in medical preparations. Definitions of key terms used in the draft guidelines are given in the glossary included in the present document.

III. Single Convention on Narcotic Drugs of 1961 and Convention on Psychotropic Substances of 1971

541. The issue of international travelers under treatment carrying preparations containing internationally controlled drugs is dealt with differently under the Single Convention on Narcotic Drugs of 1961 and the Convention on Psychotropic Substances of 1971. The 1971 Convention explicitly envisages, in Article 4, that Parties may permit the carrying by international travelers of small quantities of preparations for personal medical use, while the 1961 Convention does not contain any statement to that effect.

Article 30, paragraph 2(b), of the 1961 Convention and Article 9, paragraph 1, of the 1971 Convention require that medical prescriptions be issued by physicians to describe medical preparations that are to be used by patients. The conventions give only general indications concerning the contents of such documents, although the 1961 Convention, in Article 30, paragraph 2(b)(ii), mentions the use of prescriptions issued in the form of counterfoil books. There is a need, therefore, to describe those documents in greater detail in the guidelines, especially when they are intended to serve as evidence that medical preparations were lawfully obtained by the traveler in the country of departure.

542. It should also be understood that the carrying by travelers under treatment of medical preparations containing internationally controlled drugs from the country of departure to the country of destination does not constitute an export or import operation, that would require reporting under the international drug control treaties. The situation is instead similar to that described in Article 32, paragraph 1, of the 1961 Convention and in Article 14, paragraph 1, of the 1971 Convention, concerning the carriage of controlled substances in first aid kits. However, when a country has pursuant to Article 13 of the 1971 Convention notified that it prohibits the import into its territory of specific psychotropic substances, such prohibition will also apply to those substances when carried by travelers under treatment.

IV. Procedure for Carrying Controlled Drugs

543. The procedures related to the carrying by travelers of preparations containing internationally controlled drugs have to be consistent with national legal and administrative frameworks. Included therein are legislation and regulations related to the control of use of narcotic drugs and psychotropic substances for medical purposes and those related to the control of the cross-border movement of goods. For practical purposes, the procedures have to take into account existing regulations governing prescriptions for medical preparations containing internationally controlled drugs, as well as regulations and practices of customs authorities.

544. With regard to travelers entering the country, national regulations need to describe the document (prescription, certificate or permit, as the case may be) that will be required to confirm the licit status of medical preparations carried by the traveler, as well as the specific procedure, if any, to be followed by the traveler when entering the country. The establishment and implementation of such regulations will involve both national health authorities and customs/law enforcement authorities, for example, police and special drug law enforcement bodies.

With regard to travelers departing from the country, the national health authorities in the country of departure need to designate an authority or authorities in charge of issuing appropriate documents in the form of certificates confirming that the medical prescription held by the traveler was issued by an authorized medical practitioner and that the medical preparations were licitly acquired. This task may be entrusted to a single central authority or delegated to local authorities.

545. In states that, as a general rule, do not permit travelers (both those entering and those leaving the country) to carry internationally controlled drugs, it might be advisable to designate a competent authority able to issue, in exceptional circumstances, the necessary certificates or permits on compassionate grounds.

Documents for travelers who carry medical preparations containing internationally controlled drugs. The medical prescription is the principal document which confirms the legal authority of the traveler to possess, for personal use, medical preparations containing internationally controlled drugs. Depending on the requirements of the country of destination, and on the quantities of preparations involved, the traveler may additionally be required to obtain a certificate issued by a competent authority in the country of departure, and/or a permit issued by a competent authority in the country of destination. Travelers who travel by land and cross the territory of third countries should also ascertain the documents required by the transit countries.

V. Medical Prescription Regarding Controlled Drugs

546. Prescriptions are normally in the language of the country in which they are issued. The medical prescription should be issued in the country of departure by the patient's treating physician, taking into account the approved indications for the medical product. The prescription should indicate the name of the patient, the name of the medicinal product (usually a trademark but also the international name of the active substance), the posology and total amount of the medical preparation prescribed. The prescription should be issued according to national regulations governing the prescribing of controlled drugs, including the use of appropriate forms. The amount of the preparation prescribed should be in conformity with the principles governing good medical practice. When the prescription is issued in a country where national regulations limit the maximum length of treatment with specific types of medical preparations containing internationally controlled drugs, the physician should abide with such regulations, unless there exists a specific exemption concerning patients traveling abroad.

547. Prescriptions for narcotic drugs are usually written using counterfoil books, the original being given to the patient and the copy remaining with the prescribing physician. If the original of the prescription is retained in the pharmacy that dispensed the preparation, it is advisable for the physician to either give to the patient who intends to travel abroad a duplicate of the prescription, or issue a letter indicating that a preparation containing internationally controlled drugs was prescribed for the traveler and specifying the amount prescribed and the duration of treatment. The duplicate of the prescription retained by the traveler may contain an attestation (or stamp) from the dispensing pharmacy confirming the purchase of the product.

VI. Certificate for Controlled Drugs

548. Certificates to be issued by the competent authority of the country of departure may be required to confirm the patient's legal authority to possess, for personal use, preparations containing internationally controlled drugs. Such certificates are issued on the basis of the medical prescription identifying the patient and indicating the type and amount of preparations that he/she is permitted to carry. In case of prescriptions of unusually high amounts, the competent authority should also ascertain that the prescription is in line with the patient's needs. Certificates should also indicate the total amount of the controlled substance contained in the medical preparation, using the international nonproprietary name (INN) of the substance in accordance with relevant schedules of the international drug control conventions.

Certificates should preferably be issued in a generally used language, such as English, French or Spanish. If the country of destination so requires, the traveler should obtain a translation of the prescription, of the letter produced by the physician, or of the certificate into a language generally used in the country of destination.

549. A procedure should be established by the national health authorities indicating the competent authority (or local bodies) authorized to issue certificates confirming the legal authority of the patient to possess, for personal use, preparations containing internationally controlled drugs that he/she intends to carry abroad. Certificates may either be produced by the issuing authority or completed, on a suitable form, by the treating physician, and presented to the competent authority for confirmation (stamp, seal, and signature). The authority issuing the certificate should take due account, to the extent possible, of the types and maximum amounts of preparations containing internationally controlled drugs that travelers are allowed to carry into the country of destination. The names and addresses of authorities responsible for issuing the certificates for travelers should be made generally available to medical practitioners.

VII. Permit from the Country of Destination

550. States that require travelers under treatment to obtain a permit from the country of destination before arrival in that country should also establish suitable procedures to that effect. Such procedures should indicate the authority competent for the issuance of permits, establish the extent of medical information to be provided by the traveler, and describe any restrictions on the types and amounts of preparations that travelers are allowed to carry for their personal use. The requirement of a prior permit may apply to all types of internationally controlled substances or to specific types of substances only (e.g., narcotic drugs).

551. The guidelines consider a period of thirty days of treatment as a period of sufficient length for prescription of medical preparations for travelers. Beyond that period, it should be possible for the traveler to obtain a prolongation of treatment in the visited country, if needed. However, a longer period may be acceptable for patients treated with psychotropic substances used as anticonvulsant agents.

Annexes II and III to the guidelines include an indicative list of types of narcotic drugs and psychotropic substances contained in preparations frequently used for medical treatments. The quantities indicated in the annexes refer to the maximum total amount of controlled substance contained in the preparations for the prescribed medical treatment that may be carried by the international traveler.

552. The quantities were calculated on the basis of a thirty-day period of treatment and defined average daily doses used by INCB for statistical purposes. Those doses correspond, in most cases, to the doses recommended by WHO for drug utilization studies. In the case of substances used for the treatment of chronic or severe pain for terminally ill patients and in the case of substances used for maintenance treatment and/or substitution treatment of drug dependence, the quantities indicated were calculated taking into account doses actually used for those categories of patients. This mode of calculation may be used by countries, which, due to local considerations, need to establish maximum quantities for additional types of preparations or introduce modifications to the quantities indicated in the examples.

553. Annex II provides examples of narcotic drugs listed in Schedules I and II of the 1961 Convention and psychotropic substances listed in Schedules II and III of the 1971 Convention, and the maximum total quantities of controlled substance contained in preparations for the prescribed medical treatment allowed to be carried by international travelers. For amounts exceeding the indicated limits, the traveler should be required to possess a certificate.

554. Annex III provides examples of psychotropic substances listed in Schedule IV of the 1971 Convention and the maximum total quantities of controlled substance contained in preparations for the prescribed medical treatment allowed to be carried by international travelers. For amounts exceeding the indicated limits, the traveler should be required to possess a prescription. The possession of a prescription should not be required from travelers carrying preparations containing psychotropic substances listed in Schedule IV of the 1971 Convention in amounts not exceeding the quantities indicated in Annex III.

555. It should be understood that narcotic drugs included in Schedule IV of the 1961 Convention cannot be carried by international travelers, even if their use is permitted in the country of departure. Furthermore, prohibition of the import of specific psychotropic substances into countries that made a notification pursuant to Article 13 of the 1971 Convention (*see* the "Green List" issued periodically by INCB) will entail the prohibition of carrying by travelers under treatment of medical preparations containing such psychotropic substances.

556. It is also understood that preparations, intended for personal use, of narcotic drugs listed in Schedule III of the 1961 Convention may usually be carried by international travelers without restrictions. Finally, no prescription should be required for travelers carrying up to one retail package (usually 20 unit doses or less) of any preparation containing internationally controlled drugs.

When entering the country of destination and depending on the type of preparation and amount of controlled substances involved, the traveler should have in his/her possession the documents required by that country: medical prescription, certificate and/or permit, confirming his/her legal authority to possess, for personal use, medical preparations containing internationally controlled drugs.

557. In many countries, the traveler will not be required to spontaneously present those documents to the customs authorities. However, those documents should be in the traveler's possession during the stay in the visited country and should be available on request for presentation to the authorities. In some countries, however, the traveler may be required to present the required documents to the customs authorities on entering the country of destination. In such situations, the document is usually confirmed by an annotation of the customs officer. Travelers who travel by land and cross in transit the territory of a third country have to comply with the required procedures when entering and leaving the transit country in respect of possession of suitable documents, and, as the case may be, to their presentation to customs authorities.

558. INCB in its report for 2001 (paragraph 164) stated that it would publish information on restrictions on the carrying by travelers of medical preparations containing internationally controlled drugs. Furthermore, there is a need for mutual disclosure among countries of the following data:

(a) Information on the type of documents required for incoming travelers indicating whether a medical prescription or a letter issued by the treating physician is required, or/and a certificate or/and a permit as well as on specific language demands, if any, for those documents.
(b) Information as to whether travelers carrying internationally controlled drugs are required to present, on entering the country of destination, the above-mentioned documents for confirmation by the customs officer.
(c) Where required, the names and addresses of the authorities responsible for issuing permits for travelers carrying preparations containing internationally controlled drugs, when those are different from the competent national authorities empowered to issue certificates and authorizations for the import and export of narcotic drugs and psychotropic substances in accordance with the 1961 and 1971 Conventions (*see* Directory of competent national authorities published yearly by UNDCP).

Part XIV. Transplantation and Donation of Organs

559. The medical practice of organ transplantation has grown by leaps and bounds over the past fifty years. The major transplant-related medical advances in the last century include: successful transplantation of different kinds of organs; transplant now expanded to kidney, hearts, lungs, livers and other organs and development of cadaveric and living organ donation practices. Deciding who can donate organs has been a flexible and changing process, starting with living donors and then moving to include deceased donors. The debate about increasing and restricting the pool of eligible donors continues today. Some organs of animals have also been tried. Further, artificial organs have also been developed.

Chapter 1. Organ and Tissue Transplantation

560. Organ transplantation is a surgical operation where a failing or damaged organ in the human body is removed and replaced with a new one. Any part of the body that performs a specialized function is an organ. Therefore eyes are organs because their specialized function is to see, skin is an organ because its function is to protect and regulate the body, and the liver is an organ that functions to remove waste from the blood. A graft is similar to a transplant. It is the process of removing tissue from one part of a person's body (or another person's body) and surgically re-implanting it to replace or compensate for damaged tissue. Grafting is different from transplantation because it does not remove and replace an entire organ, but rather only a portion. Not all organs are transplanted. The term "organ transplant" typically refers to transplants of the solid organs: heart, lungs, kidneys, liver, pancreas, and intestines.

§1. Transplantation Related Law

561. Organ transplantation is the best and sometimes only form of treatment for many patients with end-stage organ failure. Organ donation and transplantation has been the subject of extensive international interest both at governmental and professional levels. This interest has been driven by two main factors. First, the shortage of organs for transplantation and the wide international variation in donation and transplantation activity and related law. Second, the need to ensure that all developments have a firm basis in legal and ethical practice with equity, quality, and safety at their core. Any comprehensive review of organ transplantation needs to consider both deceased and living donation. Indeed, while deceased donation fails to meet the need for transplantable organs in all countries, it is almost nonexistent in many countries, and it is this that has led to the ever-increasing use of living donors as a source of kidneys and more recently also livers. Many of the controversial—and unacceptable—aspects of living donation stem from this, and while interest sometimes appears to be focused on steps to stop these practices, there is also an equal emphasis on the need for all countries to work to achieve "self-sufficiency" by establishing effective deceased donation programs.

§2. International Response

562. The international response to organ transplantation has been to create two sets of global agreements: an international governmental response created through the WHA and WHO, and a professional response created through international societies spearheaded by The Transplantation Society and the International Society of Nephrology. Led by the WHO, the WHA resolved in May 2010 to endorse revised Guiding Principles on Human Cell, Tissue and Organ Transplantation. These refer to both living and deceased donation, are accompanied by a commentary, and contain eleven specific and carefully worded principles. It is stated that, "The Guiding Principles are intended to provide an orderly, ethical and acceptable framework for the acquisition and transplantation of human cells, tissues and organs for therapeutic purposes. Each jurisdiction will determine the means of implementing the Guiding Principles." The professional response to these challenges has been led by The Transplantation Society, in association with other international professional societies, through publications such as the Amsterdam Forum, the Vancouver meeting, and importantly the DOI on Organ Trafficking and Transplant Tourism.

I. WHO Guiding Principles on Human Cell, Tissue & Organ Transplantation

563. The WHO has come up with following guiding principles on human cell, tissue, and organ transplantation:

(i) Cells, tissues, and organs may be removed from the bodies of deceased persons for the purpose of transplantation if consent required by law has been obtained, and there is no reason to believe that the deceased person objected to such removal.

(ii) Physicians determining that a potential donor has died should not be directly involved in cell, tissue, or organ removal from the donor or subsequent transplantation procedures; nor should they be responsible for the care of any intended recipient of such cells, tissues, and organs.

(iii) Donation from deceased persons should be developed to its maximum therapeutic potential, but adult living persons may donate organs as permitted by domestic regulations. In general, living donors should be genetically, legally, or emotionally related to their recipients. Live donations are acceptable when the donor's informed and voluntary consent is obtained, when professional care of donors is ensured and follow-up is well organized, and when selection criteria for donors are scrupulously applied and monitored. Live donors should be informed of the probable risks, benefits, and consequences of donation in a complete and understandable fashion; they should be legally competent and capable of weighing the information; and they should be acting willingly, free of any undue influence or coercion.

(iv) No cells, tissues, or organs should be removed from the body of a living minor for the purpose of transplantation other than narrow exceptions allowed under national law.

Specific measures should be in place to protect the minor and, wherever possible, the minor's assent should be obtained before donation. What is applicable to minors also applies to any legally incompetent person.

(v) Cells, tissues, and organs should only be donated freely, without any monetary payment or other rewards of monetary value. Purchasing, or offering to purchase, cells, tissues, or organs for transplantation, or their sale by living persons or by the next of kin for deceased persons, should be banned. The prohibition on sale or purchase of cells, tissues, and organs does not preclude reimbursing reasonable and verifiable expenses incurred by the donor, including loss of income, or paying the costs of recovering, processing, preserving, and supplying human cells, tissues, or organs for transplantation.

(vi) Promotion of altruistic donation of human cells, tissues, or organs by means of advertisement or public appeal may be undertaken in accordance with domestic regulation. Advertising the need for or availability of cells, tissues, or organs, with a view to offering or seeking payment to individuals for their cells, tissues, or organs, or, to the next of kin, where the individual is deceased, should be prohibited. Brokering that involves payment to such individuals or to third parties should also be prohibited.

(vii) Physicians and other health professionals should not engage in transplantation procedures, and health insurers and other payers should not cover such procedures, if the cells, tissues, or organs concerned have been obtained through exploitation or coercion of, or payment to, the donor or the next of kin of a deceased donor.

(viii) All health care facilities and professionals involved in cell, tissue, or organ procurement and transplantation procedures should be prohibited from receiving any payment that exceeds the justifiable fee for the services rendered.

(ix) The allocation of organs, cells, and tissues should be guided by clinical criteria and ethical norms, not financial or other considerations. Allocation rules, defined by appropriately constituted committees, should be equitable, externally justified, and transparent.

(x) High-quality, safe, and efficacious procedures are essential for donors and recipients alike. The long-term outcomes of cell, tissue, and organ donation and transplantation should be assessed for the living donor and the recipient in order to document benefit and harm. The level of safety, efficacy, and quality of human cells, tissues, and organs for transplantation, as health products of an exceptional nature, must be maintained and optimized on an ongoing basis. This requires implementation of quality systems including traceability and vigilance, with adverse events and reactions reported, both nationally and for exported human products.

(xi) The organization and execution of donation and transplantation activities, and their clinical results, must be transparent and open to scrutiny while ensuring that the personal anonymity and privacy of donors and recipients are always protected.

564. A further joint initiative between governmental and professional organizations was the Resolution of Madrid, co-sponsored by the European Commission, WHO, Spanish Presidency of the EU, and The Transplantation Society. This called for all states to strive toward self-sufficiency, both by increasing organ donation activity and by efforts to reduce the burden of end-stage organ failure.

Chapter 2. Organ Donation and Malpractices

565. Generally, organs are sourced from living or dead human beings. In 1986, the first animal organ was used as a transplant in human beings. This intriguing field of study becomes more attractive to some researchers as the number of people needing organ transplants continues to grow. The first artificial heart transplant in the 1980s was closely followed by the news media and the international community. The first split liver transplant in 1996 allowed one cadaveric liver to be used among multiple transplant patients. Stem cell research is examining adult and human embryo cells in an attempt to discover how organs are developed and what stimulates their growth.

§1. Living Donation

566. Living donation makes a significant contribution to kidney (and to a lesser extent liver) transplantation programs worldwide and carries a number of advantages. Transplantation becomes elective and can be scheduled to the time the patient needs the transplant. Furthermore, the outcomes are better than if a deceased donor organ is used. However, this is at a cost, as living donation opens the door to commercialization and trafficking. Different countries have resolved these issues in different ways, depending at least in part on the availability of deceased donation, and living donor rates vary widely.

§2. Organ Sale

567. Donation is driven by the needs of patients with end-stage organ failure for transplants, and in this regard, the most important metrics are transplant rates, both in terms of the total number of transplants (from both living and deceased donors) and those for specific organs. In 2004, the WHA adopted a resolution that urged Member States "to take measures to protect the poorest and vulnerable groups from transplant tourism and the sale of tissues and organs, including attention to the wider problem of international trafficking in human tissues and organs." As of 2007, the WHO estimated that 10% of organ transplants performed worldwide involved these unacceptable activities. To address the concerns of the WHA and the growing problem of organ sales, a Summit Meeting of more than 150 international representatives of scientific and medical bodies, government officials, social scientists, and ethicists was held in Istanbul, Turkey, from April 30 to May 2, 2008. The result of these deliberations was the Istanbul Declaration on Organ Trafficking and Transplant Tourism.

The DOI calls for a prohibition of organ trafficking, transplant commercialism, and transplant tourism: "because transplant commercialism or the buying and selling of organs targets impoverished and otherwise vulnerable donors it inexorably leads to inequity and injustice and should be prohibited. The vulnerable donors are minors, illiterate and impoverished persons, undocumented immigrants, prisoners, and political or economic refugees."

§3. WHO CAN DONATE

568. For donation by living individuals the donor can be relatives who are allowed to donate including mother, father, brothers, sisters, son, daughter, and spouse. In a recent notification grandparents have been included in the list of first relatives. The first relatives are required to provide proof of their relationship by genetic testing and/or by legal documents.

I. Declaration of Brain Death

569. For declaration of brain death, two certifications from doctors are required which need to be six hours apart. Wherein, one of these doctors must be nominated by the Appropriate Authority (AA) of the government and one of them must be an expert in the field of neurology.

§4. TRANSPLANT TOURISM

570. Travel for transplantation is the movement of organs, donors, recipients, or transplant professionals across jurisdictional borders for transplantation purposes. Travel for transplantation becomes "transplant tourism" if it involves organ trafficking, transplant commercialism, or both or if the resources, for example, organs, professionals, and transplant centers, devoted to providing transplants to patients from outside a country undermine the country's ability to provide transplant services for its own population. Transplant tourism is different from medical tourism for other kinds of medical care because it involves a live donor, whose interests and well-being must be considered just as important as those of the recipient. The medical resource used in transplant tourism is an exploited live donor. Vulnerable populations in resource-poor and underdeveloped countries have become a major source of organs for so-called "transplant tourists" who can afford to travel and purchase organs. Not all recipients' travel to a foreign country is unethical to undergo transplantation. Travel for transplantation may be acceptable if the following conditions are fulfilled.

I. Dark Side of Transplant Tourism

571. Transplant tourists prevent deceased donor organs from being available for the people of the destination country because the rich tourists who pay for the organs receive preference. In addition, transplant tourists impede the development of deceased live donation that otherwise would develop in the client country. If the insurance companies of a country preferentially send patients to the Philippines or Pakistan for organs because the transplant will cost less with a meager payment to the organ vendor, deceased donation and altruistic living-related donation (in the country that the tourist resides) are affected by that systematic approach to use the poor of the destination country as the source of organs.

II. Quality and Safety

572. All transplanted human organs carry potential risks to the recipient, either from unsatisfactory organ function or disease transmission from the donor to the recipient, with malignancy and infectious diseases being the most relevant. In the case of living donors, there are also the risks to the donor, both immediate and longer term. Knowledge of these risks is a prerequisite for proper and informed consent. However, for some recipients—faced with imminent death without a transplant—even significant risks associated with a specific organ or its donor may be acceptable and better than the alternative of imminent death. From the recipient's point of view, it is therefore important to approach quality and safety in terms of the risk–benefit balance rather than by attempting to eradicate risk entirely.

573. The European Commission issued a binding directive on the Quality and Safety of Human Organs for Transplantation, for implementation by all Member States. The directive requires establishing and maintaining a framework for quality and safety that covers all stages of the chain from donation to transplantation and to identify a competent authority with the responsibility to ensure compliance with the specific requirements of the various articles of the directive. In the UK, the Human Tissue Authority is the competent authority, which has delegated some areas of its responsibility to other statutory bodies.

574. Comprehensive data collection, storage, and analysis are significant and offer several important benefits like allowing the generation of a comprehensive overview of donation and transplantation activity and supporting the development of evidence-based practice. They facilitate dissemination of learning regarding experience with rare diseases and complications and allow recipients of high-risk organs to be tracked in case subsequent follow-up is required. Registry data make an important contribution to the monitoring and comparison of individual center, help ensure equity of access to transplantation, and allow organs to be matched to highly sensitized individuals as effectively as possible.

Part XV. Euthanasia: End of Life

Chapter 1. Euthanasia

575. Euthanasia is the deliberate and intentional killing of a human being by a direct action, such as lethal injection, or by the failure to perform even the most basic medical care or by withdrawing the life-support system in order to release that human being from a painful life. It is basically to bring about the death of a terminally ill patient or a disabled person. It is resorted to so that the last days of a patient who has been suffering from such an illness that is terminal in nature or that disabled him can peacefully end his life and which can also prove to be less painful for him. Thus the basic intention behind euthanasia is to ensure a less painful death to a person who is, in any case, going to die after a prolonged period of suffering. Euthanasia may be practiced so that a person can live as well as die with dignity. It puts a person to painless death in case of incurable diseases or when life becomes purposeless or hopeless as a result of a mental or physical handicap. But the whole concept is fraught with the grave danger of misuse for getting property or other worldly gains.

§1. Defining Euthanasia

576. The term euthanasia is derived from two Ancient Greek words: "*eu*" means "Good," and "*thanatos*" means "death," so euthanasia means good death. It is an act or practice of ending the life of an individual suffering from a terminal illness or in an incurable condition by injection or by suspending extraordinary medical treatment in order to free him of intolerable pain or from terminal illness. Euthanasia is defined as an intentional killing by an act or omission, of a person whose life is considered as not worth living. It is also known as "Mercy Killing," which is an act where the individual who has no chances of survival as he is suffering from a painful life, ends his life in a painless manner. It is a gentle, easy and painless death. It implies the procuring of an individual's death, so as to avoid or end pain or suffering, especially of individuals suffering from incurable diseases. Oxford dictionary defines it as the painless killing of a person who has an incurable disease or who is in an irreversible coma. According to the House of Lords Select Committee on Medical Ethics, it is "a deliberate intervention undertaken with the express intention of ending life to relieve intractable suffering."

577. In April 2002, the Netherlands became the first country to legalize euthanasia and assisted suicide. It imposed a strict set of conditions: the patient must be suffering unbearable pain, their illness must be incurable, and the demand must be made in "full consciousness" by the patient. Patients with a life expectancy of two weeks or less are put in a medically induced coma, and all nutrition and hydration are withdrawn. The legislation has provoked a fierce debate over the "right to suicide," because assisted suicide outside of the criteria set for euthanasia is still illegal and is counted as homicide.

§2. Withholding or Withdrawing (Cessation) of Treatment

578. There is a very famous case about Aruna Shanbaug, in India, who was working as a nurse at KEM Hospital, Mumbai, India. A ward boy assaulted her on the night of 27 November 1973. He sodomized Aruna after strangling her with a dog chain. The attack left Aruna blind, paralyzed and speechless and she went into a coma from which she has never come out. She is cared for by the KEM Hospital nurses and doctors. The woman does not want to live anymore. The doctors have told her that there is no chance of any improvement in her state. Her next friend describes Shanbaug: "her bones are brittle. Her skin is like 'Paper Mache' stretched over a skeleton. Her wrists are twisted inwards; her fingers are bent and fisted towards her palms, resulting in growing nails tearing into the flesh very often. Her teeth are decayed and giving her immense pain. Food is completely mashed and given to her in semi-solid form. She chokes on liquids and is in a persistent vegetative state."

So, she, through her "next friend," moved Supreme Court of India with a plea to direct the KEM Hospital not to force feed her. And on December 16, 2009, the Supreme Court admitted the woman's plea to end her life. The Supreme Court agreed to examine the merits of the petition and sought responses from the Union Government, Commissioner of Mumbai Police and Dean of KEM Hospital. On January 24, 2011, the Supreme Court of India responded to the plea for euthanasia by setting up a medical panel to examine her. The three-member medical committee subsequently set up under the Supreme Court's directive, checked upon Aruna and concluded that she met "most of the criteria of being in a permanent vegetative state." However, it turned down the mercy killing petition on March 7, 2011. The court, in its landmark judgment, however, allowed passive euthanasia in India. While rejecting the plea for Aruna Shanbaug's euthanasia, the court laid out guidelines for passive euthanasia. According to these guidelines, passive euthanasia involves the withdrawing of treatment or food that would allow the patient to remain alive.

The verdict on her case today allows passive euthanasia in India, contingent upon circumstances.

579. The UK Court of Protection has clarified that decisions to withdraw life-support treatment to patients in Permanent Vegetative State (PVS) or Minimally Conscious State (MCS) need not always be taken with judicial approval. It was held that if, the decision has been taken by the relatives and doctors jointly, approval of the Court of Protection was not necessary.[56]

§3. No Right to Die under International Law

580. International law does not recognize a right to die and such a right cannot be inferred from the ordinary meaning of any human rights document. On the contrary, human rights documents call upon states to protect life. Of all the members of the United Nations, only four have legalized euthanasia, namely the Netherlands, Belgium, Luxembourg, and Canada.

581. Article 6(1) of the ICCPR states, "Every human being has the inherent right to life. This right shall be protected by law. No one shall be arbitrarily deprived of his life." Article 6(1) of the Convention on the Rights of the Child (CRC) states that "every child has the inherent right to life," and makes no mention of a right to death. Article 10 of the CRPD safeguards against, rather than recognizes, a right to death by stating, "States Parties reaffirm that every human being has the inherent right to life and shall take all necessary measures to ensure its effective enjoyment by persons with disabilities on an equal basis with others."

582. The UN treaties implicitly reject the notion of the right to die by including strong protections for the sick, disabled, and elderly being the people most often affected by the legalization of euthanasia and assisted suicide. For example, Article 23 of the CRC recognizes that "a mentally or physically disabled child should enjoy a full and decent life, in conditions which ensure dignity, promote self-reliance and facilitate the child's active participation in the community."

Neither "right to die" is mentioned in UN treaties nor the interpretation of these treaties over the course of several decades has resulted in a single piece of support for euthanasia or assisted suicide. On the contrary, UN treaty bodies have expressed concern regarding the practice of euthanasia in the small minority of countries where it is legal. For example, the Concluding Observations of the Human Rights Committee on the Netherlands state, "The Committee remains concerned at the extent of euthanasia and assisted suicides in the state party. The Committee reiterates its recommendations in this regard and urges that this legislation be reviewed in light of the Covenant's recognition of the right to life."[57]

---

56. http://www.livelaw.in/court-proceedings-not-necessary-withdrawing-life-support-uk-court-protection-read-judgment/.
57. 96th session, Aug. 5, 2009, at § 7.

§4. Regional Human Rights Law

583. Numerous regional human rights treaties recognize the right to life, including Article 2 of the European Convention on Human Rights, Article 2 of the European Charter of Fundamental Rights, Article 4 of the American Convention on Human Rights, and Article 4 of the African Charter of Human and Peoples' Rights –none of which mention to a "right to die." According to the European Court of Human Rights, "Article 2 cannot, without a distortion of language, be interpreted as conferring the diametrically opposite right, namely a right to die; nor can it create a right to self-determination in the sense of conferring on an individual the entitlement to choose death rather than life. The Court accordingly finds that no right to die, whether at the hands of a third person or with the assistance of a public authority, be derived from Article 2 of the Convention."[58]

584. Claims to read a "right to die" into privacy rights under Article 8 of the Convention have also failed.[59] In 1999 the Parliamentary Assembly of the Council of Europe recommended that Member States "respect and protect the dignity of terminally ill or dying persons in all respects by upholding the prohibition against intentionally taking the life of terminally ill or dying persons."[60] The Assembly stated, "Euthanasia, in the sense of the intentional killing by act or omission of a dependent human being for his or her alleged benefit, must always be prohibited."[61]

§5. Euthanasia Unethical

585. The WMA has consistently and categorically rejected the practice of euthanasia and assisted suicide as being unethical. In its Declaration on Euthanasia, adopted by the 38th World Medical Assembly, Madrid, Spain, October 1987, the WMA stated, "Euthanasia, that is the act of deliberately ending the life of a patient, even at the patient's own request or at the request of close relatives, is unethical." In its Statement on Physician-Assisted Suicide, adopted by the 44th World Medical Assembly, Marbella, Spain, September 1992, the WMA stated, "Physicians-assisted suicide, like euthanasia, is unethical and must be condemned by the medical profession."

§6. Basic Rights of a Dying Patient

586. In general the rights of a dying patient are being described as it is seen that international law does not recognize a right to die. A dying patient has certain basic rights, for example, withdrawing supporting devices to sustain cardiopulmonary

58. *Pretty v. United Kingdom* (2002) 35 E.H.R.R. 1 §§ 39–40.
59. *See Gross v. Switzerland*, Application no. 67810/10,2014 and *Haas v. Switzerland*, Application no. 31322/07,2011.
60. Recommendation 1418 (1999) § 9.
61. In Resolution 1859 (2012) § 5.

function even after brain death should be decided only by a team of doctors and not merely by the treating physician alone. A team of doctors shall declare withdrawal of support system. Such team shall consist of the doctor in charge of the patient, Chief Medical Officer or Medical Officer in charge of the hospital and a doctor nominated by the *in charge* of the hospital from the hospital staff.

I. Respect for Patient Autonomy

587. The physician must inform the capable patient and/or his family, with honesty and clarity, the poor prognostic status of the patient when further aggressive medical support appears non-beneficial. The physician is to initiate discussions on the treatment options available including the option of no specific treatment. Respect for the patient's autonomy and to act in his best interest is the basis for providing accurate information. Curative and palliative measures are coexistent but varying in degree at different phases of critical illness. Therefore, the physician must initiate discussions early with a clear expression of the patient's condition.

II. Limiting Life-Prolonging Interventions

588. When the fully informed capable patient/family desires to consider comfort care, the physician should communicate the available modalities of limiting life-prolonging interventions. In case the patient or family do not desire the continuation of life-support interventions, the available options for limiting the supports can be identified as follows:

(a) Do not resuscitate status (DNR).
(b) Withdrawal of life support: The cessation and removal of an ongoing medical therapy with clear intent not to substitute an equivalent alternative treatment. It is fully anticipated that the patient will die following the change in therapy primarily because of the underlying disease conditions.
(c) Withholding of life support: The considered decision not to start new treatment or escalate existing life-support modalities with the understanding that the patient will probably die from the underlying condition.

III. Counseling Sessions with Patient and Family

589. The physician must discuss the implications of aggressive interventions through counseling sessions with the capable patient/family, and work toward a shared decision-making process. Communication with the family is the key to making appropriate decisions and ensuring quality end-of-life care. Early and effective communication facilitates a more smooth transition from curative to palliative care, reduces the frequency of futile care and decreases the possibility of conflict and litigation between families and health care workers. The effective communication and family satisfaction include the provision of adequate time, frequent and consistent information provided by a single contact physician, adequacy of physician and nurse staffing and help from the family physician. Ensuring enough time for the family to ask questions and express themselves further enhances family satisfaction. Pending consensus decisions or in the event of conflicts between the physician's approach and the family's wishes, all existing supportive interventions should continue. The physician, however, is not morally obliged to institute new therapies against his better clinical judgment. The physician should not unduly influence the family of dying patient in decision-making.

590. The proceedings of the counseling sessions, the decision-making process, and the final decision should be clearly documented in the case records, to ensure transparency and to avoid future misunderstandings leading to litigation. Documentation implies transparency, clarity, and evidence of an evolving decision-making process that. This would be helpful to the physician to demonstrate his bona fide intentions in the event of litigation. It would provide security for the patient in case of *mala fide* intentions on the part of caregivers or his own family. It would also ensure that the patient is informed of all the therapeutic choices available and that overall management plans are spelled out for him. The overall responsibility for the decision rests with the physician and companion of the patient, who must ensure that all members of the team including the medical and nursing staff represent the same approach to the care of the patient. The physician in charge of the patient is ultimately responsible for the decision although the process requires full participation by the family and patient.

IV. Withdrawal of Life Support

591. If a capable patient and/or his family desire that life support be withdrawn, in situations in which the physician considers aggressive treatment non-beneficial, the treating team is ethically bound to consider withdrawal within the limits of existing laws. Physician's obligation to respect the patient's autonomy and to act in the patient's best interests may require not to continue futile treatment even though the legal position is unclear. In the absence of case law, the physician may be apprehensive of the potential for litigation in the future. Obtaining signed consent for withdrawal of support may be viewed as protective to the physician but as coercive to the family.

In the event of withdrawal or withholding of support, it is the physician's obligation to provide compassionate and effective palliative care to the patient as well as attend to the emotional needs of the family. For many, life-support interventions have not helped to mitigate their suffering, but have rather added the agony and burden of a prolonged dying process. Death, which we all wish to be peaceful and to occur in the presence of loved ones, has become artificial, away from the family surrounded by the paraphernalia of modern critical care. Prolonged and futile life support imposes economic strains on patients and their families. The physician's approach to the patient is generally "paternalistic" as the concept of autonomy may be weak in the prevailing cultural ethos. The physician's orientation by his training is only to a curative approach to disease. The physician is generally fearful of being accused of providing suboptimal care or of possible criminal liability of limiting therapies. Further, there is a virtual absence of ethical or legal guidelines.

592. In the case of *re quinlan*, the New Jersey Supreme Court permitted withdrawal of life-support measures for a woman in a persistent vegetative state, although her condition was stable and her life expectancy stretched years into the future. Many of the emotional issues were either a direct result of or were influenced by this case, including living wills and other advance medical directives, the right to refuse unwanted treatment, and physician-assisted suicide.

593. The US Supreme Court decision addressing the issue of removal of life support was *Cruzan v. Director, Missouri Department of Health. Cruzan* involved a young woman rendered permanently comatose after a car accident. Her parents petitioned to have her feeding tube removed. The Supreme Court ruled that the evidence needed to be clear and convincing that the young woman had explicitly authorized the termination of treatment prior to becoming incompetent. The Court ruled that the evidence had not been clear and convincing, but upon remand to the state court the family presented new testimony that was deemed clear and convincing. The young woman died twelve days after her feeding tube was removed.

594. The US Supreme Court decided two right-to-die cases in 1997, *Quill v. Vacco* and *Washington v. Glucksberg*. In *Glucksberg*, the appellate courts in New York and Washington had struck down laws banning physician-assisted suicide as violations of equal protection and due process, respectively. The Supreme Court reversed both decisions, finding no constitutional right to assisted suicide, thus, upholding states' power to ban the practice.

595. Though both cases were considered together, *Glucksberg* was the key right to die decision. Dr. Harold Glucksberg and three other physicians sought a declaratory judgment that the state of Washington's law prohibiting assisted suicide was unconstitutional as applied to terminally ill, mentally competent adults. The Supreme Court voted unanimously to sustain the Washington law, though five of the nine justices filed concurring opinions in Quill and Glucksberg. Chief Justice William Rehnquist, writing for the court, based much of his analysis on historical and legal traditions. The fact that most Western democracies make it a crime to assist a suicide was backed up by over 700 years of Anglo-American common-law tradition that has punished or disapproved of suicide or assisting suicide. This deeply rooted opposition to assisted suicides had been reaffirmed by the Washington legislature in 1975 when the prohibition had been enacted and again in 1979 when it passed a Natural Death Act. This law declared that the refusal or withdrawal of treatment did not constitute suicide, but it explicitly stated that the act did not authorize euthanasia.

596. The doctors had argued that the law violated the substantive due process component of the fourteenth amendment. Unlike procedural due process which focuses on whether the right steps have been taken in a legal matter, substantive due process looks to fundamental rights that are implicit in the amendment. For the court to recognize a fundamental liberty, the liberty must be deeply rooted in US history and it must be carefully described. The court rejected this argument because US history has not recognized a "right to die" and therefore it is not a fundamental right. Employing the rational basis test of constitutional review, the court concluded that the law was "rationally related to legitimate government interests" and thus passed constitutional muster.

V. Critical Care and Physician's Approach

597. In the context of critical care, the physician's approach to the patient has medical, ethical and legal dimensions. The medical dimensions relate to medical care and the legal aspects have not yet been properly developed. So far as ethical principles are concerned, there are four ethical principles upon which the practice of critical care is grounded. The respect for patient's autonomy has come to take precedence over the other three—namely beneficence, non-malfeasance, and distributive justice. Autonomy means that the informed patient has a right to choose the manner of his treatment. But for being autonomous the patient should be competent to make decisions and choices. In the event that he is incompetent to make choices, his wishes expressed in advance in the form of a will, or the wishes of the person acting on his behalf, are to be respected.

598. The second ground is beneficence, i.e., acting in what is in patient's interest. As the physician is expected to act in the best interests of the patient and his family, his responsibility should extend beyond medical treatment to ensuring compassionate care during the dying process. In this context, the physician's expanded goals include facilitating the dying process, avoiding or reducing the sufferings of the patient and his family, providing emotional support and protecting the family from financial ruin. This is totally different from euthanasia, which is a direct intervention by the physician to hasten the dying process by administering a lethal injection with the consent of the patient provided that the patient is capable of giving free consent and if not then by the caretaker.

599. The third ground is non-malfeasance, which means to do no harm, to impose no unnecessary or unacceptable burden upon the patient. This is subject to varied interpretation, as the same act may be construed as harmful or beneficial depending on the circumstances. In practical terms, it requires the physician not to act contrary to the patient's values and perspectives.

600. The last ground is distributive justice, which means that patients in similar circumstances should receive similar care. Physicians need to have a socially responsible behavior, which makes it their duty to make good use of the material, financial and human resources under their control. The physician may thus provide treatment and resources to one with a potentially curable condition over another for whom treatment will be futile.

Part XVI. Sterilization

Chapter 1. Sterilization and Population Control

601. Sterilization, both male and female, for family planning purposes developed very rapidly, beginning in Puerto Rico and Japan between 1940 and 1950 and continued in other parts of the world on a large scale after the mid-1950s. The legal status of voluntary sterilization around the world may not be clear, but recent developments show a trend toward liberalization of the laws. Certain countries still consider sterilization punishable under the criminal law, but there is a gap between the law and the practice. Certain countries have made the issue of consent relevant under the law while other governments are studying the question of sterilization officially. Countries with increasing population pressures are employing incentives to encourage sterilization and some have legally authorized sterilization.

§1. Involuntary or Forced Sterilization

602. Historically, involuntary sterilization, as a means of achieving genetic "strength" and implementing population control policies, has involved serious human rights violations. The most marginalized groups have been the target of these practices, which persist today and in some places are codified in law. Women continue to suffer most from forced sterilization which still occurs in many regions of the world. The people most often subjected to these abusive practices are women, especially those living in poverty, women living with HIV, women with disabilities, minority, and indigenous women, and transgender and intersex persons.

603. "Eliminating forced, coercive and otherwise involuntary sterilization," a statement released by several UN agencies, describes the history of this practice, including its use as a method of mass birth control in the latter half of the twentieth century in contravention of fundamental human rights principles of autonomy and dignity.

604. The agencies, including the UN Office of the High Commissioner for Human Rights, have produced the research, in the form of a statement for general release, to add weight to calls for States to take action to eliminate involuntary sterilization. While acknowledging "Sterilization is one of the most widely used forms of contraception in the world," the statement reaffirms that it must only be used with the "full, free and informed" consent of those undergoing the procedure.

I. Forced Sterilization Against Certain Population

605. In 2014, several United Nations agencies collaborated on eliminating forced, coercive and otherwise involuntary sterilization. This was an interagency statement which notes that forced sterilization has been used disproportionately against people living with HIV, persons with disabilities, indigenous peoples, ethnic minorities, and transgender and intersex persons. It lists the various human rights violated by sterilization without consent: rights to health, information, and privacy, reproductive rights, the right to be free from discrimination, and the right to be free from cruel, inhuman or degrading treatment or punishment. Regional and international human rights bodies have also condemned forced sterilization as a form of violence against women, as well as a violation of ethical principles. The 2014 UN publication includes an extensive bibliography of sources, cross-referenced to statements in the text.

606. Involuntary sterilization is often based on presumptions, stereotypes, and/or misinformation about the individuals at risk. For instance, coerced sterilization of women living with HIV has been linked to inaccurate information about HIV transmission. Assumptions that disabled people are asexual or sexually inactive is also used as justification for involuntary sterilization. In some countries, transgender people are forced to undergo sterilization to obtain identity documents which reflect their gender identity, as well as to access treatments such as hormone therapy or sex reassignment operations.

607. Coercive sterilization procedures continue to be used, particularly against Roma women without their informed consent and often in violation of the law. The procedure is often performed at the same time as cesarean sections or women are presented with consent forms during labor or delivery, when in great pain or duress. The statement also addresses the situation of intersex children, who are commonly subjected to treatments resulting in sterility and which the report says, "have life-long consequence for their physical and mental health." The agencies recommend that, if possible, "irreversible invasive medical interventions should be postponed until a child is sufficiently mature to make an informed decision."

608. Drawing on international human rights law, the statement says sterilization without full, free and informed consent is frequently discriminatory and in violation of several other fundamental rights, includin, the right to health, the right to privacy, the right to found a family, and the right to information. Juan Méndez, the UN Special Rapporteur on torture considered abuses in health care in a report to the Human Rights Council in February 2013.

"Medical treatments of an intrusive and irreversible nature, when lacking a therapeutic purpose, may constitute torture or ill-treatment when enforced or administered without the free and informed consent of the person concerned," the Méndez said in his report. The Special Rapporteur drew attention in particular to, "patients from marginalized groups, such as persons with disabilities, notwithstanding claims of good intentions or medical necessity."

In their statement, the UN agencies offer a set of guiding principles for sterilization procedures. Principal among them is autonomy: respect for dignity and the physical and mental integrity of each person expressed through full, free and informed decision-making. People should be able to choose and refuse sterilization, the statement says. In addition to the UN Human Rights Office, UN Women, the Joint UN Programme on HIV and AIDS (UNAIDS), the UNDP, the United Nations Population Fund (UNFPA), the United Nations Children's Fund (UNICEF) and the WHO all contributed to the statement.

II. Forced Sterilization a Crime Against Humanity

609. As per ICC Statute, crimes against humanity are "any of the following acts when committed as part of a widespread or systematic attack directed against any civilian population, with knowledge of the attack: … enforced sterilization."[62]

Forced sterilization, as a crime against humanity, must have been committed in a widespread or systematic manner against a number of targeted victims. Over 2000 persons were supposedly subject to forced sterilization across Peru. As per reports, there was an organized state policy plan. Further, the alleged existence of a state organization to commit forced sterilization proves the "systematic" element. The alleged victims were civilian population, mainly consisting in indigenous and peasant women. The perpetrator does not need to have "had knowledge of all characteristics of the attack or the precise details of the plan or policy of the State."

610. Forced sterilization involves deprivation of biological reproductive capacity, neither justified by the medical or hospital treatment of the person or persons concerned nor carried out with their genuine consent.[63] The alleged victims would have been coerced as evidenced by verbal threats invalidating their consent. Even if threat or coercion is not demonstrated, the absence of informed consent would suffice. Indeed, there were illiterate women or women with only primary school education among the alleged victims and, thus, ambiguous statements must be clarified in the investigation. These are important elements indicating the commission of the crime against humanity of forced sterilization. Identifying those who may have been responsible for these events is necessary for Peru's transitional justice.

62. ICC Statute, Art. 7(1)(g).
63. ICC Elements of Crimes, Art. 7(1)(g)-5.

Chapter 2. Sterilization and Disadvantaged Groups

611. In 1995, the International Conference on Population and Development in 1994 and the Fourth World Conference on Women brought a shift toward a rights-based approach to population policies and the provision of comprehensive sexual and reproductive health policies and programs. States agreed to support the principle of voluntary choice in family planning and to leave targeted approaches to practices such as sterilization. It led to the empowerment of individuals, especially women and enabled them to make autonomous, informed decisions about their reproductive options. Since then, international human rights norms and standards, as well as an increasing number of regional human rights standards, have consistently reinforced these principles. However, people from groups that face discrimination or social marginalization are still subjected to involuntary sterilizations as part of government strategies to reduce population growth. Women often face discrimination and coercion on multiple and intersecting grounds, because they are women, live with disability or HIV and/or belong to indigenous populations or ethnic minorities.

§1. Women Living with HIV

612. Women with HIV may choose sterilization as a contraceptive method. However, it has been documented that such women in some countries are being sterilized without their full, free and informed consent. In most of the cases, the information about prevention of vertical transmission, or regarding the ability of women living with HIV to care for their children, is inaccurate which leads to violence and discrimination, including coercive sterilization practices. In some instances, women living with HIV agree to sterilization on the basis of lack of information or misinformation about their reproductive options. The women living with HIV may be coerced to sign consent forms for sterilization procedures, as a condition of receiving antiretroviral and other HIV treatment and prenatal care for a current pregnancy, or other reproductive health services.

613. Pregnant women may be asked to sign consent forms in situations, such as during labor and while in severe pain, believing that the forms relate to authorizing a cesarean section and not sterilization procedures. In these cases, the women have not been given information on the sterilization procedure, its permanent nature, or alternative methods of contraception. In other cases, spouses or parents have also given consent for sterilization on behalf of women without their knowledge, and often on the basis of being misinformed themselves. Human rights standards recognize that women living with HIV have a right to contraception and other reproductive health services on the same grounds as all other women. These standards state that safe and affordable means of contraception should be available and that women should have the right to freely choose or refuse family planning services including sterilization services.

§2. Indigenous, Minority Girls and Women

614. Indigenous peoples and minorities are particularly vulnerable to coercive sterilization. Coercive sterilization policies and practices against indigenous peoples and minorities, particularly girls and women, have a long history across the globe. These discriminatory practices are often founded on wrongful stereotyping based on gender, race, and ethnicity. The United Nations Declaration on the Rights of Indigenous Peoples, 2007 specifically guarantees indigenous peoples' equality with respect to the enjoyment of the right to health.[64] Further, it is required that special attention shall be given to protection of rights of indigenous people with disabilities.[65] However, the population policies of some countries have targeted indigenous women from the most deprived sections of society. Efforts to meet government-mandated quotas have resulted in thousands of indigenous women being sterilized without consent. Often, indigenous girls and women are not provided with a full choice of contraceptive methods. Moreover, information is often not made available in accessible formats and in indigenous languages.

I. The Romas of Europe

615. Roma, one of the largest minority groups in Europe, has suffered severe human rights abuses, resulting in many Roma living in conditions of extreme social and economic exclusion. They have been victims of coercive sterilization policies and practices since the eugenics era, during World War II, and they remain so currently. Reports and cases brought to national, regional and international courts and human rights bodies from some central and eastern European countries show that while state-financed incentive programs targeting Roma ceased after the fall of communism, the practice of sterilizing Roma women without their informed consent, and in violation of the law, has continued. Recent decisions and reports by national and international human rights bodies describe sterilization of Roma women without their informed consent or even knowledge. Women have been presented with consent forms for the first time during labor or delivery when they are under great pain and duress. In many cases, women are not informed of the permanency of the procedure, or of alternative methods of contraception. In some instances, information is presented in complex formats, for example, using unfamiliar medical terminology, or there is misinformation, for example, the procedure is claimed to be necessary on life-saving grounds. While some states have, in recent years, strengthened their legal frameworks and policies to prevent the recurrence of these practices.

616. Human rights bodies have affirmed that the failure to provide reproductive health information and to ensure full, free and informed consent for sterilization procedures for women belonging to minorities is a violation of basic human rights,

64. Article 21(1).
65. Article 21(2).

including the right to information, women's right to determine the number and spacing of their children, the right to be free from inhumane and degrading treatment, and the right to private life. It has also been found that it is a manifestation of multiple discrimination on the grounds of gender and race. Responding to coerced sterilization of indigenous and minority women, particularly Roma women, human rights bodies have emphasized the need to take legal and policy steps to prevent such violations from occurring and ensuring effective remedies, including apologies, compensation, and restoration of fertility for victims.

§3. Persons with Disabilities

617. Persons with disabilities are very often perceived as asexual or sexually inactive. However, they are sexual beings in the same way as other people, and may also wish to become parents and should not be deprived of their sexual and reproductive rights. Various forms of control over sexual behavior and reproduction, including coercive and involuntary sterilization, are used as methods of fertility regulation for persons with disabilities, often without their informed consent. Women with intellectual disabilities are particularly vulnerable to coercive and involuntary sterilization. Similarly, men with intellectual disabilities may also be subjected to sterilization and to treatments that suppress sexual drive, sometimes including castration. Women with intellectual disabilities are often treated as if they have no control, or should have no control, over their sexual and reproductive choices; they may be forcibly sterilized or forced to terminate wanted pregnancies, based on the paternalistic justification that it is "for their own good." Human rights bodies recognize that sterilization of persons with disabilities without their consent constitutes discrimination, a form of violence and torture, or other cruel, inhuman or degrading treatment. They have called on states to prohibit such practices and adopt legislative changes clearly defining the requirements of full, free and informed consent with regard to sterilization of women with disabilities, in accordance with relevant international standards.

618. The CRPD, 2008 is intended as a human rights instrument with an explicit social development dimension. It adopts a broad categorization of persons with disabilities and reaffirms that all persons with all types of disabilities must enjoy all human rights and fundamental freedoms. It clarifies and qualifies how all categories of rights apply to persons with disabilities and identifies areas where adaptations have to be made for persons with disabilities to effectively exercise their rights and areas where their rights have been violated, and where protection of rights must be reinforced. The Convention affirms the legal capacity of persons with disabilities and their right to equality and nondiscrimination in all aspects of life, including the rights to find and maintain a family and to retain their fertility.[66] The CRPD recognizes that persons with disabilities should have access to sexual and reproductive

66. Articles 3, 5 and 23.

health services, which include voluntary sterilization and any other method of contraception, on an equal basis with others[67] and that these services must be based on full, free and informed consent.[68]

619. The Committee on the Rights of Persons with Disabilities formed under the Convention has called for states to revise laws and administrative measures and to take appropriate steps to prohibit forced sterilization and forced abortion and enable persons with disabilities to marry and found a family including providing access to sexual and reproductive health services. Various motivations for performing sterilization without the consent of persons with disabilities are not justified under the CRPD. Parents or guardians may have different motivations for persuading persons with disabilities, including those aged under 18 years, to opt for sterilization, often in the absence of full, free and informed consent. Parents or guardians may be concerned about avoiding unwanted pregnancy as a result of sexual abuse. Furthermore, enabling persons with disabilities to retain their fertility is rarely prioritized, even though less permanent contraceptive options are available. Instead of providing persons with intellectual disabilities with the necessary support to look after any children they may have, sterilization is offered to them as a way of avoiding the distress of having any potential children removed from their care.

§4. Substitute Decision-Making

620. Depending on the jurisdiction, procedures carried out on clinical rather than contraceptive grounds may or may not require court authorization. Somc states, family members, guardians, courts, review boards or tribunals are permitted under national law to take decisions on behalf of persons with disabilities; this is referred to as substitute decision-making. Article 12 of the CRPD reaffirms that persons with disabilities have the right to recognition everywhere as persons before the law and that states must ensure that persons with disabilities have access to the support they may require in exercising their legal capacity. This may include supportive decision-making where supporters, advocates, or other systems assist persons with disabilities to make their own decisions, free of conflict of interest or undue influence.

§5. Supportive Decision-Making

621. The Committee on the Rights of Persons with Disabilities has consistently urged States Parties, including with respect to sterilization, to adopt laws and policies that replace substitute decision-making systems with a supported decision-making model that upholds the autonomy, wishes, and preferences of the individuals concerned. No child, including those with disabilities, should undergo nontherapeutic sterilization, without full, free and informed consent of the child. The United

67. Article 25; 115–117.
68. In accordance with Arts. 12 and 25.

Nations Committee on the Rights of the Child has specifically addressed forced sterilization of persons with disabilities under the age of 18 as a form of physical violence. The Committee has called upon states to prohibit, by law, the forced sterilization of children on the grounds of disability and to provide these children with adequate information on relationships and sexual and reproductive health, as well as guidance and counseling.

§6. Transgender and Intersex Persons

622. In many countries, transgender and also intersex persons are required to undergo sterilization surgeries that may be unwanted, as a prerequisite to receiving gender-affirmative treatment and gender-marker changes. According to international and regional human rights bodies and some constitutional courts, and as reflected in recent legal changes in several countries, these sterilization requirements run counter to respect for bodily integrity, self-determination, and human dignity, and can cause and perpetuate discrimination against transgender and intersex persons. Intersex persons may be involuntarily subjected to so-called sex normalizing or other procedures as infants or during childhood, which, in some cases, may result in the termination of all or some of their reproductive capacity. Children who are born with atypical sex characteristics are often subjected to cosmetic and other surgeries performed on their reproductive organs, without their informed consent or that of their parents. Thus, such children are being subjected to irreversible interventions that have lifelong consequences for their physical and mental health.

623. Parents often consent to surgery on behalf of their intersex children, including in circumstances where full information is lacking. The human rights bodies, professional organizations and ethical bodies have recommended that full, free and informed consent should be ensured in connection with medical and surgical treatments for intersex persons and, if possible, irreversible invasive medical interventions should be postponed until a child is sufficiently mature to make an informed decision. It has also been recommended that health care professionals should be educated and trained about bodily diversity as well as sexual and related biological and physical diversity and that professionals should properly inform patients and their parents of the consequences of surgical and other medical interventions. Discrimination on the basis of gender identity has been recognized by international human rights bodies as a human rights violation. Human rights bodies have condemned the serious human rights violations to which transgender and intersex persons are subjected and have recommended that transgender and intersex persons should be able to access health services, including contraceptive services such as sterilization, on the same basis as others: free from coercion, discrimination, and violence. They have also recommended the revision of laws to remove any requirements for compulsory sterilization of transgender persons.

Part XVII. Dispute Settlement in Medical Field

624. There is no meaningful dispute settlement body dealing exclusively with global health disputes. Although the lack of concrete normative standards and capacity to assure effective implementation is an endemic problem in international law, it is a particularly acute problem in the economic and social arenas, including global health law. The field of health and human rights is the most discussed body of global health law. But, even here, established norms are vague or rhetorical, not backed by implementation mechanisms and are silent on important aspects of global health.

One of the most striking characteristics of the emerging global health law is the proliferation of organizations contributing to the elaboration of this increasingly complex and multifaceted field. These organizations include the UN and its agencies (primarily WHO), organs and other bodies, and international and regional institutions outside the UN system. The proliferation and patchwork development of multilateral organizations with overlapping ambitions and without any central coordinating agency creates the risk that global health law will develop in an inconsistent and suboptimal manner without a clear-cut dispute settlement mechanism. There is growing evidence of fragmentation, duplication, and inconsistency in areas of global health law-making ranging from biotechnology to tobacco control. In the WHO Framework Convention on Tobacco Control in addition to establishing limited substantive obligations in tobacco control, the Convention drafters neglected to incorporate any mechanisms to promote national action or international review, including, most glaringly, an independent monitoring system, effective dispute resolution procedures, or a mechanism for ensuring that poor states have access to the resources necessary to implement their treaty obligations.

Chapter 1. Dispute Settlement

625. Most international instruments relating to health contain few incentives or options to encourage or promote compliance. An important case in point is the new IHR, which mandate that states establish systems for national epidemiological surveillance. While such a system of global epidemiological surveillance is widely recognized as an essential component of effective global disease control, the new IHR does not provide any mechanism to assist poor states in establishing or maintaining their national systems.

§1. Right to Health and Its Implementation

626. The right to health can be found in the most basic UN documents, i.e., Article 55 of the Charter ("find solutions of international economic, social, [and] health problems"); Article 25 of the Universal Declaration of Human Rights ("standard of living adequate for … health") and Article 12 of the International Covenant of Economic, Social, and Cultural Rights (ICESCR) ("highest attainable standard of physical and mental health"). However, these declarations and treaty provisions have had little impact on state practice. The treaty body that administers the ICESCR, known as the Committee on Economic, Social and Cultural Rights (Committee), attempted to clarify the meaning of the broad declaratory language that the ICESCR uses to set out the right to health. The Committee specified core obligations to meet basic human "survival needs"—e.g., primary health care, essential food, adequate shelter, sanitation, safe potable water, and essential drugs. But after all the implementation and settling of differences has not been adequately addressed.

§2. WTO Dispute Settlement Body

627. The World Trade Organization (WTO) has established a powerful dispute resolution mechanism that, with a structured process and the capacity to enforce rulings, is an extremely rare entity in the international legal system. The WTO Member States established a WTO Dispute Settlement Body authorized to formally adjudicate trade disputes between members. This body is empowered to enforce its decisions by granting the winning party right to apply trade sanctions against the losing party if the latter fails to modify its law or policy that the body found to be in violation of WTO rules. This mandatory and enforceable dispute resolution process stands in sharp contrast to the limited implementation mechanisms established by most treaties, including those in the realm of global health. Still, establishing effective mechanisms to promote implementation and compliance with global health law norms is an enduring challenge in global health law governance.

628. An increasing number of international organizations with law-making authority and relevant mandates are serving as platforms for global health law negotiations, while others are influencing contemporary law making in this realm. The complexity of global health law governance and the need for more effective coordination of the law-making enterprise is further evidenced by the fact that so many agencies and institutions other than those intergovernmental organizations with a mandate closely related to global health are increasingly involved in global health law governance. Institutions with a stake in global health law governance include organizations, such as the World Bank and the WTO. The growing dominance of non-state actors ranging from civil society to private enterprises to foundations in global health law governance further complicates effective coordination. The proliferation of actors and institutions in the field of global health law is not serving to strengthen global health law governance but rather is leaving the field in disarray.

629. The WHO has a unique directive to provide leadership and promote rational and effective development and coordination in the evolving field of health law. The WHO Constitution envisaged an agency that would use law, and exercise powers, to proactively promote the attainment of "the highest possible level of health."[69] But the agency has never met these key expectations. The WHO did not serve as a platform for a health convention until 2003, when the WHA adopted the Framework Convention on Tobacco Control. WHO has long been chastised for its reluctance to create binding norms, despite the bold mission and sweeping powers granted in its Constitution.[70] At the turn of the twenty-first century, more than fifty years after its founding, the agency had failed to adopt a single treaty, and its two regulations on disease classification and epidemic control were largely historical and lacked real-world impact. Since that time, WHO has been far more proactive, suggesting that it may be prepared to exercise political power when necessary to avert global health crises. The critical question, however, is whether or not WHO can build on these recent achievements to deal with the most important, and intractable, health problems in the poorest regions of the world.

630. Amelioration of the enduring and complex problems of global health is virtually impossible without a collective response. The creation of international legal norms, processes, and institutions provides an ongoing and structured forum for states to develop a shared humanitarian instinct on global health. The global health law has a number of structural inadequacies and inherent challenges like vague standards, ineffective monitoring, weak enforcement—and a "statist" approach that insufficiently harnesses the creativity and resources of non-state actors and civil society more generally. Notably, international law suffers from important structural limitations that impact its effectiveness as a tool of global health governance. These limitations include challenges of timely commitment, implementation, and modification of international standards. Overall, in the absence of effective mechanisms for rationalizing and coordinating the global health law system, there are serious questions about the capacity of existing and future global health law to advance global health effectively and equitably. Thus, although members of the global community are increasingly turning their attention to the idea of international law as a tool

69. WHO Constitution, Art. 1.
70. Allyn Lise Taylor, *Making the World Health Organization Work: A Legal Framework to the Universal Access to the Conditions for Health*, 18 Am. J. L. & Med. 301–346 (1992).

for cooperation in global health and calling for codification of new instruments, developing strategies to improve standard-setting, implementation and coordination are enduring grand challenges in global health law.

§3. Medical Disputes

631. One of the main causes of medical disputes is resentment that the patient has not been provided sufficient information in order to make their own decisions. Litigation is resorted to not just for compensation but for patients to get more information about what actually happened to them. It is well understood that most medical disputes are better resolved through alternative dispute resolution (ADR) mechanisms and that these mechanisms can contribute to improving patient safety by encouraging more candid and comprehensive reporting of risks. The medical disputes and patient safety are being viewed through patient autonomy. Autonomy is dominating the discourse on medical negligence in recent years. It reached a high watermark in the recent landmark UK Supreme Court decision of *Montgomery v. Lanarkshire Health Board*,[71] in which the Supreme Court, overruling its earlier jurisprudence on the medical duty to inform, endorsed the *Australian Rogers v. Whitaker* [72] test of the prudent patient in preference to the conventional test of the reasonable doctor, established in *Bolam v. Friern Hospital Management Committee.*[73] The court, in *Montgomery,* recognized that the doctor–patient relationship had fundamentally changed, with patients now much better informed and actively involved in making decisions affecting their bodily integrity and personal autonomy.

632. In *Thomson Medical Centre* and *Hii Chii Kok* (*ACB v. Thomson Medical Pvt. Ltd and others* [74], the Court of Appeal reiterated the centrality of patient autonomy to the doctor–patient relationship. Briefly, in *Thomson Medical Centre*, the Court of Appeal, recognizing the loss of genetic affinity as a new form of actionable damage, awarded substantial damages to vindicate the claimant's autonomy interest. In *Hii Chii Kok*, the Court of Appeal adapted the *Montgomery* test for the duty to inform, holding that the materiality of a risk had to be determined from the perspective of the patients in order to respect their autonomy.

§4. Patient Autonomy

633. Some medical disputes arise out of medical negligence. The plaintiff must prove that the defendant owed a duty of care, breached that duty, and caused damage that is not too remote. However, each of these aspects of negligence becomes more complex in medical malpractice suits. The relationship between doctor and patient is of trust, vulnerability, and expectation. The medical choices are infinite

71. [2015] AC 1430.
72. [1992] 175 CLR 479.
73. [1957] 1 WLR 582.
74. [2017] SGCA 20; *Hii Chii Kok v. Ong Peng Jin London Lucien* and another [2017] SGCA 38.

and doctors have to take into account not just the patients' emotions, idiosyncrasies, and autonomy, but also the institutional culture of the medical services provider as well as the practices and policies of insurers and managed care systems. Causation in medical negligence is especially complex.

634. In *Montgomery*, the infant child suffered from cerebral palsy during childbirth. The mother, who was diabetic, was carrying a child that was larger than normal. The mother herself was quite small, increasing the risk of shoulder dystocia during vaginal delivery, as the child's shoulder might not be able to pass through the pelvis. The risk materialized with tragic consequences. It was alleged that the doctor was negligent in failing to inform the mother of the risk of vaginal delivery and in failing to perform an emergency cesarean section. In finding the doctor liable, Lady Hale, in her concurring opinion, emphasized the significance of patient autonomy: "it is now well recognized that the interest which the law of negligence protects is a person's interest in their own physical and psychiatric integrity, an important feature of which is their autonomy, their freedom to decide what shall and shall not be done with their body."[75]

635. In *Thomson Medical Centre*, the Court of Appeal dealt with complex questions involving damages in a "wrongful birth" type case. The plaintiffs (husband and wife) had a child through IVF. There was a mix-up in the donor's sperm due to the negligence of the defendant, resulting in the conception of a baby who was not biologically that of the husband. The question is whether the parents are entitled to claim damages for the cost of raising the child. This raises complex legal and moral questions with the international jurisprudence divided: some countries allow such claims and others deny them. However, even in the UK, which denies such claims, the House of Lords recognized that in these cases, the autonomy interests of the parents has been adversely affected, meriting some compensation. Again, although from a different perspective, patient autonomy is central to medical negligence discourse.

636. The Singapore Medical Council, in its revised guidelines, highlights the importance of patient autonomy, both in its foreword and within the guidelines. Section C5 states explicitly, "Patient autonomy is a fundamental principle in medical ethics and must be respected."

Section C5(3) states, "you must ensure that patients are made aware of the purpose of tests, treatments or procedures to be performed on them, as well as the benefits, significant limitations, material risks (including those that would be important to patients in their particular circumstances) and possible complications as well as alternatives available to them (emphasis added). This reflects the Montgomery/Rogers disclosure standard based on material risk. Patient autonomy is a recurrent theme affecting medical malpractice today and it has to be taken into account both in resolving medical disputes and in developing patient safety protocols."

75. *Montgomery v. Lanarkshire Health Board* [2015] AC 1430 at [108].

§5. Patient Safety

637. Lord Woolf, in his 1996 Access to Justice Report, stated, "early in the Inquiry it became increasingly obvious that it was in the area of medical negligence that the civil justice system was failing most conspicuously to meet the needs of litigants in a number of respects."[76] The Report noted that the costs were disproportionately high and that there were significant delays in resolving claims. Often, unmeritorious claims were pursued by disgruntled patients while clear-cut claims were vigorously defended by medical insurers. This is supported by US data showing that over 60% of medical malpractice claims are summarily dismissed as having no merit.[77] The Woolf Report noted that the success rate for medical negligence litigation was lower than in other personal injury litigation. Again, US data supports this, with research showing that doctors prevail in about 90% of the cases in which the evidence of medical negligence is weak and in about half the cases where the evidence of medical negligence is strong.[78] Finally, the Woolf Report noted that suspicion and animosity between parties in medical negligence litigation is generally higher than in other areas of litigation.

638. The answer to the question of whether litigation raises professional standards and patient safety is that it most likely does not. Anecdotal evidence suggests that doctors either settle claims with a nondisclosure agreement or, if they do not believe they are personally at fault, take their chances with litigation where they have a high chance of successfully defending the action. This does not encourage a culture of sharing information and learning from mistakes. Litigation is a compensation with no proven impact on patient safety, but with increasing evidence that it contributes to defensive medicine and prevents reporting of adverse incidents. Separate strategies are required to improve patient safety and to resolve medical disputes.

Patient safety is improved through systemic intervention rather than by identifying individual instances of negligence. The majority of medical errors do not result from individual recklessness or the actions of a particular group—this is not a "bad apple" problem. More commonly, errors are caused by faulty systems, processes, and conditions that lead people to make mistakes or fail to prevent them.[79]

639. The litigation serves an important function necessary as it is vital that individuals have access to courts to seek justice; the trial process, for all its weaknesses, does provide procedural fairness and legitimacy. However, for the most part,

76. Lord Woolf, *Access to Justice: Final Report to the Lord Chancellor on the Civil Justice System in England and Wales* ch. 15, para. 2 (HMSO 1996).
77. D.H. Sohn & B.S. Bal, *Medical Malpractice Reform: The Role of Alternative Dispute Resolution*, 470 Clin. Orthop. Relat. Res. 1370–1378 (2012).
78. P.G, Peters, *Twenty Years of Evidence on the Outcomes of Medical Malpractice Claims*, 467 Clin. Orthop. Relat. Res. 352–357 (2009).
79. L.T. Kohn, J.M. Corrigan & M.S. Donaldson, *To Err Is Human: Building a Safer Health System* (National Academy Press 1999).

litigation probably does more harm than good in resolving medical disputes and alternative resolution for the majority of disputes is preferable. Litigation is designed to result in a win–lose outcome. The question is whether ADR can provide a win-win outcome.

Chapter 2. Alternate Dispute Resolution

640. ADR is seen as an alternative to litigation and is increasingly being used in conjunction with litigation as a screening or settlement device. Instead of viewing arbitration and mediation as "alternative" dispute resolution, courts should promote a combination or hybrid mechanism that works best for the particular dispute. The arguments in favor of ADR are that they promote conciliation, facilitate creative settlements, and enable the parties to present explanatory rather than defensive narratives. It is described as providing a "therapeutic resolution" of the dispute, allowing parties an opportunity to explain or receive an explanation, to apologize or to forgive, and to have closure and to restore relationships. Mediation is particularly suited to disputes where the parties have an interest in an ongoing relationship. In medical disputes, often, the relationship has actually ended, so there is no interest in continuing or repairing it. Patients want an explanation and compensation, while doctors—and the institutions with which they are affiliated—want to protect their reputations and financial interests.

§1. Mediation

641. Mediation can help reframe the medical dispute away from the taking rigid legal positions and help preserve the relationship. This may lead to better outcomes for both the doctor and the patient in resolving disputes and improving patient safety. Medical disputes have unique features that make them particularly challenging for mediation. First, they may involve complex medical facts and issues of causation, making it difficult to comprehend by an untrained mediator. Second, medical disputes can involve a range of parties with conflicting interests: the medical personnel, from the referring doctor to the consultant to the nurse, the insurer, the hospital management, the patient or the next of kin, and the lawyer. Each has a different perspective, based on their professional training or institutional culture, making a meeting of minds challenging and difficult. Third, there is a power imbalance in medical disputes between the health care provider and the patient. Fourth, the confidentiality and privacy issues are unlike those in other disputes due to the sensitivity of health records and the personal nature of the information.

642. The two known biggest obstacles to the mediation of medical disputes come from doctors and lawyers. The studies of medical mediation show that most mediation takes place without the doctor being present for a variety of reasons. For example, they do not want to face their patients; they are too busy with their practice; or they just want to leave it to their insurers to settle. Sometimes defense lawyers may advise doctors not to attend mediation for fear that doctors may be too candid, leaving them vulnerable if mediation fails and the patient proceeds with litigation. Apart from discouraging doctors from attending mediation, some lawyers do not like it because mediation affects their economic interests. Mediations are much quicker, affecting the number of hours they can charge and bill. One US study showed that a lawyer spent 3.5 hours on average preparing for mediation and over 36 hours preparing for trial.[80]

643. Given inherent difficulties, mediation cannot be used more widely to resolve medical disputes. However, a commitment is to be made to genuine mediation and not merely to mediation as a means or a guise for settlement or to test the waters for litigation. At the heart of mediation is the notion that the parties own the dispute and that they are willing to work with each other to reach a mutually acceptable outcome.

The basic principles for successful medical mediation are as follows.

I. Self-Determination

644. Self-determination means the parties must be willing and voluntary participants, with the right to leave the mediation at any time. This does not necessarily preclude mandatory mediation; as one mediator observed, mandatory medical mediation is necessary to get the parties there, but once they are there, they must be free to leave at any time.

II. Impartiality

645. The mediator must be impartial in order for the parties to have trust and for the process to have credibility. In mediation, there is a power imbalance as the defense is often a repeat player and has an advantage. The mediator has to protect the patient's interest while guarding against becoming an advocate for the patient.

III. Flexibility

646. The solutions have to fit the particular dispute and the expectations of the parties. The mediator needs to be creative and parties must be willing to explore different solutions. Examples include apologies, donations to charities, free medical care and education of children.

IV. Confidentiality

647. It is vital that whatever is said during mediation remains confidential; otherwise, it will be difficult to have a full and frank discussion, as the parties will worry that what they say may be used in court if mediation fails.

80. S.J. Szmania, A.M. Johnson & M. Mulligan, *Alternative Dispute Resolution in Medical Malpractice: A Survey of Emerging Trends and Practices*, 26 Conflict Resol. Q. 71–96 (2008).

Medical disputes require respect for patient autonomy and treating the patient as an equal partner in managing his or her health issues. Giving opportunities for the individuals on either side of the dispute to present their narratives in a nonconfrontational environment is healthy. Common to both systemic strategies to improve patient safety and personalized strategies to deal with dispute resolution are good communication and transparency, which are critical to identifying risks in the health care system and to preserving the trust inherent in the doctor–patient relationship.

Selected Bibliography

Amirthalingam, Kumaralingam. "Medical Dispute Resolution, Patient Safety and the Doctor–Patient Relationship." *Singapore Medical Journal* 58, no. 12 (2017): 681–684 doi: 10.11622/smedj.2017073.

Aronowitz, Alaxis A. & Elif Isitman. "Trafficking of Human Beings for the Purpose of Organ Removal: Are (International) Legal Institutions Effective Measures to Eradicate the Practice." *Groningen Journal of International Law* 1, no. 2: Human Trafficking http://grojil.files.wordpress.com/2014/01/03-aronowitz-isitman.pdf.

Brown, Willium Y. "Its Time for a New Biotechnology Law." *Brookings*, July 27 (2011) http://brookings.edu/opinions/its-time-for-a-new-biotechnology-law/.

Gostin, Lawrence O. & Devi Sridhar. "Global Health and the Law" (May 1, 2014) https://www.nejm.org/doi/full/10.1056/nejmra1314094.

Jackson, Emily. *Medical Law, Text, Cases and Materials*, 4th edn. Oxford: Oxford University Press, 2016.

Jasmine, Cameron, "Mental Health Law: International Legal Standards and Human Rights." *Legal Dialogue,* 2017. http://legal-dialogue.org/mental-health-law.

Joly, Yann & Knoppers, Bartha Maria. *Routledge Handbook of Medical Law and Ethics*. London: Routledge, 2015.

Mabry, Tracy. "Legal Issues in Obtaining and Providing Healthcare Internationally." *Medical Tourism Magazine*, January 16, 2012 https://www.magazine.medicaltourism.com/article/legal-issues-in-obtaining-and-providing-healthcare-internationally.

Selected Bibliography

Index

The numbers here refer to paragraph numbers.

Index

Index

www.ingramcontent.com/pod-product-compliance
Lightning Source LLC
Chambersburg PA
CBHW071433230926
51846CB00001B/213
9789403547503